Early Dutch Entrepreneurship and its Contribution to Modern Economy

Anton Kruft

Early Dutch Entrepreneurship and its Contribution to Modern Economy

Aspekt 2014

Early Dutch Entrepreneurship and its Contribution to Modern Economy

© 2014 Uitgeverij ASPEKT
© Anton Kruft

Amersfoortsestraat 27, 3769 AD Soesterberg, Nederland
info@uitgeverijaspekt.nl - http://www.uitgeverijaspekt.nl

Omslagontwerp: Mark Heuveling
Binnenwerk: Thomas Wunderink

ISBN: 9789461534279
NUR: 780

Alle rechten voorbehouden. Niets van deze uitgave mag worden verveelvoudigd, opgeslagen in een geautomatiseerd gegevensbestand of openbaar gemaakt, in enige vorm of op enige wijze, hetzij elektronisch, mechanisch, door fotokopieën, opnamen of enig andere manier, zonder voorafgaande toestemming van de uitgever.

Voorzover het maken van kopieën uit deze uitgave is toegestaan op grond van artikel 16B Auteurswet 1912 j° het Besluit van 20 juni 1974, St.b. 351, zoals gewijzigd bij het Besluit van 23 augustus 1985, St.b. 471 en artikel 17 Auteurswet 1912, dient men de daarvoor wettelijk verschuldigde vergoedingen te voldoen aan de Stichting Reprorecht (postbus 882, 1180 AW, Amstelveen). Voor het overnemen van gedeelte(n) van deze uitgave in bloemlezingen, readers, en andere compilatiewerken (artikel 16 Auteurswet 1912), dient men zich tot de uitgever te wenden.

Contents

1	**INTRODUCTION**	7
1.1	Background	7
1.2	Approach and methodology of the research	14
2	**THE THEORY OF ENTREPRENEURSHIP**	17
2.1	Theory formation	17
2.2	Mainstream of entrepreneurship theory	37
2.3	Definitions of entrepreneurship	39
3	**DIMENSIONS IN ENTREPRENEURSHIP**	43
3.1	Overview	43
3.2	Dimensions and factors to be examined	44
3.2.1	Opportunity conditions for entrepreneurship	44
3.2.2	The institution development dimension	46
3.2.3	Socio-cultural dimensions	47
3.2.4	Personal characteristics of entrepreneurs	50
3.2.5	The research model	55
4	**A CURSORY VIEW ON ENTREPRENEURSHIP PRIOR TO TRADE CAPITALISM**	59
4.1	First traces of 'Dutch' entrepreneurship	59
4.2	International developments influencing Dutch entrepreneurship	69
4.3	The emergence of the 'trade capitalist' entrepreneur	77
5	**OPPORTUNITY CONDITIONS FOR ENTREPRENEURSHIP**	81
5.1	Geography, land and water	81
5.2	Labour	86
5.3	Capital	90
5.4	Technology	96
5.5	The market	98
6	**INSTITUTION DEVELOPMENT**	111
6.1	The period of economic take off (1350-1580)	111
6.2	Institution development during economic supremacy (1580-1670)	124
6.3	Institution development during the decline of the economy (1670-1815)	147
7	**SOCIO-CULTURAL ASPECTS AFFECTING ENTREPRENEURSHIP**	155
7.1	Socio-cultural developments during economic takeoff (1350-1580)	155
7.2	Socio-cultural developments during economic supremacy (1580-1670)	161
7.3	Socio-cultural developments during economic decline (1670-1815)	175
8	**ENTREPRENEURIAL CHARACTERISTICS**	179
8.1	Identity of entrepreneurs	179
8.2	Orientation of entrepreneurship: expansion and innovation	193
8.3	Entrepreneurial traits	205

9	**ENTREPRENEURSHIP DEVELOPMENT DURING TRADE CAPITALISM AND ITS CONTRIBUTION TO MODERN TIMES**	**255**
9.1	Evaluative remarks on entrepreneurship during trade capitalism	225
9.1.1	General	225
9.1.2	Opportunity conditions for entrepreneurship	227
9.1.3	Institution development	234
9.1.4	Socio-cultural aspects of society affecting entrepreneurship	238
9.1.5	Entrepreneurial characteristics	242
9.1.6	Final remarks	251
9.2	Entrepreneurship during Manufacture- and Industrial Capitalism	252
9.2.1	The start of the new kingdom of The Netherlands	253
9.2.2	Manufacture capitalism (1815-1900)	255
9.2.3	Industrial Capitalism (1900-1970)	259
9.3	Entrepreneurship during Total Capitalism (as from 1970)	262
9.3.1	Opportunity conditions for entrepreneurship	263
9.3.2	Institution development	267
9.3.3	Socio-cultural aspects of society affecting entrepreneurship	272
9.3.4	Entrepreneurial characteristics	277
9.4	Modernity of early Dutch entrepreneurship	284

BIBLIOGRAPHY 295

INDEX 313

FIGURES AND TABLES 317

1. INTRODUCTION

1.1. Background

Dutch historians that do research on 'entrepreneurship' are of the opinion that entrepreneurial history of early modern times remains sharply underexposed. This seems to be true for both the traditional philological historiography concerning trade and industry, and the more theoretically-oriented school of economic history that has evolved in the past few decades.[1] In their views, one of the themes to expand upon includes the use of elements from a variety of social theories, which may point the way to a broadly conceived entrepreneurial history that comprises not only economic but also social, political, religious and cultural dimensions.[2] Therefore, the purpose of this study is to apply the above-mentioned dimensions to an analysis of early Dutch entrepreneurship during the early-modern period, i.e. mid-14th century till the beginning of the 19th century.

The entire history of Dutch entrepreneurship as of early modern times, say 1350, till the year 2000 may be sub-divided into four different periods with its own character. The period 1350 to 1815 is very much characterized as a period of mainly trading activities. Obviously, also productive activities took place during that time, such as shipbuilding, cheese making, beer production and the like. However, the main emphasis of that period was on international trade, which is the reason why we call this era the '*Trade Capitalistic Period*'. The period thereafter, running from 1815 to 1870/1880, is mainly characterized as an era in which manufacturing was emphasized, obviously following the developments of the Industrial Revolution around 1815. We call it the period of '*Manufacture Capitalism*'. Then follows the period of '*Industrial Capitalism*', running from 1880 to approximately 1960/1970. This period signifies the use of modern production techniques, such as electricity, chemicals, electronics, etc. Finally, the period we now live in can

---
1 Lesger and Noordegraaf, *Entrepreneurs and entrepreneurship in Early Modern times*
2 Ibid., p.1

be called the period of '*Total Capitalism*', with its modern forms of globalization, digital networks, software, communication gadgets, etc.[3].

Next to making an analysis of entrepreneurship during the '*Trade Capitalistic Period*' of 1350 to 1815, this study we will furthermore try and make an attempt to work out the relationship between '*Trade Capitalism*' and the modern era of the '*Total Capitalistic*' system. How did '*Trade Capitalism*' influence '*Total Capitalism*'? It is striking how advanced the trade capitalist period was in its innovations and developments, many of which today are still common practice. Indeed, much of what entrepreneurs all over the world are doing now is a direct derivative of what in this early modern period was established. Making dynamic use of the comparative advantages of the geography of the Netherlands, Dutch entrepreneurs combined the country's opportunity conditions with their experiences and knowledge, and thus established a first form of the 'marketization of the economy'. By producing products and services for the worldmarket in an emerging money economy a first form of capitalism – *Trade Capitalism* – was born. This type of economy – marketization - was a fundamental breach with the preceding period and made other forms of capitalism possible, including *Manufacture Capitalism*, *Industrial Capitalism* and *Total Capitalism*. This study shows that capitalism did not start at the time when large-scale industrialisation took place in the 19th and 20th century Clearly, the industrial revolution was not the start, but a *next* manifestation of capitalism, which was made possible because of the preceding trade capitalistic form, the form in which Dutch entrepreneurs were particularly instrumental.

---

3   The question arises whether these periods can be termed 'capitalism'. Fernand Braudel remarks in the introduction of his study about '*Civilization, Economy and Capitalism*' that the word 'capitalism' in its full and explosive meaning appears relatively late in the 20th century. Should this term then be considered as an anachronism if we use it for the periods prior to the 20th century? Braudel does not see any problem in using this term. According to him historians invent words and labels in order to indicate the specific problems in a specific period, such as Renaissance, Humanism, Reformation, etc. Therefore he could not resist using the term 'capitalism', in spite of the many images and heated discussions it caused and is still causing. In this study, we follow the same reasoning as a justification for also using the term 'capitalism' for the period prior to the 20th century.

In this book, important features that led to *Trade Capitalism* will be analyzed and will include dimensions related to the nature of the opportunity conditions, institutional developments and institutional structures around entrepreneurship of both the private and public sector. Also, social-cultural aspects which influenced entrepreneurship will be discussed, such as legitimacy of entrepreneurship, mobility, social integration, and ideology. Finally, issues related to the characteristics of the entrepreneurs, such as their identity, their orientation, whether or not they were expansionist and/or innovative, their risk management and problem-solving abilities, will be dealt with.

Of course we know that 'the entrepreneur' does not exist. According to Baumol the entrepreneur strives for wealth, power and prestige, and each entrepreneur does this in his or her own way, depending on the background of that person, including education, training, personal characteristics, experiences, social conviction, religion, and ethnic or cultural descent. But despite all these personal differences there are basic patterns of entrepreneurship that distinguish them from other professions in society, such as health care professionals, civil servants, educators, or military personnel, etc.

That economic activity hasn't changed much in its core principles over the last five to seven centuries as can be illustrated by the example of the weekly public 'farmers' market. Still, on fixed days, in various towns and villages in Europe and elsewhere, market traders hit the road with their vehicles, offload their merchandise at the various market places and, according to a schedule, set up their booths and are ready to do business. They show their products often with handwritten pricetags on pieces of cardboard taken from the very boxes in which the merchandise was packed. If customers find the merchandise too expensive, they can start haggling. Prices are in first instance fixed, based on quality, design and scarcity, but will be reduced as soon as products are insufficiently sold, and approach their expiration date/time (perishables), or if a competitor has lower prices. Five, six, seven centuries ago things worked exactly in the same way. Also back then one found similar merchants on local markets according to an exhibitor schedule: also in that period they went from one market place to another; also in that same period municipal authorities established the places where the markets could be held, as well as established the rules regarding general market operations. Also back then the consumer would haggle about the price. Possibly the only difference to present-day market place activities is the transportation of merchandise, which now is fully motorized, and the cooling installation of the stalls that sell cheese, fish or other fresh produce.

Looking at the basic business patterns of how merchandise is marketed now in comparison to five centuries ago, it is all about: 'competitiveness' (the right relationship price/quality/design); 'competition' of colleagues or other marketing channels; forces of 'supply and demand' (in case of scarcity a *sellers-market,* in case of large surpluses of supply a *consumer market*); and 'innovation' (in production techniques, products and services). Similarly, innovation existed in the 17th century as well, e.g. as regards to beer production (think of the Czech invention of Pilsner beer), shipbuilding, fisheries, dairy, textile and ceramics production, etc. Finally, also in centuries past entrepreneurs had to cope with the vagaries of business life: foreign competition, piracy, opening up new markets, promoting products in hostile environments, lack of credit, and so on.

What did change in the period 1350 – 1815 was the increase of globalization of business. The initial focus on the village and city shifted to the region and later, because of the good water roads, shifted to an even wider, provincial level, then to a European level and, finally, trading became a global phenomenon. This shift in focus took place in the 15th and 16th centuries, and became even more pronounced in later periods. The construction of sea-going vessels, the compass and the famous discovery journeys opened up unprecedented markets. Dutch traders opened international trade offices in Russia, around the Mediterranean, in the Baltic States and other places in Europe. In the wake of these developments, also trade posts and colonies *outside* Europe were founded, initially for the supply of raw materials and later to be used as markets for finished products. In the meantime, the dominant trading areas in Europe shifted from the city-state of Venice, through Champagne in France to the Southern Netherlands, where cities like Bruges, Ypres, Ghent and later Antwerp became leading economic centres. With the emergence of the money economy, these and other nearby international markets became increasingly important for Dutch entrepreneurs, since purchasing power in these areas increased dramatically and thereby also the demand for new and innovative products. This motivated the Dutch entrepreneurs to set sail with their own sea-going vessels, which had been developed over a long period of time, whilst using their navigation expertise, which had been developed over many centuries on the North and Baltic Seas. In addition they could make use of the favourable geographic situation of the country at the crossroads between East and West (from Germany to England) and between North and South (from the Baltic countries to countries at or nearby the Mediterranean).

This was a major economic break with the past. Whereas previously the market had become regionalised, it now obtained a more international, global, character. Instead of producing merchandise for well-known target groups in selected regions as was done by entrepreneurs in the Southern Netherlands (Antwerp, Bruges, Ghent, etc.), entrepreneurs in the Northern Netherlands changed the mode of production drastically into that for the world market. This shift obviously required different tools and instruments, specifically in the area of 'institution development': legal structures, appropriate business- and financial services, transparent taxation, etc.

This study will focus on how entrepreneurship in the Netherlands, specifically during *Trade Capitalism* (1350-1815), took shape and what tools and instruments entrepreneurs developed in order to sustain entrepreneurial growth and to become and remain competitive in the international market. In doing so, the entire period of *Trade Capitalism* will be split up into three sub-periods. The first sub-period runs from 1350 to 1580 and is considered to be the upbeat to the 'first modern economy', as is phrased by the historians De Vries & Van der Woude. In the second sub-period, running from 1580 to approximately 1670 (the so-called Dutch "Golden Age"), this first modern economy reached its absolute zenith.[4] It was a period in which both trade and manufacturing in bulk commodities played a significant role in the economy, which had a strong international character but an equally strong growing domestic consumer market. During the then following third sub-period, from 1670 to 1815, we see forms of economic stagnation and a gradual decline in trade in the Netherlands. At first, manufacturing in the country remained quite stable, albeit with many fluctuations in the various manufacturing subsectors. But in the latter part of this period, as from approximately 1770, it changed dramatically for the worse. Wars with Spain, France and Britain to curtail Dutch free trade operations during that era had stagnated the supply of raw material. In addition, high wages and taxation discouraged investments in productive enterprises. What finally aggravated the situation thoroughly were the political situation (1795 Patriotic movement) and the ultimate annexation of the Dutch provinces into the Napoleonic Empire. Trade as from 1795 was at an absolute low ebb.

Perpendicular to each of these three periods, four dimensions related to the functioning of entrepreneurship will be applied so as to assess the entrepreneur's standing in practice. These are 1) identifying and making optimal use of 'opportunity conditions', 2) institutional development in which the government played an important role, 3) socio-cultural aspects affecting entrepreneurship, and 4) specific personal characteristics of the entrepreneur (see figure 2 in chapter 3). Each of these four dimensions include a number of factors which will help us to arrive at an optimal assessment of changes in entrepreneurship during the three periods of *'Trade Capitalism'*. These 'change in entrepreneurship factors' will be elaborated in chapters five to eight.

Prior to the start of *'Trade Capitalism'* (1350), from approximately 1000 to 1300 a preceding period of an escape from economic

---

4   Vries, J. de & A. van der Woude, *Nederland 1500-1850; De eerste ronde van moderne economische groei*, Amsterdam 1995. The argument runs that Dutch trade capitalism was not a follow-up of the type of economy characteristic of those of the Italian city states, Bruges and Antwerp as seen so far by the majority of economic historians, but that it marks the beginning of a modern economy, in which the Industrial Revolution was just one of the phases and not the beginning of it. (see chapters 13 and 14)

medieval backwardness can be identified. During this period international business flourished in the northern part of Italy with the Arab world, England and the Low Countries. By the standard of those days, a number of these businesses even became 'super companies', having branch networks in these foreign markets and organizing international fairs in order to optimize their business results in their large scale commodity trading. This was achieved by applying sophisticated techniques of management control (double entry bookkeeping) and an innovative way of transferring money (bills of exchange). However, at the start of the period marked as *Trade Capitalism* (around 1350), we see in Europe a general decline in business dynamics, caused by the Great Pestilence, famine and endemic warfare. It meant severe depopulation, as well as disruption and disorder of European societies, although in The Netherlands the consequences of these disasters were far less as compared to other regions in Europe. Nonetheless, the development of entrepreneurship during the first stage of *Trade Capitalism* in Northern Europe must be understood against this background. As Hunt and Murray state: '...European business was able to adapt to the groundswells of change in ways that are both consistent and continuous with business enterprise of the previous era. And business enterprise did more than only survive; entrepreneurs took advantage of new opportunities, even among the disasters of this period'.[5] These opportunities were indeed seized by these entrepreneurs in the North Sea delta area of the Rhine, Scheldt, Meuse and Yssel rivers - the Low Countries. The historical description of entrepreneurship during the era running from 1000 - 1350 will be dealt with in chapter four.

The preceding chapter 2 will deal with 'theory formation of entrepreneurship', as has been developed over the past few decades by political economists, sociologists and social-economic historians on the notion 'entrepreneurship', a term first coined around 1734 by the French business man Richard Cantillon. In addition we will study the research done and views developed by multilateral development organisations such as the International Labour Organisation (ILO), in their drive to promote entrepreneurship in

---

5 Hunt, E.S. & J.M. Murray, *A History of Business in Medieval Europe, 1200-1550*, Cambridge 1999, p 128

developing economies. Once we have operationalized the current views on successful entrepreneurship by today's standards, we will turn to chapter three to describe in detail the four earlier-mentioned 'change in entrepreneurship' dimensions. These will be used as an analytical tool through which the performance of entrepreneurship will be examined during the three selected sub-periods within the *Trade Capitalism* period (1350-1815).

Finally, in the last chapter, chapter 9, a summary will be provided of the results of the research related to entrepreneurship over the three selected periods on the basis of the analytical framework (see figure 2 in chapter 3). Each of the four dimensions will be discussed and a number of conclusions on the entrepreneurs' performance and functioning will be drawn. Likewise, an effort will be made to indicate to what extent instruments adopted by the entrepreneurs from that period have left traces in the present time. It may be interesting to see what similarities exist in the land of entrepreneurship between the first Golden Age and the current second one: between *Trade Capitalism* of 1350-1850 and *Total Capitalism*, in which total global economics, internationally operating financial institutions, the formation of the European Union, the end of the cold war (and ideology[6]), the collapse of the centrally guided economies have brought new opportunities for western businesses and, not in the least, free trade and the "marketization" of society.

1.2. Approach and methodology of the research

As mentioned before, the ultimate aim of this study is searching for, and comparing, determining exogenous and endogenous factors, which caused the growth and development of entrepreneurship in the Netherlands during trade capitalism. The approach and methodology applied to achieve this, is by first working out the state of the art of present-day entrepreneurship. This entails both an identification and general analysis of current theories and views and visions of socio-economic researchers and historians on major aspects in the development of entrepreneurship as well as an analysis of all major and minor

---

6   Fukuyama, F., *The End of History and the Last Man*, New York, 1992

characteristics or features that make up the fabric of entrepreneurship as currently perceived. The analysis of the characteristics, ultimately leading to a working definition of 'entrepreneurship', will include 1) Identity, 2) Orientation and 3) Personal traits of the entrepreneur, - in fact a further break down of the fourth dimension (specific characteristics of the entrepreneur), mentioned above:

- *The identity of entrepreneurs* includes factors such as: individual vs. collective, mainstream vs. outsider, family vs. non-family, socio-economic origin, religious orientation, old vs. new, private vs. public;

- *The orientation of entrepreneurship* includes factors such as: is the entrepreneur expansion-driven, innovation-driven;

- *The personal traits of entrepreneurs,* including factors such as: risk-management, need to achieve or initiative, self-perception, independence, etc.

The then remaining three dimensions to be assessed during each of the three selected sub-periods of '*Trade Capitalism*' encompass:

- *Opportunity conditions.* This dimension includes factors as: quantity of factor inputs, quality of factor inputs, size and composition of markets;

- *Institution development.* This dimension includes government measures related to protective-, promotional- and corrective factors exercised by the nation-state and initiatives from the private entrepreneurial sector to set up institutions in order to facilitate cooperation among various actors in the economy, as well as to reduce uncertainties;

- *Socio-cultural dimension.* This includes factors such as: legitimacy of entrepreneurship, social mobility, marginality, social integration, security, ideology, need for achievement.

(See also figures 2 and 3, of chapter 3.2.5: The research model)

Due to the length of the period, it would be nearly impossible to study all relevant authentic sources about the period 1350 - 1815. Instead, selected authentic sources have been consulted, whereas the main focus of the research was on making an analysis of most recent national and international literature of various scientific disciplines, so as to identify points of reference related to the objective of the study. In order to arrive at a maximum objectivity of the research, the existing literature studied has been chosen with extreme care, considering a well-balanced diversity in terms of differences in interpretation of historical events, as well as representation of different schools of thought.

2. THE THEORY OF ENTREPRENEURSHIP

2.1. Theory formation

According to a number of researchers in entrepreneurship and entrepreneurial behaviour, the very reason for an entrepreneur to carry out the function of 'entrepreneurship' is to realize personal aims and preferences, such as wealth, power and status, in which profitability and continuity of the enterprise are imperative instruments in achieving these objectives.[7] In other words, 'entrepreneurship' is not an end in itself, it is considered to be a means to an end, 'the quality of acting as a go-between or agent matching supply and demand'.[8]

Obviously, there is an extremely close linkage between performing entrepreneurship on the one hand and the performer (the entrepreneur) on the other. In 1925, Joseph Schumpeter dealt with the question whether entrepreneurs constitute a class, or just people carrying out a profession. He wrote that, although entrepreneurship is not a profession, people carrying out this occupation could indeed be seen as a class in the sense where researchers consider them as certain economic subjects, though with very different forms of lifestyle. It is not a class in terms of a social phenomenon in the context of 'class formation', 'class struggle", etc. The fulfillment of the entrepreneurial function provides status for the successful entrepreneur and his family. It can also mark its specific lifestyle, moral and aesthetic value system in the society where it is active.[9] As Schumpeter held, in case the entrepreneur or their descendants are successful, they will rise into the capitalistic class, however, one does not - from the outset - belong to it or to

---

[7] Lesger, 'Ondernemen en Ondernemerschap' in: Davids, *Kapitaal, ondernemerschap en beleid'*, p. 58, referring also to Weber's classification in class, party and status in: M. Weber, *Wirtschaft und Gesellschaft: Grundriss der erstehenden Soziologie* II (Tübingen, 1976, chapter 3 and 4. See also: Baumol 'Entrepreneurship'

[8] Hunt, E.S. & J.M. Murray, *A history of Business in Medieval Europe, 1200-1550*, Cambridge 1999, p. 132

[9] J. Schumpeter, 'Theorie der Wirtschaftlichen Entwicklung, eine Untersuchung über Unternehmergewinn, Kapital, Kredit, Zins und den Konjunkturzyklus, Berlin 1926, p.116, 117, taken from T.J. Kastelein, *Groei naar een industriële samenleving*, p. 294

any other definite class. As a matter of historical fact, entrepreneurs come from all classes, which at the time of their emergence happen to exist.[10]

Inherent to to-day's entrepreneurship is that it must balance opportunities with threats, as they are part and parcel of an economic, political, institutional and socio-cultural environment which can not be controlled by the individual exercising entrepreneurship. How to deal with these opportunities and threats in the best possible manner is very much dependent on the personal qualities of the entrepreneur. Visions about the relationship 'entrepreneur and entrepreneurship' was lacking in the classic or neo-classic theory formation of economy. The emphasis was primarily put on technical and mechanical aspects in the sense that the early writings about economy dealt for the greater part with issues like demand and supply, in which there was hardly room for autonomous actions of individual entrepreneurs in economic processes. This absence was even more strengthened by a further de-personification of the economy due to increased quantification of the same in the period following World War Two.[11] Nonetheless, in spite of the absence or the marginal role of the entrepreneurs as such in economic theories, he certainly played an important role in the development and growth of the economy, as was recognized by quite a number of researchers over the past few centuries.

Early theory formation on entrepreneurship must be seen against the background of nation-state building, which started at the end of the Middle Ages in very divers forms. Many of the new nation-states had a dual purpose: 'to build up economic power to strengthen the state and to use the power of the state to promote economic growth and enrich the nation'.[12] Without the gold and silver mines of the New World from which Spain drew its riches, a nation could

---

10 J. Schumpeter, 'The Entrepreneur as an Innovator', from Business Cycles: A Theoretical, Historical, and Statistical analysis of the Capitalist Process, Vol. I, p 102-109, in: E. Dale, *Readings in Management*, p. 7-11
11 Lesger, Ondernemen en Ondernemerschap, p. 57, 59
12 Cameron, R., *A Concise Economic history of the world; From Palaeolithic times to the present*, Oxford 1997, p. 130

accumulate these precious metals only by selling more merchandise to foreigners than it bought from them.[13] Hence, economic nationalism was the driving force for these countries in their aim to become a strong nation-state. As a reaction to economic nationalism or 'Colbertism', as it was later characterised, physiocracy, favouring internal free trade, was briefly *en vogue* in France during the 18th Century. Turgot, a French economist and statesman became specifically known when in 1776 he submitted as the Controller General of Finance his famous Six Edicts to the Royal Council, in which he argued for the abolition of the *corvée*, the suppression of commercial monopolies, and taxation of the nobility. His publication resulted in his forced resignation. The significance of this school of thought was primarily its orientation towards free trade and abolition of monopolies, allowing entrepreneurs to do business in a more or less competitive environment.

It was also, during this precise period, that the French business-man and banker Richard Cantillon (1680-1734) used the term "entrepreneur" for the first time in the modern meaning of the word, borrowing it from the battle field, where a military commander leading troops into battle was called an 'entrepreneur'.[14] His *Essai sur la nature du commerce en général* was published in 1755, 21 years after his death. This document can be considered as the first theory of entrepreneurship. He recognised three classes of economic agents: landowners, entrepreneurs and employees. Cantillon's entrepreneur exercised business engagements in the face of uncertainty. This view would much later, in 1965, be elaborated upon with Knight's publication *Risk, uncertainty and profit*. In the 1980s the International Labour Organisation (ILO) expressed similar views[15]. In the realm of the physiocrats the entrepreneur

---

13 Ibid., 130-131. Adam Smith characterised these forms of economic nationalism as the mercantile system, although in later studies by Gustav von Schmoller, mercantilism was assessed not to be an economic policy but in its innermost kernel was nothing more but 'state-making and national-economy-making' at the same time. Jean-Baptiste Colbert, principal minister under Louis XIV was a staunch supporter and implementer of this form of economic nationalism, also characterised as 'Colbertism'.

14 Hunt, E.S. & J.M. Murray, p. 132

15 Meredith, G.G., R.E. Nelson, P. Neck, *The practice of entrepreneurship*, International Labour Office, Geneva, 1982

was indeed a quantity to be taken seriously, as also the economist Jean-Baptiste Say (around 1800) remarked - copying the notion 'entrepreneur' from Richard Cantillon – stating that 'the entrepreneur shifts economic resources out of an area of lower into an area of higher productivity and greater yield'.[16] The ideas of Say, can also be seen as an understanding of the 'innovative capacity' that entrepreneurs should posses, in order to contribute effectively to the national economy.

Although Adam Smith had indeed contacts with the French physiocrats, his *Wealth of Nations*[17] published in 1776, only mentions the 'merchant' or 'manufacturer' to indicate the function of the entrepreneur. And although Smith wrote about a host of subjects related to the economy, he did not contribute in any form to theory-formation in the field of entrepreneurship. His merchants and manufacturers were only used in order to describe the economic processes and, clearly, his 'invisible hand' did not really allow interventions from the merchant, or entrepreneurial class. David Ricardo, another influential economist, often mentioned in conjunction with Adam Smith, did not develop theories related to entrepreneurship either. And the same can be said about Karl Marx, who approximately a century later than Smith (1867) wrote *Das Kapital*[18]. Although quite influential for entrepreneurs in the political-economic sense, also Marx did not contribute either to the development of entrepreneurial theory formation.

In the 18th and 19th centuries a lot of research was carried out in fields not directly related to the entrepreneurial person, but was related to methods and ways for manufacturing - and later industrial entrepreneurs, to help them manage their business affairs more effectively. The 19th century marks the 'Industrial Revolution', whereas the latter part of the 18th century can be seen as the prelude to it, a period in which 'economies of scale' became an important feature in the execution of businesses. And, although micro, small- and

---

16   Economist: Survey Innovation in Industry, Feb. 20th, 1999, p 6
17   Smith, A., *An Inquiry into the Nature and Causes of the Wealth of Nations*. Edited edition Toronto, 1937
18   Marx, K., *Het Kapitaal; een Kritische Beschouwing over de Economie; deel 1: Het Productieproces van het Kapitaal.* Translation by: Lipschits, I., Bussum 1970

medium-sized businesses have always been with us, much attention at that time was given to the phenomenon of larger companies, which - due to their complexity - were far more difficult to manage for the entrepreneur than smaller ones. As a consequence, we see a good number of researchers quite active in this period in developing scientific methods to support the entrepreneur in managing their large enterprises. In their view, the entrepreneurs were seen as 'managers' of complex businesses, rather than 'traders', and that therefore more weight was given to the fact that an entrepreneur should be some-one making use of modern scientific methods in production, in the application of inputs (in particular the factor labour) and not in the least in specific management methods.

So, in the 18th century a few Frenchmen carried out that type of research, among them M. Charles Augustus Coulomb, who made early experiments and observations on the amount of workmen could do in a day. His observations were first published in 1781 and republished in 1809 and 1821. It provided a support to the entrepreneur on making an effective use of the factor labour. In Coulomb's words: '...Thus the whole question reduces itself to a search for a way to combine the different degrees of force, speed and of time, so that a man with equal fatigue may furnish the greatest quantity of action'.[19] Others, such as M. Schulze and F. Gerstner made similar studies in 1773 and 1831 respectively.[20] These researchers were the predecessors of the school of thought that became know as 'Scientific Management'. Although much of the research was done in the later part of the 19th century, the subsequent publication appeared in the early 1960s.

To understand the research related to the advocacy of a systematic approach to the use of the factor labour, it might be helpful to briefly sketch the career of Frederick W. Taylor (1856-1915). Instead of starting his studies at Harvard for which he had already been admitted, he accepted in 1874 a job as a lathe operator, be-

---

[19] Hoagland, J. H., Charles Babbage: His life and Works in the Historical Evolution of Management Concepts (PhD dissertation) Ohio State University, Columbus, Ohio, 1994 in: Dale, E., *Readings in Management; landmarks and new frontiers,* New York 1965, p. 114

[20] Ibid. p. 113-114

cause of health problems. Within six years of starting in 1878, at the Midvale Steel Company, he progressed through the ranks of ordinary labourer, via floor supervisor, head maintenance and repair, head of the design department, head technical departments and, finally, to Chief Engineer. In the meantime, when his sense of sight improved, he followed courses at the university and got a degree in machine engineering.[21] Obviously, Taylor was known with all details of what actually happened on the work-floor and knew that his former colleagues frustrated systematically the production volume. He was also aware of a lot of animosity between workers and the management. Hence, Tailor wanted to replace inefficient work methodologies with 'objective scientific' norms for workers, instead of using subjective estimates. Simultaneously, he wanted to take away the existing animosity between worker and entrepreneur, as described in his publications.[22] As a manager/intrapreneur, Taylor's vision on entrepreneurship was formed on the work-floor going through all production departments. His idea, apparently, was that entrepreneurship can only be successful when applying new scientific and innovative methods, and therefore should be open to innovations of this kind. Another pioneering researcher of this kind, albeit it in a different scientific method, was Henri Fayol (1841-1925). He graduated in 1860 as mining engineer and joined the Commentry-Fourchambault Company, where he became Managing Director in 1888 and when he retired in 1918 he remained until his death the position of Director of the Company. As a very successful top manager of a public enterprise, he maintained that his success was not the result of any outstanding personal quality, but was due to the consistent application of certain management principles. These, which he outlined in his book *Administration industrielle et général* in 1916.[23] As with Taylor, also in Fayol's view, the successful top-manager/intrapreneur is the person who has the

---

21 Keunink, D. & D.J. Eppink, *Management en Organisatie; Theorie en Toepassing,* Leiden 1985, p. 451-453
22 Taylor, F.W., The Working Man and Labour Unions, from a series of lectures given at the Harvard Graduate School of Business Administration, Boston 1909-1914, in: Dale, E. Readings in *Management: landmarks and new frontiers,* New York 1965, p. 118-123
23 Fayol, H., *General and Industrial Management,* London 1949, p. 5-20

ability to make use of newly developed scientific methods. As we shall see in the following paragraph this idea seamlessly corresponds with that of Schumpeter, albeit focussed on the person of the entrepreneur, rather than on his function.

The first most explicit study about entrepreneurship was written in 1934 by the Austrian-American economist/sociologist Schumpeter, who visualised the entrepreneur as the key figure in economic development. He regarded entrepreneurship as 'the primary cause of economic development'[24] and also delineated its distinguished features and suggested societal conditions that promoted its appearance. Innovation, the carrying out of new combinations of the factors of production, constituted the entrepreneurial function for him, and these combinations comprised the qualitative economic changes, which he regarded as the essence of economic development.

The entrepreneur's role, according to Schumpeter, is not necessarily an entrepreneur in the original sense of the term, i.e. the man who undertakes the financial risks of a business, or the founder (although he often is). Instead he is the man who introduces new ways of doing things. Only entrepreneurs, he believed, can be said to produce true profits. Because of their innovations their costs are lower than those of others in the same industries; yet they can charge the same going price and thus achieve a net gain greater than is customary in their fields. This does not mean that businesses, that continue to do things in the same old way cannot make a 'profit' in the ordinary sense of the term, only that Schumpeter considers these profits to be more in the nature of quasi-rent or interest than true profits.

Schumpeter was the first to challenge classic economists, seeking to optimise existing resources within a stable environment, treating any disruption as an external force on a par with plagues, politics and weather. As Schumpeter saw it, a normal healthy economy was not one in equilibrium, but one that was disrupted by technological innovation, a process which he termed 'creative destruction'. Entrepreneurs created new wealth by destroying existing market

---

[24] P.H. Wilken, *Entrepreneurship; A comparative and Historical Study.* New Jersey, 1979, p. 57

structures. This view was confirmed by other researchers who had noticed 'long waves' of economic activity, notably a Russian economist, Nikolai Kondratieff, who drew attention in 1925, using data on prices, wages and interest rates, as well as industrial production and consumption drawn from France, Britain and the USA. Each of these long business cycles was unique, driven by entirely different clusters of industries. Typically, a long upswing in a cycle started when a new set of innovations came into general use, as happened with water power, textiles and iron in the late 18th century; railway and steel in the mid 19th century; and electricity, chemicals and the internal-combustion engine at the turn of the 20th century.

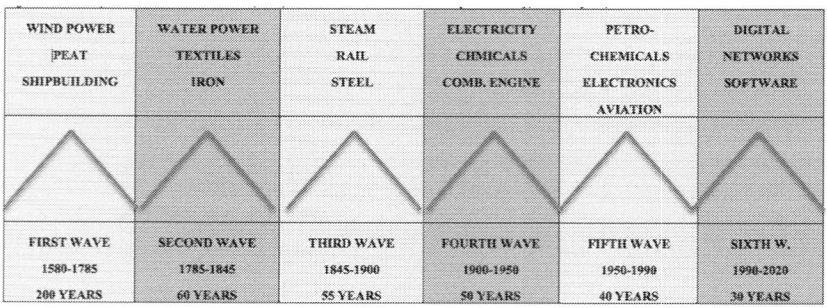

Figure 1: Schumpeter's waves acceleration; adapted from the Economist Survey in industry, February 20, 1999

The entrepreneur's role, as Schumpeter saw it, was to act as ferment in this process of creative destruction, allowing the economy to renew itself and bound onwards and upwards again.[25]

Other studies followed suit, each of them emphasising specific traits related to entrepreneurship. Approximately at the same time of the writings of Schumpeter, the sociologist Max Weber wrote his "Protestant Ethic". He articulated the significance of the Protestant - in particular the calvinistic - ethics for the entrepreneurial emergence and spirit.[26] The ideological/religious orientation con-

---

25 Economist: Survey Innovation in Industry, Feb 20, 1999, p. 7 and 8
26 M. Weber, *The Protestant ethic and the spirit of capitalism*. New York 1958 (originally published 1930)

stituted an organised set of beliefs about the world and enjoyed its adherents to behave in the mode as Weber described as 'worldly asceticism'.

As Weber put it: 'The fight against sex and wealth as expressly testified by the great apologist of Quakerism, Barclay, as well as by the Puritans, is not a fight against the rational acquisition of property, but against the irrational use of it. It was against ostensible forms of luxury as they were seen as a form of extreme abundance, instead of God's desired rational and utilitarian use of the same for the purposes of life of the individual and the community. The religious appreciation of restless, continuous, systematic, secular professional work as the absolutely highest ascetic means, should indeed conceivably be the most powerful lever of the specific view of life, which we denote here to be the 'spirit' of capitalism'.[27]

'The 'calling', which it incorporated, when heeded by its followers, resulted in the saving and the investment of capital and in entrepreneurial behaviours, although that was not its manifest intent'.[28] The major critique on his publication was related to his argument that protestantism had created capitalism[29], to which Weber responded that it would indeed be 'a foolish and doctrinaire thesis as that the spirit of capitalism (...) could only have arisen as the result of certain effects of the Reformation, or even that capitalism as an economic system is a creation of the Reformation... on the contrary'. He stated furthermore 'we only wish to ascertain whether and to what extent religious forces have taken part in the

---

27 M. Weber, Soziologie, Weltgeschichtliche Analysen, Politik, Alfred Kröner Verlag, Stuttgart 1965, p 370, taken from T.J. Kastelein, *Groei naar een industriele samenleving*, p. 65-66
28 Wilken, 1979, p. 14
29 Even in their most recent (1999) publication *A History of Business in Medieval Europe, 1200-1550*, the historians Hunt and Murray are still at odds with Weber's ideas, which 'are explicitly antithetical to our central argument, that the "spirit of capitalism" was alive and thriving throughout most of the Middle Ages', and they continue, 'Recognising the necessity of trade and traders to the proper functioning of human society, the church increasingly accepted the notion of unpredictability of gain and compensation for losses or 'damages' as legitimate practices....It is therefore important to stress that the church before 1550 (start of the Reformation) was neither prohibitionist with regard to business, nor was it an adherent of laissez faire; rather it stood in a kind of productive tension with the more unbridled forces of entrepreneurialism' p. 242-3

qualitative formation and the qualitative expansion over that spirit in the world, and what concrete aspects of our capitalistic culture can be traced to them.' In view of the tremendous confusion of the described interdependent influences among the material, the forms of social and political organisation, and the ideas current in the time of the Reformation, Weber commented 'we can only proceed by investigating whether and at what points certain correlations between forms of religious belief and practical ethics can be worked out. At the same time we shall as far as possible clarify the manner and the general direction in which, by virtue of those relationships, the religious movements have influenced the development of material culture'.[30]

In 1961 a very influential study appeared from David McClelland, titled *The Achieving Society*, followed in 1971 by his *Motivating Economic Achievement*. McClelland can be considered as the main representative of the "need-achievement" theory, another attempt to explain entrepreneurship. The theory holds that individuals having personality characteristics with a high 'need achievement', are especially likely to behave entrepreneurially. Therefore, if the average level of need-achievement in a society were relatively high, one would expect a relatively great amount of entrepreneurship in that society. Hence, entrepreneurship becomes the link between need-achievement and economic growth. Consequently, McClelland advocates increasing the level of need-achievement in a society in order to stimulate entrepreneurship, thus economic growth. The distinctive characteristics of high need achievements, as worked out by McClelland are: 'a) a preference for moderate risks and a propensity to work harder in such situations; b) a belief that one's personal efforts will be influential in the attainment of some goal and pleasure derived from this belief; c) a tendency to see the probability of success in attaining a goal as being relatively high; d) a need for feed-back regarding success or failure of one efforts; e) the capacity to plan ahead and to be particularly aware of the passage of time; f) an interest in excellence

---

30 Weber, M., Protestant Ethic, p 91-92 in: Hughes, H.S., *Consciousness and Society; The Reorientation of European Social Thought 1890-1930*, New York 1977, p. 319-320

for its own sake'.[31] In addition, he suggests that individuals with high need-achievement will not be motivated by monetary incentives, but that monetary rewards will constitute a symbol of achievement for them. Achievement will be their primary reward and in this he links his theory with that of the Protestant Ethics theory of Max Weber, which in his view should be seen as a special case of the need-achievement thesis.

There has been substantial criticism on the need-achievement thesis, which can be categorised into three main classes. 'First it has been claimed that the correlations between need-achievement and economic growth which McClelland found for the countries he studied are spurious. Second, there have been a variety of methodological criticisms, particularly of his indicators of economic growth and need-achievement. And third, he has been criticised for failure to consider negative evidence'.[32] In spite of that criticism, scholars do not belief that it has completely demolished the need-achievement theory; hence it is being treated as a potentially significant psychological factor promoting the emergence of entrepreneurship.

However, all modern theories that had been developed in the course of the first part of the 20th century had little effect on the growth of entrepreneurship. The economic growth of industrial nations of the world appeared to be driven by large industrial firms, whereas small firms were being driven into failure by the economies of scale of large firms. Entrepreneurship seemed to be a dead or dying phenomenon. Not the least of these pessimists was Schumpeter himself, who argued in his 1942 book *Capitalism, Socialism and Democracy* that entrepreneurship could not survive in the face of the ever larger industrial firms that monopolised innovation through well funded and organised research and development laboratories. This belief continued to flourish after World War II, since simple observations of industrial activity in the 1940s through the 1970s showed industrial firms growing ever larger, even to such an extent that John Galbraith in 1967

---

31   Wilken, 1979, p. 17
32   Ibid., p. 18

proposed that capitalist societies would evolve into three powerful groups, i.e. big businesses, big governments and big labour unions. Galbraith's 'new industrial state' was in fact devoid of entrepreneurs.[33]

Nonetheless, evidence gradually began to emerge that new firm formation and growth was an increasingly important part of overall economic activity and growth. In 1979, David Birch of the Massachusetts Institute of Technology (MIT) published statistics showing that from 1969 through 1976 entrepreneurs of small firms created over 81% of the net new jobs in the US economy. Subsequent research by the US Small Business Association revealed that entrepreneurs of small firms produced a disproportionate share of the net new jobs from 1976 through 1988.[34] The same pattern could also be observed in Western European countries, where flexible and innovative companies and entrepreneurs also played a leading role in the transition from a managerial- to a more entrepreneurial economy. Obviously, this caused renewed research in the phenomenon 'entrepreneurship'.

Since the 1960s Peter F. Drucker (Austrian born American) carried out fundamental research in the field of management, which comprised the development of management practices at various levels of the businesses, including that of the owner-manager-entrepreneur. In his book *Management,* Drucker identified two entrepreneurial and basic functions to be carried out in an enterprise, i.e. marketing and innovation.[35] In the years before World War II until the 1950s, marketing management and market-research were hardly developed, due to the fact that there was a relatively scarcity of product choice and a relatively low purchasing power as a result of both less developed economies in the West and the absence of consumer credit instruments. Products for these reasons were 'sold', rather than 'marketed'. However, the more mature the economy became,

---

33 Galbraith, J.K., The New Industrial State, New York, 1967, in: Bruce A. Kirchoff, 'The Dynamics of Ambitious Entrepreneurs' in EIM publication *Entrepreneurship in the Netherlands; Ambitious entrepreneurs: the driving force for the next millennium,* Zoetermeer, 1999, p. 4
34 Ibid., p. 4
35 Drucker, P., *'Management',* New York, 1977, p. 57-62

the more the purchasing power continued to increase, as well as the diversity in product ranges through innovation and fiercer competition. Hence, in order to survive as an enterprise, the entrepreneur required improved skills of a marketeer. So, in the words of Drucker: Marketing and innovation produce results; all the rest are 'costs'. Drucker is the first who made the linkage between marketing and innovation as two qualities, which are inextricably intertwined. Market-research and marketing, of which 'sales' is just one of its elements[36], are strong stimulators for innovation, i.e. in the development of new products or services, and - as a consequence - may also stimulate the use of newly developed raw materials (chemicals) or even other - more appropriate - organisational structures. In its turn, 'innovation' has to be marketed in order to bring it to the attention of the consumer. The entrepreneur is therefore seen as someone making use of opportunities, which the market offers and in doing so, whilst combining marketing and innovation smartly, he will acquire wealth, power and prestige.

The importance of the marketing concept is found back in the work of I.M.Kirzner. In his *Competition and Entrepreneurship*, he states that the entrepreneur should not be seen as disrupting the equilibrium in the market place, but as the one who benefits from the lack of that equilibrium, and by doing so promotes a new equilibrium.[37] As Kirzner remarks: '...the crucial element in entrepreneurship is the ability to see unexploited opportunities whose prior existence meant that the initial evenness of the circular flow was illusory - that, far from being a state of equilibrium, it represented a situation of disequilibrium inevitably destined to be disrupted'.[38] As Lesger rightly notices, Kirzner's stand means that both the innovators - the ones who first recognise profits of an 'above-equilibrium price' -,

---

36 Marketing in this sense comprises the so-called 4 Ps, i.e. Production (the right type of product to be manufactured), Price (setting a competitive price, which provides a reasonable profit), Promotion (the way the product will be advertised for what segment of the market) and Place (the type of distribution channel through which the product can be obtained); see also: Kotler, Ph., Marketing Management; Analysis, Planning and Control, New Jersey, 1980, Chapter 4, Assembling the Marketing Mix.
37 C. Lesger, *'Ondernemen en Ondernemerschap,* p. 61
38 I.M. Kirzner, *Competition and entrepreneurship*, Chicago/London, 1973, p127. Taken from C. Lesger, p. 61

as well as the imitators are considered to be entrepreneurs. We are talking here not so much of Schumpeter's 'creative destruction', but of a (perpetual) process to try to restore the market equilibrium. In conclusion, Kirzner differs from Drucker in that the former emphasizes creativity in the sense of being alert of market opportunities, whereas the latter sees the two elements - marketing and innovation - as the dual intertwined functions of entrepreneurship.

Frank Knight followed another avenue of that renewed research in entrepreneurship. In 1965 he described entrepreneurship primarily as a 'risk-taking' activity. As mentioned before Knight's publication *Risk, uncertainty and profit,* made a clear distinction between risk and uncertainty. In taking risks, he held that the probabilities of future events are known e.g. through analysis of the past experiences. Therefore, risks can be insured, which therefore looses its character of 'uncertainty', and hence will be of less influence on the profitability of the enterprise. Contrary, in case of 'uncertainties', the probabilities of future events are not known since each situation in which these occur is unique. Such a real 'uncertainty' cannot be insured. Subsequently, there are consequences for profits and losses, hence for undertaking entrepreneurial activities.[39] Also Von Mises (1881-1972) qualifies 'uncertainty' to be the basic feature of the economy. However, he goes that far as to consider any economic actor to be an entrepreneur. Decisions about the production process, such as the choice of the most appropriate technology, the marketing function and other matters, which are usually ascribed to the entrepreneur, are in his view, the work of a 'promoter'.[40]

Interestingly, in the 1980s the International Labour Organisation (ILO), also presented the view that entrepreneurship was to a great extent determined by the 'risks' (in general), which the entrepreneur was willing to take; in that view ILO did not distinguish between Knight's elements of 'uncertainty' and 'risk'. Nonetheless, their view is quite interesting as it was based on empirical research carried out throughout the world, with a strong emphasis on entrepreneurship development in both developing- and emerging

---

39 C, Lesger, *'Ondernemen en Ondernemerschap'*, p. 59
40 C. Lesger, *'Ondernemen en Ondernemerschap'*, p. 59

economies. Since emerging economies are generally more insecure as compared to developed economies, the view as expressed by ILO in their publication *The practice of entrepreneurship*, was that entrepreneurs were basically 'risk-takers', albeit "calculated' risk-takers.[41] Entrepreneurs enjoy the excitement of a challenge, but they don't gamble. According to the authors, 'entrepreneurs avoid low-risk situations because there is a lack of challenge and avoid high- risk situations because they want to succeed. They like *achievable* challenges'.[42] Another important feature of being entrepreneurial, as shown by ILO, is the somewhat idealistic notion that the entrepreneur should provide something of value to others. 'If you (the would-be entrepreneur) work to help other people, to raise their standards of living and to improve on their lives, you (the entrepreneur) will be serving the needs of society. This is the meaning of being an entrepreneur'.[43] One can hardly escape the impression that the latter view has emerged as a consequence of the overall objectives of the ILO, i.e. to improve the political, human and economic standards of the world.

This view was sharply criticised by William Baumol. In an article which he wrote in 1990 for the journal of Political Economy with the title *Entrepreneurship: Productive, Unproductive, and Destructive*[44], he held the basic hypothesis that, 'while the supply of entrepreneurs varies among societies, the productive contribution of the society's entrepreneurial activities, varies much more because of their allocation between productive activities such as innovation, and largely unproductive activities such as rent seeking or organised crime. This allocation is heavily influenced by the relative payoffs society offers to such activities'.[45] This implies, according to Baumol, that policy can influence the allocation of entrepreneurship more effectively than it can influence mere supply of entrepreneurship. For his study he used historical

---

41 Meredith, G.G., R.E. Nelson, P. Neck, *The practice of entrepreneurship,* International Labour Office publication of ILO, Geneva, 1982, p. 25-36
42 Ibid., p. 27
43 Ibid., p 7
44 W.J. Baumol, in Journal of Political Economy, 1990, 98(5):893-921; copyright to Journal of Business Venturing II, p 3-22
45 Ibid., p 3

evidence from ancient Rome, early China and the Middle Ages and Renaissance in Europe. His study settles with the idea that entrepreneurship would only exert to achieve positive effects to the economy and society at large. Periods of economic stagnation or decline are most of the time explained as a decrease in entrepreneurial spirit and mentality or in number of entrepreneurs. Baumol, however, points out that these explanations are based on an incomplete understanding as to what the entrepreneur envisages, which is not the well-being of society, but rather his own well-being.

> *'...entrepreneurs are always with us and always play some substantial role. But there are a variety of roles among which the entrepreneur's efforts can be reallocated, and some of those roles do not follow the constructive and innovative script that is conventionally contributed to that person. Indeed, at times the entrepreneur may even lead a parasitical existence that is actually damaging to the economy. How the entrepreneurs act at a given time and place depends heavily on the rules of the game - the reward structure in the economy - that happen to prevail.* [46]

In Baumol's view, the entrepreneur is the person who is ingenious in finding ways that add to his own wealth, power and prestige and it is therefore to be expected that not all of them will be overly concerned with whether an activity that achieves these goals (wealth, power, prestige) adds much or little to the social product, or for that matter, even whether it is an actual impediment to production. Posing himself the question what influences the flow of entrepreneurial talents among Schumpeter's innovative activities to be undertaken by the entrepreneur, Baumol proposes to extend that list with innovations that are not necessarily productive, e.g. an innovative form of rent-seeking. Finally, Baumol is of the opinion that there are 'identifiable means by which the rules of the game can be changed effectively (…), there exist (in principle) testable means that promise to induce entrepreneurs to shift their atten-

---

46   Ibid., p 6

tions in productive directions, *without any major change in their ultimate goals*.[47]

This approach corresponds handsomely with the issue of institutional change and economic performance, as illuminated by North in his *Institutions, Institutional Change and Economic Performance* (1990). He holds the view that institutions that are able to create the enabling (legal and commercial) environment for organisations and their entrepreneurs, are at the very core of the economic performance in a country. However, it should be noted that, apart from institutional changes that could be implemented right away in adapting Baumol's rules of the game, it should be noted that institutional changes might also include adaptations in culture which, according to North, takes a relatively long period of time, if it can be changed at all.[48] North develops an analytical framework for explaining the ways in which institutions and institutional change affect the performance of economies and businesses. His central focus is on the problem of human cooperation and coordination, particularly related to actions, which permits economies to capture the gains from trade that were the key to Adam Smith's Wealth of Nations.[49]

In his study North makes a crucial distinction between institutions and organizations. Institutions (local- and supranational governments, agencies, etc.) provide the basic structure by which human beings, including entrepreneurs, throughout history have created order and attempted to reduce uncertainty in exchange. These institutions can be formal, like e.g. the creation of the Constitution (at a certain time) or usury law, including property rights, bankruptcy laws, which are developed over a period of time. They can also create informal regulations, such as conventions and code of behaviour depended on culture, which is developed over a relatively long period of time. In addition, there

---

[47] Ibid., p 20; measures of deregulation and more rational anti-trust rules can do a lot, as remarked by Baumol and as a matter of fact already applied in a number of countries with transitional economies.
[48] D.C. North, *Institutions, Institutional Change and Economic Performance*, Cambridge, 1998
[49] Ibid. , p. viii.

are organisations, distinct from institutions, which include political bodies (political parties, a city council, a regulatory agency), economic bodies (enterprises, firms, trade associations, cooperatives, etc), social bodies (churches, clubs, athletic associations), and educational bodies (schools, universities, vocational training centres, etc.). The institutional framework fundamentally influences what types of organisations come into existence and how they evolve, are fundamentally influenced by the institutional framework. Conversely, the types of organizations influence how the institutional framework evolves. Looking specifically at enterprises, these engage in purposeful activity and in that role are agents and shapers of institutional change. Enterprises are designed by their creators (the entrepreneurs) to maximise wealth, income, or other objectives defined by the opportunities afforded by the institutional structure of society. In the course of pursuing these objectives, enterprises incrementally alter the institutional structure. These alterations, however, are not always productive, which is reason why institutions vary widely in their consequences for economic performance. Some economies develop institutions that produce growth and development, whereas other economies develop institutions that produce stagnation. A case in point as demonstrated by North is the historical development of England and Spain: in the former an institutional framework evolved that permitted the complex impersonal exchange necessary for political stability and to capture the potential economic gains of modern technology. In the latter, personalistic relationships where still the key to much of the political and economic exchange. They are neither a consequence of an evolving institutional framework that produces neither political stability nor a consistent realisation of the potential of modern technology.[50]

North also puts emphasis on the issue of "transaction costs", where he states that the cost of products is not only limited to the character of the goods (quality, quantity, composition, distribution, etc.) but also relates to guarantee that all parties stick to the rules of the transaction, as well as to the enforcement of the same. Together with the technology employed to create goods, institutions

---
50   Ibid. , p. 117

determine transaction and transformation costs and hence the profitability and feasibility of engaging in economic activity. Low transaction costs are essential for the development of a sound economy and North allocates a central role to institutions in decreasing these costs, as they diminish uncertainty and are able to create a stable (but not necessarily efficient) structure to human interaction.[51]

Getting back to the development of entrepreneurship, the mutual relationship between institutions and organizations is underscored particularly, when the entrepreneur has to carry out specific activities in order to achieve his business objectives. This may include devising and discovering markets, to evaluate products and product techniques and to make an optimum use of the ability and guide the actions of their workers or employees. The kind of information and knowledge required by the entrepreneur to deal with, are in good part dependent on a particular institutional context. That context will not only shape the internal organization and determine the extent of vertical integration and governance structure in an enterprise, but will also determine the pliable margins that offer the greatest promise in maximising the enterprise's objectives. Therefore, we need to examine the institutional context to see what kind of demand from entrepreneurs exist for different kinds of knowledge, skills, intermediary support structures, financial instruments, legal and fiscal incentives, and the like.

In a way, North confirms the findings of Paul Wilken who made an historical comparative analysis of entrepreneurship in 1979 under the title *Entrepreneurship; A Comparative and Historical Study*. He formulated an analytical approach for determining the significance of entrepreneurship in socio-economic change and development and analysed both economic and non-economic (social, political and psychological) conditions active in the emergence of entrepreneurship. In the study he analysed comparatively five different societies that achieved industrialisation during the 18th and

---

51 Ibid., p.6. As Lesger rightfully remarks, the addition 'but not necessarily efficient' is important, as there may be institutions that are indeed able to diminish uncertainty, however, hardly allow transactions in an efficient manner (over-bureaucratisation or repressive government institutions). See: C. Lesger, *Ondernemen en ondernemenrschap* p. 70 in: Davids. C.A. c.s., Kapitaal, ondernemerschap en beleid (Amsterdam 1996)

19th centuries (England, France, Prussia, Japan and the USA) and one that did not (Russia). His main findings where that the development of entrepreneurship did not take place independently and that economic and non-economic factors each constituted necessary conditions for the emergence of entrepreneurship. The comparative analysis underpinned specifically the importance of the role of the state in creating an enabling environment for growth and development of entrepreneurship. This conclusion is analysed by North in a more explicit fashion when he holds 'institution development' - often a state-related activity - to be an important determinant for the entrepreneur to create a business organization as a vehicle to carry out entrepreneurship.

Finally, the Dutch-based Economic Institute of Small and Medium Enterprises (EIM) did research in entrepreneurship. In its most important publication on the topic *Entrepreneurship, Economic Growth and What Links Them Together,* the authors elaborate on entrepreneurship at the individual level, at the firm level and at the aggregate level of industries, regions and national economies. 'At the individual level entrepreneurship requires certain skills and attitudes, but predominantly it implies action. Entrepreneurial action takes us to the firm level. Entrepreneurs need a vehicle by which they can transform their ambitions into actions. A small firm, in which the entrepreneur has a controlling stake, provides such a vehicle. A larger firm mimics smallness (using organisational forms like business units), to introduce corporate entrepreneurship'.[52] At the aggregate level, according to the authors, a process of competition between various new ideas and initiatives, such as innovative actions, takes place, continuously leading to the survival and emergence of the most viable firms and industries. In this they also relate the dynamics of the processes to cultural values, incentives, competition rules and institutions, hence are quite close to North's viewpoints.

---

52 Wennekers, S., Roy Thurik & Folkert Buis, *Entrepreneurship, Economic Growth and What Links Them Together*, Strategic Study EIM, Zoetermeer, 1997, p. 7

2.2. Mainstream of entrepreneurship theory

When going through nearly three centuries of research into mainstream views of entrepreneurship theory formation, five major mainstreams can be recognised. These five mainstream views are complementary and as we have seen many researchers cover more than just one aspect.

The first view, represented by Cantillon, Knight, Von Mises and the ILO, emphasizes the entrepreneur as the *'risk-taker'*. A differentiation is made between risk and uncertainty. 'Risk' in the entrepreneurial meaning is a unique event and therefore offers profit (or loss) opportunities for the entrepreneur, whereas uncertainties are events which are insurable, hence not belonging to the domain of the real risk-taking entrepreneur. The ILO introduces the notion of 'calculated' risks, indicating that risk in the entrepreneurial sense should not be perceived as a form of gambling.

The second mainstream view, represented by Schumpeter, Drucker, Baumol, puts the *innovative ability* of the entrepreneur central in entrepreneurship. It concentrates on the entrepreneur as an agent of creative destruction. It centres on the innovative function of entry (emerging entrepreneurs) and exit (bankruptcies). This function implies that markets (unconsciously) seek equilibrium, but that due to entry and exit, such equilibrium is never attained. In this mainstream view the entrepreneurial entry (emerging enterprises) and exit (bankruptcies) is seen as a constant search for the best product and process specification for a particular moment in time (trial and error). Drucker adds to it the notion of *'marketing'* as being a function inextricably intertwined with innovation, whereas Baumol emphasises also the unproductive- and even, for the society, harmful entrepreneurial activities to the ones already identified by Schumpeter.

The third mainstream view, represented by Kirzner, and partly both Drucker and Baumol, emphasises the *relationship between the entrepreneur and the market*. The entrepreneur is not seen as the person to disrupt the equilibrium of the market, but the one who benefits from the opportunities offered due to the lack of that equilibrium. The relationship signifies a process of constantly trying to restore a new equilibrium. Entrepreneurs combine resources to fulfil currently unsatisfied needs or to improve market inefficiencies or deficiencies.

The *psychological tradition*, represented by Weber and McClelland, focuses on religious zeal and the psychological need for achievement can be considered the fourth mainstream view on entrepreneurship. It suggests, that individuals with high need-achievement will not necessarily be motivated by monetary incentives, but that monetary rewards constitute a symbol of achievement for them.

Finally, the fifth mainstream view is related to *institution development*, strongly represented by North and to some lesser degree also by Wilken, Baumol and EIM. Institutions connect the past with the present and the future so that history is the sum of many incremental steps of institutional evolution in which the historical performance of economies - and development in entrepreneurship - can only be understood as a part of a sequential story. Institution development also includes the 'rules of the game' (procedures, regulations, laws, etc.) as set by governments or other representative bodies that emerged voluntarily from the enterprising private sector, such as employers' organisations, trade associations, and the like.

Next to the traditions in entrepreneurial theory formation, there is also another way of looking at entrepreneurship, by defining the typology of the same. In a research carried out in 1984 by SMO[53] among approximately 4.100 entrepreneurs in eleven countries, the two authors distinguished three types of entrepreneurs: person-oriented, enterprise-oriented entrepreneurs, and those that hold the middle ground between theses two[54]

The SMO researchers framed the first typology as *'person-oriented'* entrepreneurship, which stands for someone who is particularly dutiful and industrious with a high sense of responsibility towards his or her dependants, the family. They make reliable productions, are notorious problem solvers and are looking for security; their behaviour is usually risk avoiding. Entrepreneurs belonging to this category are good marketeers and are generally matured and older

---

53 Stichting Maatschappij en Onderneming, The Hague
54 Huisman H & W.J. de Ridder, *Vernieuwend Ondernemen*, SMO publication, The Hague, 1984 p. 24-31

people. In the 'Schumpeterian' sense they are more 'managers' than they are 'entrepreneurs'. According to the survey, 29% of Dutch entrepreneurs are 'person-oriented', whereas 44% is risk avoiding. (In the USA these figures were 31% and 21% respectively; for Germany the figures were 37% and 48%, and for the UK: 38% and 19%)[55]

The second typology is described as *'enterprise-oriented'* entrepreneurship, in which the attainment for family wealth and achievement is less outspoken. Their most important feature is the search for adventure. They are the real 'Schumpeterian' entrepreneurs, who are looking for opportunities and challenges; they are risk-takers and are often highly innovative. Entrepreneurs belonging to this category are relatively young, are less planning oriented and are usually active in young businesses. The survey indicated that 37% of the Dutch entrepreneurs were 'enterprise-oriented', whereas risk-taking attitudes were found with 22% of them. (In the USA these figures were 30% and 38% respectively; for Germany these figures were 21% and 13%, and for the UK: 23% and 35%)

The third typology holds the *middle between the two other categories*. According to the survey, they represent in the Netherlands 34% of those that are both 'person-oriented' and 'enterprise-oriented', whereas a same percentage (34%) hovers between risk-taking and risk-avoiding, the ones that probably only take 'very' calculated risks, in the way as described in the ILO publications.

2.3. Definitions of entrepreneurship

In the wake of theory formation on entrepreneurship, various authors as well as actors in the field of entrepreneurship development (researchers, trainers, advisers, business development agencies and the like) have tried to summarise their findings in working definitions. The advantage of defining entrepreneurship is of course that one concentrates in a few sentences the very core of entrepreneurship, hence makes it recognisable vis-à-vis other professions. Furthermore, it may also distinguish, exclude or include certain currents or schools

---

55   Ibid., graph 1, p. 30

of thought in the notion 'entrepreneurship'. For the purpose of this study we have therefore made an inventory of the most prevailing definitions of entrepreneurship, with the objective to select and/or adapt one that will be used during this particular study.

The definition used by the International Labour Organisation says: *'Entrepreneurs are people who have the ability to see and evaluate business opportunities; to gather the necessary resources to take advantage of them; and to initiate appropriate action to ensure success*[56] The emphasis in the definition is on evaluating business opportunities in the market in view of limiting the risk-taking factor as much as possible ('calculated risk' principle). It does not take innovative aspects into consideration, which have proven to be so important in entrepreneurship.

Entrepreneurship as defined by OECD (Organisation for Economic Cooperation and Development) is defined as: '*the dynamic process of identifying economic opportunities and acting upon them by developing, producing and selling goods and services*'.[57] This definition has a very strong bias on the importance of marketing as more or less the sole determinant of successful entrepreneurship and may be too narrowly defined for the purpose of this study.

For his study on entrepreneurship, Paul Wilken used the definition in which entrepreneurship is *'the combining of factors of production to initiate changes in the production of goods'*.[58] This definition lacks references to major functions as we have seen, i.e. Innovation and marketing and therefore would not serve the purpose of this study as well.

American researchers, Hébert and Link have proposed a synthetic definition of who an entrepreneur is and what he does: *'the entrepreneur is someone who specialises in taking responsibility for and making judgmental decisions that affect the location, form and the use of goods, resources, or institutions'.*[59] This definition does not give sufficient attention to the dynamics of perceiving and creating new economic

---

56 Meredith, G.G., a.o., *The practice of entrepreneurship*, p. 3
57 Taken from Sander Balje a.o., as quoted in: Is Dutch entrepreneurship Dynamic Enough, in :'*Entrepreneurship in The Netherlands*' , EIM publication, Zoetermeer 1998, p. 35
58 Paul Wilken, p 60
59 Wennekers, S., R. Thurik, F. Buis, *Entrepreneurship, Entrepreneurship, Economic Growth and what Links Them Together*, EIM Publication, Zoetermeer, 1997, p 19

opportunities and the competitive dimensions of entrepreneurship.

We are turning now to the definition, which has been developed by EIM. It sees entrepreneurship as *'the ability and willingness of individuals, both on their own and within organisations, to:*

- *Perceive and create new economic opportunities (new products, new production methods, new organisational schemes and new product-market-combinations);*

- *Introduce their ideas in the market, in the face of uncertainty and other obstacles, by making decisions on location, form and the use of resources and institutions;*

- *Compete with others for a share of that market.'*[60]

Entrepreneurship as it has been defined in the EIM definition is operational at the individual level. It implies personal traits or attitudes such as open-mindedness and alertness, courage and acceptance of risk, ambition and perseverance. It also requires many skills, among them marketing. Most indispensable however are the entrepreneurial functions, particularly in the field of autonomous decision-making and innovation.

This study does not follow the opinion as expressed by Von Mises, who considers everyone to be an entrepreneur who, in one way or another, is involved in the economic process.[61] In this book, though, activities in primary agricultural production will not be dealt with, although it is appreciated that also in the farmers' communities the notion of entrepreneurship is certainly not at all misplaced. What may be essential in carrying out entrepreneurship is 'adding value' to either raw materials, semi-finished products and finished products, including trade and all other sorts of services, such as transport, packaging, printing, but also information technology, consulting- and training services, thus those activities

---

60   Wennekers, S., R Thurik, F. Buis, *Entrepreneurship, Economic Growth and What Links Them Together*, EIM Publication, Zoetermeer 1997, p. 5
61   Lesger, p. 59

related to forward- and backward linkages. Hence, central in this research will be the entrepreneur who is starting and running his or her business; the person who each and every time has to make the decision in what way to employ investments for innovations, and what risks to take in the market that may highly affect the financial position of himself and his firm.

By doing so, the definition of entrepreneurship as has been developed by EIM will be used, since all the important ingredients of entrepreneurship have been taken into consideration. Hence the definition to be employed in this study will be to consider entrepreneurship as *the ability and willingness of individuals, both on their own and within organisations, to: a) perceive and create new economic opportunities (new products, new production methods, new organisational schemes and new product-market-combinations); b) introduce their ideas in the market, in the face of uncertainty and other obstacles, by making decisions about location, form and the use of resources and institutions; c) compete with others for a share of that market.*

3. DIMENSIONS IN ENTREPRENEURSHIP

3.1. Overview

In the previous chapter five mainstreams views in the theory formation of entrepreneurship have been identified. These are related to:

1. *Uncertainty and risk* that confront the entrepreneur on a daily basis and his way in the decision-making processes as well as the way he deals with it.
2. *Innovative actions* to be undertaken as an entrepreneur in order to distinguish his business organization from others, hence to deal effectively with competition.
3. *Market-orientation* as an indispensable element to determine the success or failure of a business.
4. *Psychological factors* such as belief-systems or need for achievement (ambition) motivating the entrepreneur.
5. *Institution development* and performance created by governments and entrepreneurs themselves -directly or indirectly - in order to regulate cooperation and reduce uncertainties.

An addtional theoretical approach was presented which was related to *the orientation of the entrepreneur* to either the persons for which he is working, or the orientation towards the enterprise for which he or she feels responsible. In the person-oriented entrepreneurship, the entrepreneur has a high sense of responsibility towards the dependants, the family or the workers. Such includes also a highly industrious and dutiful standard towards the fulfilment of the tasks be performed. Enterprise-oriented entrepreneurship inclines to the search for adventure, innovation, marketing, uncertainty, in fact, the entrepreneurship as Schumpeter saw it. A third distinction was the mix between the person- and the enterprise-orientation.

The above mentioned five mainstream views plus the three 'orientation' approaches towards entrepreneurship have been converted into 4 dimensions of theory formation, which will serve the analytical tools for analysing 'Early Dutch Entrepreneurship'.

These four dimensions are:

1. Opportunity conditions,
2. Institutional development, either initiated by the state or by the private business sector,
3. Dominant socio-cultural factors affecting entrepreneurship and
4. The personal characteristics of entrepreneurs.

Each of these four dimensions can in its turn be subdivided into a number of factors or characteristics to be examined during the three historical sub-periods of trade capitalism. This will provide us with an image of entrepreneurship in that specific time frame. By doing so we hope to identify the qualitative difference in dimensions at play from one historical period to another, and in what way these have contributed - in a positive or negative way - to the growth and development of entrepreneurship in each of the selected historical periods. The research may provide a deeper insight into the historical process of developing entrepreneurship; an entrepreneurship that economists see as the key element of economic growth and development.

3.2. Dimensions and factors to be examined

The four dimensions[62] as are mentioned above will be analysed by applying a number of factors or characteristics, as will be elaborated in the now following paragraphs. In the chapters 5, 6, 7 and 8 all these sub-factors – at least those that are relevant - will be applied when analysing each of the three sub-periods of trade capitalism.

3.2.1. Opportunity conditions for entrepreneurship

---

62 The concept of applying dimensions in measuring entrepreneurship is taken from: Wilken, P.H., Entrepreneurship; A Comparative and Historical Study, Norwood, 1979

Obviously, opportunity conditions in a certain region are of prime importance in the development of entrepreneurship. When assessing these opportunities one has to look to various factors, that determine the degree of economic development, such as the following:

Quantity of factor inputs

Economists have identified four factors of production: land, labour, capital and technology, which constitute inputs for the entrepreneurial role.[63] In this study, 'technology' is meant to be the actual techniques used to produce a good. The demand for and the supply of these production factors are highly correlated with the quality of entrepreneurial performance. Subsequently, this determines to quite some extent the significance of the level of success or failure in entrepreneurship for the entire economy.

Quality of factor inputs

The major effect from the quality of factor inputs will be upon productivity, which will influence the cost per unit produced by the entrepreneur. The greater the quality of factor inputs, the greater their productivity, the lower the cost per unit. The degree of productivity of technology, labour and raw material will be of greatest significance and an important determinant in the level of performance of the entrepreneur.

Size and composition of markets

The market size and composition will be major determinants of the amount of reward an entrepreneur can anticipate in a situation. Normally, the greater the size of the market, the greater the potential reward is. But market composition must also be taken into account. The effective demand of the market for manufactured goods or services must be appropriate for the goods and services that an entrepreneur is able to produce. And the number of competitors vying

---

63 The Schumpeter factor 'innovation' should be part of that but will be dealt with separately as part of the personal characteristics of the entrepreneur (see 3.2.4)

for that market will be a significant factor as well. Possible responses of entrepreneurs to this situation may be to try to increase the size of the existing market by cutting the cost of their goods, by improving their quality, by diversifying into the production of goods more in accord with the taste of the market (innovation). Another approach of the entrepreneur may be to find new markets either within an untapped segment of their own society or in other societies (exports). If entrepreneurs make any of these responses, then it is probable that entrepreneurship will have a positive causal influence on economic growth and development in general and to their personal benefits, such as power, wealth and prestige in particular.

3.2.2 The institution development dimension

Institutions, the rules of the game in a society at a given time, affect the performance of the economies, hence the performance of the entrepreneur. Through devised constraints, such as constitutions, laws and conventions, it shapes the interaction between human beings and reduces the uncertainties of everyday life. Through legislation, it can influence opportunity conditions, related to capital, labour, raw materials and the market. In addition, it may also influence socio-cultural factors, which are supposedly significant for the emergence of entrepreneurship, such as pronouncements and policies to provide entrepreneurship their legitimacy or to (actively) support an ideology conducive towards entrepreneurship. Finally, the state may exert certain power-political values, by e.g. waging territorial wars, for the sake of territorial gain only, which may damage economic and socio-economic conditions temporarily or for even a long period of time. The governmental role has been described as being one of three possible types, i.e.: protective, promotional and/or corrective. A government may protect the entrepreneurs within a society from competition, e.g. by allowing monopolies; it may directly or indirectly promote entrepreneurial behaviour, e.g. by creating an appropriate legal system; or it may correct deficiencies, e.g. through infrastructural improvements as road, canals, etc., in order to enhance the accessibility of markets.

It should be noticed, though, that the role of the government in this regard is not always necessarily positive. Instead of protecting entrepreneurs, it may attack them; instead of promoting entrepreneurship it may create barriers to it; and instead of correcting deficiencies in the economic system, it may reinforce them; instead of levying reasonable tax, it may excessively extract revenues from them. Hence, both positive and negative aspects of the role of the government need to be considered. Obviously, the government's role in institution development is a top-down process.

In addition, institutional development also takes place as a bottom-up process in society by various peer groups, among them entrepreneurs, for the purpose of serving their specific own interest. Private sector institutions, which also have an influence on the transactional costs of business organisations, include intermediate support organisations for enterprises, such as e.g. employers'- and trade organisations, labour unions, branch organisations, training-, consulting- and research institutions, innovation- and technology centres, and the like.

3.2.3 Socio-cultural dimensions

Culture, as defined by Hofstede[64], is the collective mental programming which distinguishes one group or category of people from another. This programming influences patterns of thinking, which are reflected in the meaning people attach to various aspects of life and which become crystallised in the institutions of society. This does not imply that everyone in a given society is programmed in the same way: wide differences between individuals will be found. Statements of culture do not describe 'reality': rather they refer to a construct derived from the observation of differing behaviours and attitudes from systems of values. In this respect a number of socio-cultural factors have been identified. These are directly correlated with entrepreneurial development in a society. The degree of importance, attached to each of these norm and values, may

---

64 Hofstede, G. , *Culture's Consequences; International Differences in Work-Related Values*, London 1980.

however vary from one historical period to the other, as values and norms tend to change over time. Hence, important factors of the socio-cultural dimension include the following ones.

Legitimacy of entrepreneurship

This describes the degree of approval or disapproval of entrepreneurial behaviour as part of the norms and values within a socio-cultural setting. A normative system, which determines the degree of legitimacy of entrepreneurship, will be a significant factor in the probability of the emergence of entrepreneurship, because entrepreneurs will be more likely to emerge in settings in which the legitimacy is high.

Social mobility

This factor involves the degree of mobility, both social and geographical, and the nature of mobility channels within a situation. It refers to the "openness" and "flexibility" in role relationships within the social structure of a society. Existing elites may play a significant role in influencing the degree of mobility. Typically, they will attempt to maintain their position against entrepreneurs attempting to be upwardly mobile.

Marginality

A prominent argument presented by many scholars is that entrepreneurship is often promoted by social marginality. Individuals or groups on the periphery of a given social system are believed to provide the personnel to fill entrepreneurial roles. They may be drawn from religious, cultural, ethnic, or migrant minority groups. Their marginal social position is generally believed to have psychological effects, which make entrepreneurship a particular attractive alternative for them. In situations in which entrepreneurial legitimacy is low, mainstream actors will be attracted to non-entrepreneurial roles, and entrepreneurial roles will be relegated to "marginals".

Social integration

However, if marginality is too great, so that individuals or groups are too far removed from the network of relationships within a social system, then entrepreneurship will not be promoted. According to scholars in this field, it appears that social integration will facilitate entrepreneurship if there are ties to groups or societal sectors that are supportive of entrepreneurship.

Security

This factor may have either economic or socio-economic bases. This type of security essentially involves protection from uncertainties, social disapproval, and political interference. Although entrepreneurship includes taking 'calculated risks', these risks mainly refer to the financial and economic results of doing business. It seems reasonable, though, that if individuals are fearful of losing their economic assets or being subjected to various negative sanctions, they will not be inclined to increase their insecurity by behaving entrepreneurially. Hence, negative business results may have a negative effect on entrepreneurship performance.

Ideology

Several prominent sociological theorists have stressed the importance of some kind of entrepreneurial ideology. Weber's Protestant Ethics is a case in point. Wilken defines an ideology as 'a comprehensive organised set of beliefs regarding the nature of the world and the behaviour that should be enacted within it'[65]. An ideology supportive of entrepreneurship may be specially oriented to entrepreneurial behaviour, or its content (e.g. a religious ethic, or philosophical conviction) may indirectly, and perhaps unintentionally, encourage individuals to behave entrepreneurially.

Need achievement

---

[65] Wilken p. 14

According to McClelland, distinctive characteristics of a high need-achievement in a society are, if individuals have:

1. a preference for moderate risks and a propensity to work harder in such situations,
2. a belief that one's personal efforts will be influential in the attainment of some goal and pleasure derived from this belief,
3. a tendency to perceive the probability of success in attaining a goal as being relatively high,
4. a need for feed-back regarding success of failure of one's efforts,
5. the capacity to plan ahead and to be particularly aware of the passage of time,
6. an interest in excellence for its own sake.

If the average level of these need-achievement characteristics in a society is relatively high, one would expect a relatively high amount of entrepreneurship in that society. In addition, McClelland suggests that a society with a high need-achievement will not primarily be motivated by monetary incentives, but that monetary rewards constitute a symbol of achievement[66].

3.2.4 Personal characteristics of entrepreneurs

This dimension includes major characteristics, which are believed to be strong determinants in the behaviour and significance of entrepreneurship. The first characteristic is that of *'identity'*, explaining who carries out the entrepreneurial role; providing insight into the socio-cultural background of the entrepreneurs. The second characteristic is the *'personal drive'* of the entrepreneur; it refers to the degree of expansionism in terms of extending the existing market or developing new ones. It also refers to the degree of innovative capacity, related to markets and the deployment of labour and capital. Finally, the *personal traits* of

---
66   McClelland 1961 in Wilken p. 17

the entrepreneurs, constituting entrepreneurship are to be considered as well.

Identity of entrepreneurs

Below a number of aspects can be distinguished in clarifying the identity issue of entrepreneurs.

Individual vs. Collective. The entrepreneurial role may be carried out by one individual, or it may be divided among a number of individuals, or it may be carried out by a corporate actor (an organisation). The transition from individual to collective entrepreneurship has been a major historical trend, representing a response to capital limitations of individual actors and to increases in capital requirements for many entrepreneurial actions[67]. So the causal significance of entrepreneurship in a certain historical period may be due to a greater or lesser willingness of individuals to join others in entrepreneurial endeavours.

Mainstream vs. Outsider. The 'outsider' can be a foreign entrepreneur, born in and a citizen of a society other than the one in which he plays the entrepreneurial role. But he can also be a person coming from a non-dominant minority group in the society in which he acts as an entrepreneur. In various studies it has been suggested that 'outsider'-entrepreneurs will be more willing to take risks because of their marginal situation, as compared to the 'mainstream'-entrepreneur.

Family vs. Non-family. Extensive literature suggests, that entrepreneurs belonging to the same family are likely to be non-expansive and non-innovative. Much of this literature refers to the "family firm", which Hagen describes as being operated for the benefit of the family, managed by the senior family member, dependent on relatives for capital, and recruiting managerial personnel only from within the family membership[68]. The failure of talent to be inherited

---

[67] Due to the emergence of small businesses and globalisation there has been a trend during the 'Total Capitalism' period of 'clustering', in which entrepreneurs are co-operating in processing, producing and marketing these products or services so as to increase their competitiveness. However, forms of clustering also took place in other 'capitalistic' periods

[68] Hagen, E. E., *The Economics of Development*, Homewood, Ill.: Dorsey, 1968 , in Wilken 1979, p. 67

or the lack of interest in entrepreneurship among future generations of the family, are believed to be the main reasons for this negative entrepreneurial orientation.

Socio-economic origin. Merchants often have been regarded as especially likely to become industrial entrepreneurs, because of certain advantages they bring to the entrepreneurial role, such as capital, knowledge, networks of business contacts, and the ability to perceive and exploit opportunities. Likewise the merchant involved in international trade will bring in international contacts, as well as more capital. Also artisans and craftsmen are occupational categories likely to turn to industrial entrepreneurship. The relationships between these occupational origins and entrepreneurship suggest that the emergence of entrepreneurship requires that an individual has certain resources, that transform the situation in which he finds himself into a favourable opportunity condition.

Religious orientation. In view of Weber's emphasis on the Protestant Ethic as a promoter of entrepreneurship, it is conceivable that the emergence of entrepreneurship may be attributable to a preponderance of entrepreneurs with a Protestant religious orientation. Hence religion as an expression of an ideology is considered to be an important facet of the entrepreneurial identity.

Old vs. new. There have been some suggestions that old entrepreneurs, those with relatively many years of entrepreneurship, may be somewhat less expansive and innovative as compared to those, who are new in their entrepreneurial role.

Private vs. Public. It also has been suggested that public entrepreneurship (related to state-owned enterprises) tends to be less expansive and innovative than entrepreneurship by private individuals. Private entrepreneurs are generally not commanded to respond by any higher authority but rather react to the advantages and opportunities created by the market.

Orientation of entrepreneurship

Entrepreneurs in the production of goods and services may initiate two basic types of changes. These may be either quantitative or qualitative. The term '*expansion*' refers to quantitative changes, or changes in the amount of goods and services produced. The extent to which entrepreneurs initiate such changes in a society will show up in indicators of economic growth in that society. The term '*innovation*' is used to indicate qualitative changes in the production of new goods and new services, or changes in the manner in which goods or services are produced. It refers to the 'newness' of a certain change as explained below.

Expansion. This orientation may refer to either starting the production of goods and services or enlarging the existing production of the same; these could be phrased as 'initial'- and 'subsequent' production respectively. In that sense we speak of 'starting' and 'existing' entrepreneurs. Closely linked with expansion is 'capital widening' in society, indicating the increase of capital required to finance the expansion. Absence of capital widening may be working as a brake upon the expansion wanted, in spite of the entrepreneurial orientation.

Innovation. This include, first of all the 'factor innovations', encompassing innovations either in the fields of financial instruments, labour innovations related to changes in either the supply of labour or its productivity, material innovations including the procurement of a new source of material, or the adoption of a material that has not yet been used before in the production of goods. Secondly, it includes 'production innovations', such as the application of an invention, as well as the mode and process of production. The latter often refers to changes in the form of the organisation. And finally, it includes 'market innovations'. This may refer to product innovations (diversification), following the demand of different segments of the market. It also includes the development of a new market, in terms of either a new category of consumers or a new geographical territory. In summary: factor innovations will increase the supply and productivity of land, labour and capital; production (technological) innovation will increase the supply of technology and very likely increases its productivity as well; market innovations will increase the size of the market and its composition. The three together will improve the competitiveness of the industry or enterprises vis-à-vis others.

Entrepreneurial traits

As has been described in the previous chapter, entrepreneurship as promoted by the EIM is the ability and willingness of individuals, both on their own and within organizations, to:

- Perceive and create new economic opportunities (new products, new production methods, new organisational schemes and new product-market-combinations);
- Introduce their ideas in the market, in the face of uncertainty and other obstacles, by making decisions on location, form and the use of resources and institutions;
- Compete with others for a share of that market

These qualities are based on a number of underlying entrepreneurial traits, which have been identified by Isobel van der Kuip[69]. These include:

- *Need for achievement,* which is evident in an individual's desire to compete with some standard of excellence and success in performance. The need for achievement and 'motivation' are considered to be the two sides of the same coin.
- *Risk taking*, as entrepreneurs are found to have an inclination to take calculated, moderate risks. They tend to avoid both excessively high and low risks situations not based on chance, but on skills. It could also be described as exposing oneself to loss and disadvantage in return for a higher reward in case of success.
- *Positive self-concept,* which includes self-confidence as well as self-sufficiency and a positive image of one's own abilities and achievements. Self-confidence is related to a realistic estimate of the entrepreneur's abilities and a realistic response to the market.

---

69   Kuip, van der I., Early development of entrepreneurial qualities; The role of initial education, Zoetermeer 1998, p 13-14. See also: Patel, V.G., Developing Indigenous Entrepreneurship: The Gujarat Model, in: Neck P.A. and Nelson R.E. (eds.) *Small enterprise development: Policies and programmes,* International Labour Organisation Geneva, 1987, p. 111

- *Initiative and independence.* As such people not only show initiative but also independence in their day-to-day behaviour. They like to act autonomously, rather than follow direction and ideas of other people.
- *Problem solving and creativity*; having a tendency to approach problems in a creative way. According to Torrance there are four main components related to creativity: 'fluency', defined as the ability to produce a large numbers of ideas/alternative solutions; 'originality', the ability to produce uncommon new ideas/alternative solutions; 'flexibility', the ability to shift from one approach to another and finally 'innovation, defined as the ability to define or perceive in a way that is different from the usual way.[70]
- *Hopeful about the future,* meaning an optimistic attitude and view on the future as regards new opportunities, chances and possibilities for further growth of the business and profitability.
- *Opportunity seeking*; the search for or identification of unfulfilled needs in the marketplace and the generation of ideas to satisfy that need by products or services.
- *Time-bound planning* in their actions, whilst setting goals, which can be described as defining objectives that can be reached by allocating entrepreneurial effort; enterprise is all about reaching goals creatively, independently and autonomously.

3.2.5. The research model

On next page follows a graphic representation of the research model as explained above. Per each of the three periods of *trade capitalism* (economic take off, economic dominance, stagnation & decline) the four dimensions as described in this chapter have been plotted. These main dimensions and its factors will shed light on the per-

---

[70] Quoted in EIM publication *"Early development in entrepreneurial qualities'*, Zoetermeer 1998, p. 13

formance of entrepreneurs in each of the thee sub-periods, whereby the entrepreneurial characteristics (identity, orientation and personal traits) will be analysed and looked upon in more detail, since these are considered to be the main focus of this study.

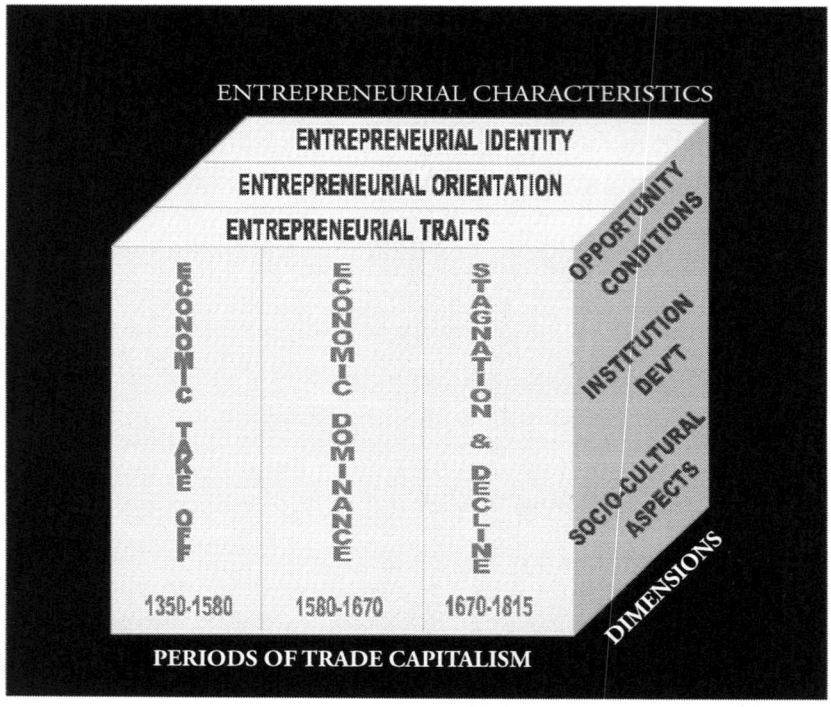

Figure 2: Research model

A further breakdown of the factors of each of the dimensions mentioned in the box (figure 2) will be shown in the table on the next page. In this chapter (3.2), a description and explanation was provided of each of the factors, which will be applied to each of the 3 selected periods of the trade capitalistic period under research.

Table 1: Break down of factors related to the four dimensions of the research

OPPORTUNITY CONDITIONS	CHARACTERISTICS ENTREPRENEURS
1. Quantity of factor inputs (land, labour, capital, technology) 2. Quality of factor inputs (land, labour, capital, technology) 3. Size and composition of the market	14. Identity • Individual vs. Collective • Mainstream vs. Outsider • Family vs. Non-family • Socio-economic origin • Religious orientation • Old vs. New • Private vs. Public
INSTITUTION DEVELOPMENT 4. Protective 5. Promotional 6. Corrective	
SOCIO-CULTURAL ASPECTS OF SOCIETY 7. Legitimacy of entrepreneurship 8. Social mobility 9. Marginality 10. Social integration 11. Security 12. Ideology 13. Need achievement	15. Orientation • Expansion • Innovation 16. Entrepreneurial traits • Need to achieve • Risk taking • Positive self concept • Initiative and independence • Problem solving • Hopeful about future • Searching environment • Time-bound planning

Before embarking on the analysis of entrepreneurship during '*Trade Capitalism*' the emergence of entrepreneurship prior to that period will be examined in the next chapter 4. This will provide a base line of entrepreneurship performance for the chapters 5, 6, 7, and 8 respectively.

4. A CURSORY VIEW ON ENTREPRENEURSHIP PRIOR TO TRADE CAPITALISM

In this chapter an effort will be made to try and identify the 'baseline' of entrepreneurship in The Netherlands at the start of Trade Capitalism - for this study determined around the year 1350. Obviously, entrepreneurship didn't start in 1350; hence, in order to analyse the factors that ultimately led to the development and growth of entrepreneurship during Trade Capitalism, it is necessary to know the state of affairs at the start of that period by not only investigating how the entrepreneurship emerged, but also to find out where it came from. In addition it is important to identify the relevant surrounding factors (political, technical, economical) determining the quality of the entrepreneurial climate at that time. To that end the result of a cursory survey will be presented below, entailing entrepreneurial development in the delta area of The Netherlands, encompassing the rivers Scheldt, Meuse, Rhine, and Yssel, in the period prior to Trade Capitalism. In a separate section the same effort will be made regarding regions situated outside the Low Countries, that affected the state of the affairs of Dutch entrepreneurship at the start of the period under research.

4.1. First traces of 'Dutch' entrepreneurship

Following the agricultural revolution in the delta around 4000 BC, first forms of division of labour and entrepreneurship can be detected, in the sense that some people decided to become craftsmen and to produce textiles and pottery and, undoubtedly, needed to 'negotiate' a reasonable quantity of food in exchange for the delivered crafts. This barter trade intensified when sedentary agriculture became common practice around 2800 BC when new groups, known as the 'beakers people' entered the delta. They developed and used, around 1500 BC, very simple wooden ploughs and cultivated a variety of agricultural products, such as millet, barley and oats.

Horses were used for both personal transportation and as draught animal for carts. Obviously this entailed entrepreneurial initiatives and efforts in both the manufacturing of these carts (wheels, axes, etc.) and the mobilisation of non-human energy (horsepower) for economic purposes.

Next to first forms of artisanship or manufacturing, initial signs of the development of 'international' or interregional trade, can be traced at that time as well. Black beads from England, ceramics from Silesia and even products from Egypt found their way to the delta. Although one cannot speak of any form of pro-active importation of these products, the mere existence and the barter trade in these products must have further stimulated forms of emerging entrepreneurship. Together with the artisans the proto-entrepreneurs were the innovators of new or diversified products, who moreover acted as a hinge between the outside world and their own communities or societies. This also entailed the skilful development of the art of 'negotiating' in getting approximately the same amount of exchanged food, non-food or other services for their communities, as compared to what they delivered in their barter to the outside world. Obviously, production, manufacturing and trade included the notion of 'taking initiatives and risks', which are distinct phenomena of entrepreneurship. After all, raw materials had to be obtained at such conditions that it had to be 'profitable' for them to convert these into ready-made utensils to be traded in their own community or elsewhere. And those who were trading had to negotiate a 'profitable' exchange of other products, taken into consideration their efforts in transporting these products, including the risks they ran and eventual 'investments' to be made in ships, horses, carts or other means of transportation.

Nonetheless, the population at that time was predominantly busy in keeping themselves alive with agricultural occupations, such as animal husbandry, cultivation and fisheries. Any form of manufacturing and trade at that time can only be considered as mere peripheral. The real first commercial revolution started at the arrival of the Romans when, around 50 AD, they took the river Rhine as the border of their empire. The establishment of Roman garrisons stimulated local agricultural production, trade of local and foreign products and brought centres of innovations to the tribes populating the delta. A very specific innovation was the establishment of Roman villas, which were relatively large agricultural enterprises, run by Romans. These functioned as collection centres from where trading in various crops took place; in addition they also introduced new products and technologies from back home.

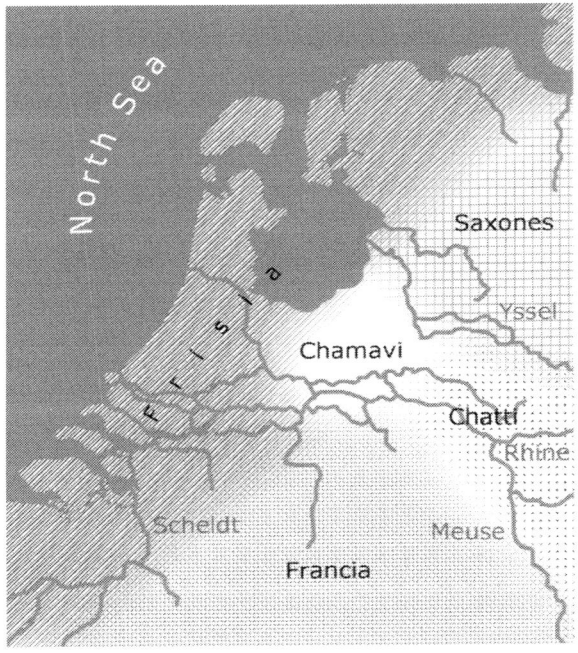

The Delta during Roman Times with the rivers:
- Rhine
- Meuse
- Yssel
- Scheldt

From that time improvements were made in the infrastructure of the delta area, albeit mainly for military purposes. Obviously, a good infrastructure is a prerequisite for trade, manufacturing and for that matter also for the development of entrepreneurship. Natural rivers were artificially improved and made better navigable, or were sometimes extended with canals.[71] In addition, land-roads for fast transportation of armies were constructed from south, via east to the west in the delta, connecting towns such as Maastricht

---

71   E.g. the "fossa Drusiana", the nowadays Vecht and the "fossa Corbulonis", the nowadays Vliet in: Uytven, R. van, Oudheid en Middeleeuwen, in Stuijvenberg, J.H. van (ed), *De economische geschiedenis van Nederland*, Groningen 1977, p. 2-3

with Tongeren, Heerlen, Cologne, Nijmegen and towns even down south in the nowadays-German territories (Mainz, Worms, Strasbourg) up to settlements such as Katwijk at the mouth of the river Rhine. Furthermore, there was also quite some coastal traffic, developing cities or harbours such as Katwijk, Domburg and Aardenburg. The Roman garrisons attracted trade and craftsmen, which led to a relatively strong urbanisation of, in particular Maastricht, Nijmegen, Heerlen and Utrecht. Innovations and new social conditions in these towns - growth poles in itself - brought opportunities that were recognised by the more entrepreneurially oriented people. Finally, the introduction of money by the Romans completed the environment for accelerating entrepreneurial activities in and around the area of the North Sea delta.

Because of the existing and improved infrastructure, continued urbanisation and increasing productive activities, international trade started to come off the ground. Corn from England, as well as other products, was transported, such as wine from France, ore from Sweden and oil from Spain. Transit trade, as a consequence of the infrastructure in the delta became an important feature for the entrepreneurs. Earthenware and bronze of the upstream Rhineland went to England, France and Scandinavia. Excavations have proved that during that period (150-250 AD), there was a pretty busy trade between the Roman garrisons and the Frisians, just north of the big rivers in hides and skins, fishery products, cattle and slaves. All of this served as a basis for the first substantial growth in entrepreneurship of the western part of the Dutch territory at a later stage i.e. from the 7th to the 9th century. This can probably be considered to be the very first foundation of 'trade-capitalistic entrepreneurship', being the effort or talent involved in combining or organising the 'factors of production' i.e. land, labour and capital.[72]

After the Romans left their garrisons around the year 250, urbanisation became considerably less and even decreased to quite some extent. This decline coincided with invasions of German tribes and with an increase of the water level along the coast. This all resulted in a temporary decline in entrepreneurship. Nonetheless,

---

72   Cameron R., *A Concise Economic History of the World*, New York, 1997, p. 9

the relatively good land- and river infrastructure in the delta kept on stimulating transport, interaction and exchange of merchandise, hence entrepreneurship. This continued entrepreneurship, together with the technical advantage in the regions where there had been strong Roman presence before, resulted in a comparatively strong commercial growth. Friesian entrepreneurs, in particular, were the most important accelerators of this growth in trade around the 7th century. Due to their specific geographical situation the Frisians and among them also Anglo-Saxons, had developed over the years a fearless proficiency in navigation for fishing and trade, which was unrivalled at that time. They navigated the Dutch rivers and the seacoasts to England and the Baltic states. Small wonder that the Frisian entrepreneurs were widely known for their cloth, made of local wool, which they also exported. Apart from products from England, Scandinavia and the Rhineland, also products from the Mediterranean began to arrive via the river Rhine. This created a very stimulating environment for would-be entrepreneurs, who around this time witnessed an expansion in a variety of products as well as with a subsequent expansion in new markets. All of this required constant improvements in the shipbuilding industry and these innovations in its turn activated other entrepreneurs in gradually establishing supporting industries as well, such as the manufacturing of rope, sails, hammers, etc., thus sowing the seeds for the development of later independent proto-industries.

The Viking raids in the 9th century diminished to some extent the advanced economic development of the Frisian entrepreneurs, traders, navigators and craftsmen alike. Their dwindled domination caused the economic emergence of other regions in the delta which were not or not that much affected by the raids, notably those just southwest of Frisia. The city of Tiel became an important trading centre and the coins they minted were used in the German territories, which underpins the growing relationship between market and minting: 'no mint, no market', as a well-known dictum went, already at that time. Because of their geographic situation along the Rhine and not in the least the presence of entrepreneurs who seized the opportunities, Tiel became a hinge between trade from the Rhineland and England. But also other cities became part of that commercial development, such as Utrecht -proclaimed again to become the Bishops' town, which had four flourishing year markets. And markets were the key to the economic development. They made the beginnings of agricultural- and along with it, artisan specialisation possible.

In addition to the closely related re-emergence of towns, new roads over land were developed and new canals were dug (Vaartse Rhine), which improved the traffic between the northern part of the German territories and Flanders in the south of the Netherlands. Deventer came up quite strongly and Maastricht revived after a period of relative insignificance after the Romans had left. Dordrecht became an internationally known centre for trans-shipment and functioned as the link between river trade and sea trade. The harbour of Middelburg obtained its importance due to its locations along the Dutch coast, but also as an entry to the river Scheldt, which ran through Antwerp and other cities further down south.

An important aspect of these flourishing 'modern' cities, was that they in most cases originated from initiatives and actions taken by entrepreneurs, who established collection- and trade points for regional and interregional commerce rather than being a creation of emperors, counts or dukes. This can be seen as a first form of institutionalising trade. However, the mere awarding of urban privileges by the local political leaders fitted neatly into the context of the steady seigniorial drive for greater profits. Recognising cities by the nobility was indeed akin to encouraging peasant colonisation of wastelands, stimulating entrepreneurs in investing in mills and ovens, and using the proceeds to obtain the trappings of noble life. So their demand for luxuries both began and completed the circle, for if peasants supplied the surplus, it was the merchant who converted it into money, traded that money for the desired luxury goods, sold these items to the lord, who then profited from the role of entrepreneur.[73] The first developments in the history of Dutch entrepreneurship were nothing more than a nearly infinite number of variations on this simple theme.

---

73   Hunt, E.S. & J.M. Murray, *A History of Business in Medieval Europe, 1200-1550*, Cambridge 1999, p. 28

Artisans, specialised providers of goods and services primarily to the local community, were self-employed individuals, masters of a trade, drawing on family members for additional labour as needed and training at least one of their offspring to take over the business in due course. In order to avoid or reduce their risks as entrepreneurs, a good number of artisans and traders in this period founded entrepreneurial associations for mutual protection. These associations were also developed for exchanging business information, as well as for the sake of concluding cooperation in business deals, which were too large for single traders, artisans or entrepreneurs to handle. Hence, the Frisians developed with the Swedes a so-called 'guild' and the traders from Frisia, Flanders and the Rhinelanders erected another association. A few more associations came to life in Groningen, Utrecht, Deventer and Tiel, which brought together masters of the same trade in combinations that became known as guilds and whose main purpose was to meet the pressure of increasing competition and to ban imports.

But also political leaders (the nobility in the rural areas) became involved in supporting the entrepreneurial sector of their societies. They saw that trade could be used to produce tolls, taxes, and tariffs for a steady flow of cash to buy military resources, rewards for followers, and symbols of prestige. The flow of money also provided the means for the rulers to build the administrative structures, often manned by businessmen, which enabled them to tighten control and enhance their power over their subjects. Businessmen, for their part, saw in the dukes, counts and emperor the means to the secure environment they needed to carry on predictable and profitable business operations. For instance, in Flanders of the early 12th century, the local government stimulated land reclamation and drainage work, which made many of the rivers (far more) navigable, hence facilitated trade to a great extent. Philips of Alsace directly participated from 1160 to 1180 in implementing a master plan to link interior towns as Bruges, Ypres and Saint-Omer with coastal ports, where docking facilities for large boats could be provided. And in 1180 a monumental dam was built ten kilometres northeast of Bruges, allowing access to the North Sea via the new port city of Damme.

Another example of mutually beneficial cooperation between government and entrepreneurs was the promotion of the county of Holland at the expense of Flanders. Duke Floris V tried to make Dordrecht a competitor of Bruges by offering in 1277 merchants from various other trading cities incentives when making use of Dordrecht instead of Bruges as a market place for their products[74]. Likewise was the effort of the Duke to provide living quarters in Dordrecht for local weavers, as these were seen as producers of drapes and cloth in competition with Bruges, which in fact had quite some fame in that trade and attracted many merchants from all over the delta. In addition, Floris V concluded a coalition with the King of England, Edward I, which finally resulted in establishing the English wool market in Dordrecht, when in 1294 some tension arose between England and Flanders.

All these efforts to make Dordrecht an important market seemed to have been in vain, when in 1295 the wool market was redirected again to Flanders, as this was more convenient for the English traders in doing business with their usual clients from the counties of Flanders and Brabant. What really made a difference for the trading-entrepreneurs in Dordrecht, was the decision of the Duke in 1299 to grant the city the right to force all transporters of merchandise, in particular wine, oats and timber, to offer their merchandise to the Dordrecht market first. At that time also entrepreneurs from Middelburg did a lot of business with England and when the Duke of the counties of Holland and Zealand negotiated with England, he was then escorted and assisted by business delegates (entrepreneurs) of Dordrecht, Middelburg and some other cities, which were involved in the England trade. Likewise, the Duchess Margaretha of Flanders gave support to promote international business with the eastern part of Europe, when she granted in 1252 and 1253 privileges to German merchants from the Hanse, originating primarily from Cologne, Bremen, Hamburg and Lübeck.[75] Their contacts with entrepreneurs from the delta facilitated not only import and export, but also brought innovations

---

74   Uyten, R. p. 13
75   Dollinger, Ph., *De Hanze; opkomst, bloei en ondergang van een handelsverbond*, Utrecht 1967, p. 59-61

to both the region (Bruges) and to the enterprising sector, be it for manufacturing or trade.

In the 13th century, one can identify in the Dutch speaking territories two important regions with relatively larger urban centres: a southern region along the big rivers and a northern region along the Frisian coast, where navigation took place from and to the North Sea as well as the Zuyder Sea. The connection between these two areas ran through the canal Vecht near Utrecht. Commercial expansion of Flanders to the Baltic and the Rhineland was mainly realised by making use of this connection and, similarly, traffic from the Northern part of the German territories made use of the same waterways.

In concluding which factors were instrumental in stimulating entrepreneurship in this part of the world, the answer must first be sought in the unprecedented infrastructure of waterways and the nearby sea. These were linked to the geographical position of the delta, laying in the centre of quite many other trading peoples, such as the British, Scandinavians, the Balts, Germans and the Franks. These, indeed, made the area around 1300 probably the strongest economic growth centre in the whole of Europe, potentially capable of taking over the dominant position of the Italian city-states, which ultimately took place in the 16th century. The delta functioned in the economic process of those days as a hinge between the Northern- and Southern-, as well as between Eastern- and Western parts of the European territories. This transit trade brought innovations of new products and new markets and stimulated the emergence of a class of entrepreneurs involved in the production of food products (fish, meat and dairy products), utility goods (cloth, ceramics, tiles, skins), transport means (ships), including all gear and accessories (sails, paint, rope) for both the domestic and foreign markets. In addition, entrepreneurship developed in trading and shipping merchandise. What once started as the technology transfer from the Romans and the barter trade was now growing into the production of a manifold of products for many different markets. Logistics improved by digging new canals connecting different waterways, and by doing so also connected different markets.

Second, apart from the invasions of the Vikings, there were at that specific time not yet that many social disturbances in terms of wars and other forms of upheaval, which characterised later periods. The merchants were flexible enough to transfer their business to other cities if the Vikings would make life difficult to them. Moreover, times of danger as well as other contacts are in quite some cases incentives to new inventions, stimulating entrepreneurs in producing improved or new products for the market.

Third, political leaders were supportive in the economic growth of their regions by being quite promotional and protective to the entrepreneurial class. The dukes apparently understood the importance of supporting entrepreneurs by making alliances with other rulers in Europe and by issuing ordinances geared towards generating business either in trade (market places) or in transportation (exemption of toll), hence creating a business environment which was conducive for economic growth. Their stimulating and supportive role was also quite apparent in developing fairs and markets beyond a local level. In Flanders, for example, a cycle of fairs came into existence around the mid 11th to the early 12th century, with the encouragement of the count. 'These were eventually five in number, shared among Ypres, Lille, Mesen, Torhout and later Bruges, each lasting thirteen days in a staggered cycle from late February through to the beginning of November, with two to four weeks in between to allow for travel'.[76] The symbiosis between entrepreneurs and political leaders, despite common animosity between the two were, if not explicitly, implicitly two sides of the same coin and generated wealth to both of them.

A fourth factor was the introduction of money and various financial instruments as initially developed in the city states of Italy, which strongly stimulated international business contacts between the northern and southern part of Europe. Specifically when the Champagne Fairs gradually declined in importance, quite a number of Italian financial specialists established themselves in Bruges and contributed greatly to the city becoming the financial centre of the west, favouring entrepreneurship in the Southern Netherlands tremendously.

---

76 Hunt & Murray, p. 25

Additional factors of the emergence of entrepreneurship were specific entrepreneurial traits such as inquisitiveness, initiative- and risk taking, as well as some form of self-confidence, knowing they could meet the international trading challenges because of their experience and know-how in navigation and shipbuilding. These factors, and why particularly they were developed in the Netherlands, will be dealt with in some greater detail in the section that follows next.

4.2. International developments influencing Dutch entrepreneurship

The long distance trade of Medieval Europe was essentially demand-driven. The prime objective of entrepreneur or merchants engaged in this activity was to seek imports of which they knew would be attractive to their local customers. Initially they did not look for outlets for exports of local produce to foreign markets, but as they gained experience, they began to see opportunities for a two-way trade.[77] Under the simplest circumstances these entrepreneurs worked for their own account. Their entire capital consisted of the stock of goods they carried. These entrepreneurs became essential in the organisation of trade and business operations. They did not only market the products, but also furnished the raw materials, supplied most of the capital requirements, and often became the town's capitalists, financing industries and acting as money changers and lenders, specifically after the business innovations, as described below (bill of exchange and double-entry bookkeeping), were introduced in their business operations.[78] Among them a form of partnership came into use: one merchant, perhaps too old for the rigours of travel provided that capital for another, who actually undertook the voyage. 'Profits were divided, usually three-fourth for the sedentary

---

77 Hunt & Murray, p. 54
78 According to Jaques Le Goff, in the 13th century the separation between the functions of merchant-banker-usurer, often carried out by one and the same person, was very vague, reason why the merchant had much difficulty in many parts of Europe to be recognised as an honourable person (see: Le Goff, J., *De woekeraar en de hel; Economie en Religie in de Middeleeuwen*, Amsterdam 1996, p. 82-83)

capitalist and one-fourth for the active partner'.[79] It also happened that single entrepreneurs, who could not afford their own ships, might lease an entire ship from an established ship-owner and then retail the space in it to other merchants. There was indeed no lack of creativity from the side of the entrepreneurs. The merchants at that time, whilst running great risks, often got prosperous and, as we have seen throughout all ages, prosperity is quickly converted into power, which eventually resulted in the merchant's domination of many city councils.[80]

Medieval business was driven by the continuous demand for luxuries for the elite. And when the elite of the north, including those of the Netherlands, began to have the desire and, more importantly, the means to acquire exotic goods from the Mediterranean region, the inhabitants of the seaport towns, adopted the role of middlemen.[81] This coincided with the further development and growth of the regional markets and fairs, which became the outlets for more specialised, rarer commodities, whose customers came from proportionately greater distances. An interesting case in point is the Champagne Fair, as Hunt and Murray so sharply describe, 'which reached its apogee in the 13th century, situated across the most important overland routes connecting the Low Countries/England axis in the north with the Italian/Mediterranean trading network in the south, hence a favoured meeting place for southern and northern European entrepreneurs and merchandise. These long-distance merchants were trading in exotic, high value and easily portable wares. The southerners (Italians) brought with them a range of articles from the western and eastern Mediterranean prised by the increasingly affluent elite in the north (The Netherlands). In return the northern merchants offered an array of woollen textiles, from ordinary to luxury, finished and unfinished; but their total value was inadequate to balance the demand for southern goods. That balance was largely made up by silver, both bullion and coin and was made

---

79 Cameron, R., p. 66
80 Florence provides an excellent example in the 1290s, when the wealthy merchant class, the *popolo grasso*, effectively disbarred the old nobility from municipal office and assumed control of the city government for several decades. (Hunt & Murray, p. 55)
81 Hunt & Murray, p. 23

available in ample quantities from the new and exceptionally rich mines at Freiberg'.[82] But payment in 'cash on the nail' was quite troublesome, because of the large amounts that had to be carried in bullion or coins and, not in the least, because of security reasons. In this connection, the international fairs developed a payment system based on credit instruments called '*lettres de foire*'. These documents - some sort of bills of exchange - recognised sales of merchandise, but often specified payments to be made at a later fair, when the total debits and credits for a season would be computed as well as a final reckoning – in different coinages - made between buyers and sellers. Virtually all of the business of the Champagne Fairs was conducted by means of this credit instrument - the bill of exchange. These were endorsable and could be transferred from one party to another and were eventually used purely as financial instruments. Obviously, entrepreneurs did no longer need to do large and cumbersome shipments of specie. Instead it promoted the Champagne Fairs as financial clearing houses for long-distance 'international' trade between the north and the south of Europe.

A business financial innovation, which first transformed medieval commerce in Italy and had great impact on the effectiveness and efficiency of entrepreneurs in the northern commercial regions of Europe, was to increase the availability of capital by spreading risks. The earliest techniques appeared in Genoa and Venice during or even before the 12th century and were focussed on risk dispersal, through establishing shareholdings or consortia for the required investment to be made, mainly in the shipping industry. Likewise was the invention of double-entry bookkeeping, when in the late 13th century entrepreneurs were increasingly facing complex transactions, which required a better control system. In its turn, these two innovations stimulated the emergence of the banking system. These banks were established by a number of merchants, who changed from moneychangers to merchant-bankers by executing payments and credits in the accounts of their clients. At a much later stage these banks also took deposits for safekeeping, which inevitably led to providing extension of credit by means of overdrafts.

---

82   Hunt & Murray, p. 28-31

Apart from organisational, institutional and financial innovations, there were also a number of technical innovations. With the widespread construction and use of watermills[83], milling as women's work had practically disappeared by the 11th century. This provided opportunities to women to be more productive for the household and field work, tending animals, brewing beer and ale and, not in the least, to be highly involved in cloth-making. Other major innovations in the production process made by entrepreneurs were the spinning wheel and the horizontal loom, which saved labour in the fields that was then redirected to more specialised activities. Initially, this activated the establishment of textile workshops in the rural areas. However, these workshops and apparent dominance of women in cloth making disappeared when cloth production became more specialised. This production moved around the 13th century to the towns where entrepreneurs (often former merchants) started relatively large-scale manufacturing units, making use of the scale of economies resulting in lower prices and larger markets. Clearly, this innovative way of production could, to a great extent, be materialised because of the availability of credits as a consequence of the earlier described financial instruments that had been developed over time.

Another type of innovation that took place in the 12th and 13th century, having a great impact on Dutch trade capitalism, was the large scale commercial fishing in the 12th century. At that time the herring became the quarry of English and German fishing fleets that ranged across the North and Baltic Sea. But it was not until the 13th century, when Lübeck merchants both financed Baltic fishing fleets and provided vast quantities of salt needed to preserve the catch, that herring became the highly wanted food commodity, which it retained for many centuries thereafter. Obviously, this type of fishing (as well as international trade navigation) had a tremendous innovative impact on the design, development and ultimately on the manufacturing of ships, which would find its apogee during the heydays of Dutch trade capitalism.

---

83   In the year 1086 the agents of William the Conqueror counted in England 5624 watermills in some 3000 villages (Cameron, p. 71)

There was a wide variety of towns and cities in Europe in the period prior to Dutch trade capitalism, where entrepreneurs carried out their activities. 'First, in the small market towns throughout most of Europe the leading entrepreneurs enjoyed a modicum of self-government but exercised little control of affairs beyond their immediate environs. Second, merchants and artisans in the royal cities of Paris and Barcelona retained a limited degree of independence but were directly subject to the sovereign and his officials. Third were the self-governing commercial-industrial towns, such as Ghent and Bruges in the Southern Netherlands and Lübeck in northern Germany. Businessmen there, essentially controlled by local politics, had the authority to deal with committal overlords, but were subservient to them. Finally, there were the truly independent city-states like Venice, Genoa, Florence and Sienna. Businessmen in these cities managed not only local politics, but also foreign policy, which they directed to further their interests, projecting their power by force or cash or sometimes as a combination of both'.[84] Hence, in the whole of Europe we see the strong symbiosis of government and entrepreneurs, although it should be noted that in the Low Countries this symbiosis was of a different character as compared to other parts of Europe. Nobility in the Low Countries – as a result of the feudal society - had its prime basis in the rural areas, rather than in the cities. The bourgeois, being mainly entrepreneurs and merchants, instead governed the cities. Therefore the cities and the bourgeois, on the one hand, and the rural based nobility, on the other, lived in a somewhat mutual dependency, each in charge of their own power base.[85]

It was also during this period that a specific form of collective entrepreneurship developed. Forms of cooperation among entrepreneurs started which ultimately led to the highly regulated guilds. These guilds, business associations of artisans carrying out the same profession, dated back from the 13th century. It is only in the 14th

---

84   Hunt & Murray, p. 77
85   Kleinpenning, J.M.G., Profiel van de derde wereld: Een inleiding tot de geografie van onderontwikkeling, Assen 1978, Chapter XVI

century, the period in which they acquired political power, when they got the rights which are considered to be typical for the artisan guilds. These rights included the so-called 'guild coercion', i.e. that only members of the guild were allowed to exercise a certain profession, including a strict regulation of the professional education or training. After one started as an apprentice, one could become a companion and finally a master, only after the assessment of a so-called 'master piece' one had to make.[86] These forms of institutional development among entrepreneurs also took place in other parts of Europe, albeit far more intense as compared to the Northern Netherlands. In other parts of Europe, the guild organisations reacted sharply to changes in the economy, tightening their regulations so as to control the supply more effectively in cartel terms. They restricted output, enforced working rules, and restricted new members to the sons or relatives of diseased masters.[87]

Another form of business cooperation was the Hanse, a medieval German merchant organisation, established around 1150. Eventually, it included almost 200 cities and towns and was not formally organised until 1367, although it had proceeded by many years of informal cooperation among German merchants in foreign cities. It owed its beginning to three factors: a) the newly created cities in the Baltic, b) increased autonomy in the Rhineland and in other German cities, and c) the common goals among these cities of opening up new trade territories and excluding non-German competitors. By 1300, they had German quarters (Kontors) not only in the north and east, but also in the two major trading cities of the west of Europe, Bruges and London. At that time they were trading in furs, timber and other forest products, and in the important food commodities, fish and wheat. This 'federation of many cities, towns and communities' lasted for nearly 500 year, till they were challenged in the mid 17th century by the Dutch entrepreneurs from Amsterdam and Holland in the fishing industry, strongly supported by the government of the Republic.[88]

---

86   Jansen, p. 197
87   Cameron, p. 76
88   Dollinger, Ph., *De Hanze; opkomst, bloei en ondergang van een handelsverbond*, Utrecht 1967, p. 455-462. See also Hunt & Murray p. 86

As we have seen from the studies of Douglas North in chapter 2, the issue of 'institution development' is very important to entrepreneurs, as it should create an enabling environment to effectively carry out their business activities. At the beginning of the 13th century four of these developments had taken place. 'First, the *Corpus iuris civilis* of Emperor Justinian had been rediscovered towards the end of the 11th century and gradually clarified during the 12th century. Second, (...) sovereigns of regions and governments of city-states began to initiate and codify legislation, often specifying that the enactment had the consent of the populace. Third was the formation of the law schools, beginning at Bologna, where masters and students studied, interpreted, and disseminated the texts of both canon law and civil law, compiling many of the civil codes. And finally, canonical and civilian lawyers were radically revising their attitudes toward private property, making it a sacrosanct principle deriving from natural law'.[89] The legal framework emerging from these four developments initially took place in Italy, but had its direct impact at the business ethics and procedures of entrepreneurs in the northern commercial regions of Europe as well. This was more or less the legal scene in 1350 at the start of trade capitalism in the Netherlands.

In their study *A History of Business in Medieval Europe 1200-1550*, Hunt and Murray arrive at two conclusions as regards the development of business organisations from Europe's High Middle Ages to approximately 1350. 'The first is that while business units at (...) 1200 were small, simple and particularistic, business itself was extremely complex, requiring multiple transactions among numerous business units to transform raw materials into finished goods and to move products from place to place. This business complexity was costly and inhibiting to trade'. Their second conclusion was that 'there was an unmistakable trend throughout the 150 year period (up to 1350), towards larger and more complex units co-incident with a move towards simpler business processes'.[90] These business processes were indeed recognizable in the cities of Bruges and sometimes later also in Antwerp in the Southern Netherlands. And these can indeed be considered as the up-beat to an accelerat-

---

89   Hunt & Murray, p. 96-97
90   Hunt & Murray, p 73-74

ed improvement of business organisations as was achieved in the Northern part of the Netherlands during the period of Dutch trade capitalism, particularly during its zenith between 1580 and 1670.

We will end the description of the period before the start of "Trade Capitalism" with the scrooges of famine, pestilence and war that plagued the countries in Western Europe and had an immediate effect on entrepreneurship. Many crops failed due to weather changes in the 1300s, which seem to have led to increased rainfall and colder temperatures in the north, increased drought in areas in the south, and general instability in both. And although it was most manifest during the 1320s and '30s, it had a direct effect on later periods, as population losses due to famine were insufficient to redress the imbalance between population and declining crop yields. As Hunt and Murray remark: 'Allowing for wide variation of extent and tempo, it can be said that the age of agrarian growth and stability had ended across Europe by 1350'[91]. The Black Death or Great Pestilence, was indeed another "plague" affecting all centres of international commerce, Christian and Islamic alike. Many Italian cities suffered 50 to 80 percent mortality, and although the cities of Flanders were less severely affected by the plague of 1347-52, they were not as fortunate as once believed and suffered heavily during the outbreaks of the 1360s. And finally there were the wars: the repeating hostilities between the French and the English. There were the intermittent but vicious local conflicts and civil wars in Flanders, Germany, Scandinavia, and the Iberian and Italian peninsulas. Of special significance to Mediterranean commerce directly, and indirectly also to the entrepreneurs of Western Europe in general, were the loss of the last Christian outposts in the Holy Land, the great naval struggles between Genoa and Venice, and the push of the Ottoman Turks into Europe proper.

What did it all mean for European business after 1350? First, it meant severe depopulation from one third to one half by the year 1400. Second, it meant disruption and disorder. The development of Dutch entrepreneurship as from 1350 with their international

---
91 Hunt & Murray p. 126

contacts must be understood against this background of adversity. So what had changed was nothing less than the ecological and political conditions so instrumental in Europe's great expansion and the escape from economic backwardness of the Early Middle Ages. Apart from the fact that the northern regions of the Low Countries suffered considerably less from famine, pestilence and warfare than other parts of Europe, Dutch entrepreneurship in the meantime had been developed to a point of taking advantage of newly emerging business opportunities. This eventually gave rise to *Dutch Trade Capitalism,* as will be explained in the following four chapters.

4.3. The emergence of the 'trade capitalist' entrepreneur

Trade Capitalism may be defined as the period in which the merchant-entrepreneur started to dominate the economy. In the period of *Dutch Trade Capitalism* (1350-1815) he combined commercial activities with direct interventions in the production process, whereas in the period prior to approximately 1350, the entrepreneur was merely a merchant, a trader or peddler or a combination of the three. He was the one who traded in local surpluses and made profits due to regional price differences. The newly emerging entrepreneur, though, started to reorganise the production in such a way that it generated surpluses for which there was a profitable domestic- or international market. He tried to make profits by producing goods or services as cheaply as possible. By doing so he could offer the merchandise below regular market prices, subsequently securing his sales and profits, hence could achieve continuity in his business.[92]

The now following chapters discuss four dimensions of entrepreneurship as described in the previous chapter, i.e. 1) '*Opportunity Conditions for Entrepreneurship*', which includes quantity and quality factor inputs, such as labour, land, capital and markets; 2) '*Institution Development*', which includes issues related to governmental organisations and private sector institution building;

---

92 See also: JL van Zanden, Arbeid tijdens het handelskapitalisme; Opkomst en neeergang van de Hollandse economie 1350-1850, Bergen, 1991, p. 16

3) '*Socio-Cultural Aspects of Society Affecting Entrepreneurship*' and 4) '*Entrepreneurial Characteristics*', such as identity (individualism, mainstream or outsider, religion, etc.), orientation of the entrepreneur (expanding, innovative, inclination to withdrawal, etc.), and the many personal traits that characterised the entrepreneur of that time.

Each of these four dimensions will be described taken into consideration three timeframes within the period 1350-1815. These are, firstly, the 'incubation-period' of the emerging capitalistic-oriented entrepreneur, running from 1350 to 1580 and which can largely be regarded as the up-beat to Dutch economic supremacy, or to speak with Rostow: 'the period of creating the pre-conditions for take off into self-sustained economic growth'[93]. Then follows the period between 1580 to 1670, during which Dutch entrepreneurs brought the economy to its peak, becoming the strongest economic power in Europe and, finally, the period between 1670 and 1815, when Dutch entrepreneurs felt the strong competition of other nations, leading first to stagnation and, subsequently, to a decline of trade and manufacturing, particularly after 1795 when the Republic ultimately got occupied by the French during the Napoleonic era. Hence, the analysis in the next following chapters will be carried out along the research items as indicated in figure 3. Obviously, the years indicating the three sub-periods are not sharp divisions of what happened precisely in these periods, but is an approximation, indicating the main entrepreneurial performance of these periods.

---

[93] W.W. Rostow, *The stages of economic growth, a non-communist manifesto*, Cambridge 1971, p. 6-9

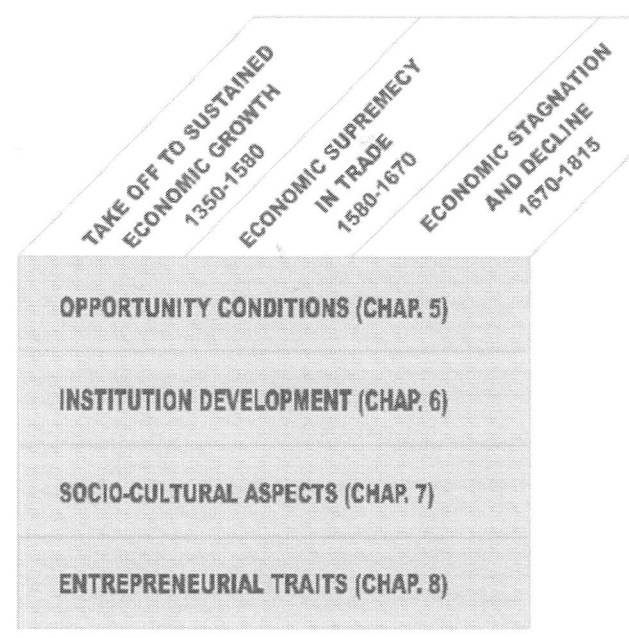

Figure 3: Research focus of next chapters

In the now following chapters 5, 6, 7and 8, each of the 4 dimensions as described in chapter 3 will be dealt with per each of the 3 sub-periods (see the above figure 3). All to these 4 dimensions belonging factors and sub-factors as were identified in chapter 3, will be described and analysed as well. (See also figures 2 and 3)

The Netherlands at around 1620

5. OPPORTUNITY CONDITIONS FOR ENTREPRENEURSHIP

As elaborated in chapter three, the mentioned opportunity conditions, such as land, labour capital, technology and markets, are of prime importance in the development of entrepreneurship. In assessing these opportunities one has to look at various factors, determining the degree of economic development, such as the quantity and quality of factor inputs and the size and composition of markets. Below follows a descriptive analysis of their importance for the emergence of modern entrepreneurship, which is covering three phases of *Trade Capitalism,* i.e. the period of economic take-off (1350-1580), the period of economic supremacy (1580-1670) and finally, the period of stagnation and subsequent economic decline (1670-1815).

5.1. Geography, land and water

Use and development of infrastructure during take off (1350-1580)

Land, water and its geographic situation proved to be important quantity factor inputs for the development of Dutch entrepreneurship. In the 13th century, three broad regions in the Netherlands had become important grids of logistics and trade. The first region was that of the cities in the north and east that had connections with the Hanseatic League, such as Kampen, Zwolle, Hasselt, Deventer, Zutphen, Stavoren, Bolsward and others. The second region was that of the southern cities along the big rivers, the Rhine and Meuse, where entrepreneurs from cities like Nijmegen, Roermond and Zalbommel were able to develop upstream and downstream trade from England to Germany and *vice versa*. Entrepreneurs from some of these cities became even that much successful in their trade that they managed to establish staple markets, for example in Nijmegen in 1394 and Roermond in 1372. Dordrecht became the most famous of them, where entrepreneurs ran a staple market since 1338. It became a market place were many foreign business people met. Its decline, however, was due to the increase of traffic between the Zuyder Sea and the Zeeland delta. This was reason why entrepreneurs/merchants from these areas redirected their routes via Holland, in order to avoid Dordrecht and the toll-payment. Obviously, this made their merchandise less costly and more competitive.[94] The third geographical and trading region consisted of cities of Holland and Zeeland. A group of enterprising people like ship-owners, farmers and fishermen, founded the city of Amsterdam around 1270. This resulted in the abolition of tolls in the entire county of Holland and was one of the reasons for Amsterdam's fast emergence as an important trade harbour for the Netherlands. Situated along the Zuyder Sea, being a safe port and free from tolls, many merchants and entrepreneurs preferred Amsterdam to other harbours. Hence, in less than two centuries, around the middle of the 14th century, Amsterdam merchants and entrepreneurs developed the city. From an amalgamation of land and water in the river Amstel, they developed Amsterdam into the most important Hanse port in the Netherlands. Situated at the crossroads East-West and South-North, Amsterdam entrepreneurs developed a distinct flavour for doing business abroad. Entrepreneurs from Delft, Haarlem, Gouda and Leyden who were also involved in foreign trade, particularly in the Baltic, were much more focused on supplying the relatively strong urbanised large cities in the Republic. Like Amsterdam also Middelburg, situated at the entrance of the Scheldt to Antwerp, developed international trade, for instance with England from which it got the right in the latter part of the 14th century to establish a staple market for wool. Also their trade with France in wine and grain was of great importance. An interesting expansion of international trade as a result of its geographic position took place when merchants and ship-owners developed back-load business for mass merchandise they collected from the Baltic (grain, timber). Also at that time, entrepreneurs were trying to cut cost in order to both meet competition effectively and optimise profits. Hence, since 1425 they connected the trade between the southwest of Eu-

---

94   R. van Uytven, p. 20-27

rope with that of the east by transporting wine and salt from France to the Baltic.[95] Obviously, entrepreneurs in Holland and Zeeland could benefit enormously from the sea-faring experiences of numerous skippers, possessing centuries of inherited skills in sailing at surrounding and neighbouring seas. Apparently, entrepreneurs were smart enough to make use of that inborn strength by applying this skill in the strongly emerging economy of North-Western Europe.

Most importantly, land - although short in quality and quantity - proved to be the major element and accelerator as well of the ever-increasing economic growth and development of entrepreneurship. The profitability of Dutch agriculture had already been attested by continuous efforts to create new land by reclaiming it from the sea, by draining lakes and marshes, and by planting peat bogs after the peat had been removed for energy use. This activity started in the Middle Ages, but it increased substantially in the 16th and 17th centuries, and was especially intensive in the period of rising prices for farm products. Building dikes and carrying out draining activities required large capital investments. To that end, urban entrepreneurs formed companies to reclaim land, which they sold or rented to farmers. Likewise, peat production became a big thing in the Netherlands and provided the country with the required energy on which the entrepreneurs built the economy and kept it going. The three reasons why the exploitation of peat was important were that it was a unique entry to cheap energy. Next, the exploitation provided a lot of employment and, furthermore, it caused an extension of the canals for transporting the peat, which could also be used for other economic purposes, particularly in opening up markets. The first steps for intensifying the exploitation took place in 1530. Investments were made by companies of entrepreneurs who were founded in 1546 for the specific purpose of peat exploitation. Since 1550 there was even a consortium of Antwerp entrepreneurs, investing in the venture. A year later, wealthy merchants and artisans of Frisia started their own peat exploiting company and the same took place in Groningen in 1565. Quoting De Vries & Van der Woude in assessing the ultimate blessing of the

---

95 R. van Uytven, p. 27-30

use of peat, 'Dutch cities and rural areas were - at any 17th century measure - a triumph of human ingenuity that nature had deployed in favour of the economic interest'[96]. And it was already during the 16th century, and before, that entrepreneurs took massive measures to exploit the peat, as well as to found institutional structures to finance the exploitation, which from an energy point of view was quite visionary given the upcoming proto-industrial production.

At that juncture, Europe's commercial centre of gravity had, for a variety of reasons, been shifted west- and northwards. First, entrepreneurs had acquired the means to bypass the middlemen of the eastern Mediterranean in their quest for luxuries from the East. Secondly, there was a significant improvement in overland transportation routes through Germany and France to the north. And, finally, there were the growing needs of the larger political units in the west and north that attracted capital and enterprises of increasing size.[97] As discussed in the previous chapter, the geographic conditions of the delta during the Middle Ages gave rise to sea- and river navigation and to fishery, as well as to trade with England, Norway and especially with the Baltic states. In the 15th century important sea-faring contacts were extended to France, Portugal and Spain. Dutch supremacy in sea faring was underlined by the Danish Sund tolls of 1557, which showed that 60%.[98] of the cargoes conveyed from the Baltic to the west in that year were carried in the holds of Dutch merchant ships. The supremacy of Dutch skippers/merchants was to become the foundation of the Amsterdam financial and commercial hegemony well before the 17th century. The geographical position and infrastructure of Holland made a successful appeal to the creativity and initiative of their entrepreneurs. They made an advantageous use of these in such a successful way, that Amsterdam became the international business centre for the whole of Europe during the then following centuries.

---

96   Vries, J. & Van der Woude, p. 59-61
97   Hunt & Murray, p. 203
98   Hunt & Murray, p. 236. See also Wenneker p. 385: around 1650 this percentage increased to 71.

So, in the second part of the 16th century the volume and intensity of trade in mass merchandise increased. As a result the trade cities in the northern Netherlands got their competitive edge of having better waterway connections for the transportation of mass merchandise to the hinterland as compared to the transportation connections of Antwerp. Hence, entrepreneurs in the Northern Netherlands had been building a far larger merchant fleet then their counterparts in the Southern Netherlands. The fleet was even that big that the city of Amsterdam in 1596 could write to the Estates General that entrepreneurs in the Republic had exceeded the number of ships from those of France and England together. Dutch entrepreneurs found themselves in such a very advantageous position, that in a period of great expansion of traffic by sea, it was only *they* who had the biggest economic factor at their disposal, i.e. the required tonnage for sea transportation. Entrepreneurs in the already ancient shipbuilding industry took care for expanding the fleet in numbers and through technical innovations also improved its efficiency. Pretty soon, the English could not cope effectively with the competitive Dutch entrepreneurs and had not only to abandon their Baltic trade, but also the Nordic timber trade, the Archangel trade, as well as the whale fisheries near Spitsbergen.[99] These were all lost trades, however, created a lot of resentment with English entrepreneurs, who ultimately convinced their government in the 17th and 18th century to go to war with the Netherlands, apparently for them the only way to contain Dutch entrepreneurs in their successful free-trading practices.

Use and development of infrastructure during economic supremacy (1580-1670)

The importance of land and water, i.e. the geographical position of the Netherlands at the crossroads of East-West and North–South with good navigable rivers along the relatively busy North Sea, giving access to the Mediterranean and the Baltic Sea, has extensively been discussed in the previous sub-period (1350-1580). In addition, the exploitation of peat had created a fine grid of canals, which brought the production centres closer to the domestic markets. Over a peri-

---
99   J.G. van Dillen, in: Vaderlands Verleden, p. 342-3

od of less than 35 years (1631 to 1665) construction took place of 658 kilometres of canals with towing paths.[100] Also the road system improved considerably during that period.[101] Next, also a different type of infrastructural construction works of quite some magnitude took place. Between 1500 and 1815 a total number of approximately 2.700 polders, adding 250.000 ha of agricultural area were reclaimed and according to De Vries & Van der Woude half of these between 1590 and 1650.[102] The reclaimed land was mostly used for either extensive farming or animal husbandry, producing also luxury products for the domestic and international markets such as cheese and butter. These reclamations were generally financed by both entrepreneurs/investors from the cities and farmers with one overriding motive: the desire for making profits. Two other significant developments were connected to the investments in a better infrastructure. The first was the increasing high population growth throughout the delta region and the concentration of that growth in the cities. This led to entrepreneurial measures to improve the division of labour, resulting in higher productivity. Secondly, traditional farming was pushed aside in favour of a more market-oriented approach with specialised cultivation of produce and dairy in the rural (reclaimed) areas, for which entrepreneurs had found profitable markets.[103]

During the later period of trade capitalism (1670 to 1815) when the economy declined, no significant opportunity conditions for entrepreneurs in the area of infrastructural works could be recognised, apart from the continued reclamation of land by creating polders from lakes and marshland.

5.2. Labour

Use and development of labour during take off (1350-1580)

---

100 J. de Vries & A.M. van der Woude, p. .54
101 P.W. Klein, De Zeventiende Eeuw (1585-1700, in: J.H. van Stuijvenberg, (ed), *De economische geschiedenis van Nederland,* Groningen 1977, p. 91
102 J. de Vries & A.M. van der Woude, p. 49/50
103 P.W. Klein, De Zeventiende Eeuw, p. 87/88

As described in the previous chapter, there was around this period severe depopulation as a result of famine, pestilence and warfare. The numbers were indeed startling: in 1340 there were roughly 74 million Europeans; in 1400 is had gone down to 52 million, and there was little chance for survival of two other generations still to come. However, around the year 1450 a sustained period of population expansion took place in Europe, in particular in the Netherlands, where also the urbanisation was probably the highest all over Europe.[104] By the end of the 16th century about one-third of the population of Flanders and almost half of that of Holland lived in towns and cities, obviously giving a boost to entrepreneurship. At that time, towns functioned primarily as commercial and administrative- rather than industrial centres. Many manufacturing activities, as in the textile and metallurgical industries (weaponry), took place in the countryside. The handicrafts, practised in the towns, were usually organised in guilds, with extensive apprenticeship requirements and restrictive entry. The rural migrants to the towns, though, rarely had the skills or aptitudes necessary for urban occupations. These people formed a *Lumpenproletariat*, a pool of casual, unskilled labour, frequently unemployed, which supplemented their meagre earnings by begging and petty thievery.[105]

The size of the population around 1500 in the area of the northern Netherlands must have been around 0.9 to 1 million[106], which means a density of 30 persons per km². The variation per area, however, was quite high; 37 persons per km² in Holland, 25 in Frisia and 16/17 in the eastern part of the Netherlands. The density of the population was for the standards of those days quite high and became higher, because of increasing urbanisation, taking place in the delta area. This was partly due to the fact that the entrepreneurs in the towns managed to get the administration convinced to forbid the rural areas to carry out activities in trading and manufacturing,

---

104 Hunt & Murray, '...it is estimated that 10 percent of Europeans lived in cities in 1500, some 12 percent resided there in 1600, with Italy at 17 percent and the Low Countries at 25 percent' p. 227
105 R. Cameron, p. 99
106 J.A. Faber, p. 120, table 1

which were competitive to their own businesses.[107] However, the main reason of urbanisation must be sought in an increase of international activities, particularly, navigation at a time when trade was not yet the predominant economic activity. As the delta was situated at the vital European crossroads of the North-South and East-West axis, obviously many people were involved in navigation. This resulted, specifically around the fishery- and navigation businesses, a network of many other supplying and processing industries, like shipbuilding, timber production, fishing-nets and sail-cloth manufacturing, and the like. This high degree of urbanisation stimulated businesses to a high extent, as entrepreneurs could increase both productivity (a better division of labour as compared to rural manufacturing) and benefit from an increase of purchasing power, although there was a lot of poverty in the towns as well[108]. The high degree of urbanisation also provided the entrepreneur with a relatively large labour force, which had a decreasing effect on wages as compared to other urban centres in Europe, where there was a shortage of urban labour. This led to a higher competitiveness of Dutch products, specifically in the export markets. In conclusion, at the beginning of the 16th century there was a high degree of urbanisation and a well-developed infrastructure, which were favourable circumstances that made economic expansion relatively easily and rapidly possible.[109]

Use and development of labour during economic supremacy (1580-1670)

The growth of the population did not only take place as a result of normal demographic developments. Also foreign immigrants mainly established themselves in the cities, resulting in productive labour increase. Between 1600 and 1800 an approximate number of 500.000 foreign immigrants settled permanently in the Netherlands. Another 500.000 trans-migrant workers - those who only worked in the country for a small number of years -, were mainly

---
107 R. van Uytven, p. 20
108 In the early 1500, the poverty numbers in the cities varied between 23% (Amsterdam) and 40% (Hoorn). See Uytven, p. 20
109 Vries, J. de & A.M. Van der Woude, p. 82-95

active as sailors for the Dutch East-Indian Company (VOC). A third group consisted of seasonal labour, in particular for the whale hunting, peat exploitation, merchant fleet and agrarian sector. This latter group numbered after 1650 approximately 30.000 workers annually, staying for an average period of 4 months. It is estimated that for Holland the foreign labour contribution hovered between 15 to 20%.[110] These were very high figures, taken into consideration the fact that the total population in the Republic at that time did not exceed 2 million (approximately double the number of inhabitants in 1500). The strong economic development in the Republic attracted new immigrants and rural labour for the expanding enterprising sector. And as has been discussed in the previous section of this study, the fundamentals in society for everyone to benefit from the economic development, were in place as can be illustrated by the emergence of Leyden as the major textile city in Europe. Entrepreneurs from Leyden in manufacturing of cloth and drapery made the city one of the biggest industrial centres in Europe and probably in the world. Within a period of 40 years the population of the city increased from 12,000 to nearly 45,000 in 1622. With the arrival of the Flemish weavers around 1580, local entrepreneurs, with the assistance of the city government developed a textile industry, which ultimately included 125 different professions. These were united into seven main trades, which manufactured more than a 100 different qualities of fabrics for the world market. Technical innovations supported the increasing specialisation and differentiation such as the so-called ribbon mill, which stimulated large-scale production requiring a lot of labour. Due to the availability of immigrants, individual entrepreneurs were able to exploit in 1610 already more than 45 of these mills. Also the textile paint production improved, specifically by making use of a new dye, called indigo.[111] All these are excellent examples of opportunities, which were perceived by individual entrepreneurs with an orientation towards expansion and innovation.

In addition, also city governments were very supportive to the entrepreneurial class. They developed in many cities incentives,

---

110 J. de Vries & A.M. van der Woude, p. 95-106
111 P.W. klein, De Zeventiende Eeuw, p. 97

such as protective and promotional institution development. Taking all these developments into consideration it is clear that with the increasing availability of financial instruments, the entrepreneurial activity in the Netherlands was strongly on the increase. And as is known from recently carried out research, countries with a high level of entrepreneurial activity have a relatively high level of economic growth.[112] In sum, immigrant labour, politically or economically motivated, was widely available and indigenous entrepreneurs could employ that labour in the strongly expanding economy to the benefit of both the local entrepreneurs and workers, including immigrants.

Specifically different opportunity conditions for entrepreneurs related to labour during the latter stage of trade capitalism (1670-1815) were non-existent as a result of economic stagnation and the ultimate decline of the economy

5.3. Capital

Access to and deployment of capital during take off (1350-1580)

The increase of the circulation of money, minted from silver coming from the mines of Central Europe, together with the increase of commercial activities in the Netherlands, caused around 1540 an inflationary effect on the prices of food and other commodities. Inflation increased even more, when in the course of the Spanish war with the Netherlands (1568-1648) more silver, mined in South America, was coming into the direction of the Netherlands for maintaining the Spanish armies against the Dutch. Apart from inflation and the subsequent price increases in grain and livestock, the ultimate result was in fact a large flow of money into the Netherlands proper. This created the conditions for improving the construction of dikes in order to protect the country from regular floods that plagued many regions in the centuries before (Elisabeth flood in 1421) and at times

---

112 P.D. Reynolds (ed.)., Global Entrepreneurship Monitor; 2000 Executive Report, London, 2000, p. 45

brought severe damage to the economy. It was also the period of reclaiming land, which in many cases was financed by well to do entrepreneurs and merchants, investing their money productively in new land and by doing so created more business opportunities for themselves.[113] These entrepreneurs had been able to diversify farming and manufacturing, which became increasingly market-oriented and cost effective, so that by the middle of the 15th century they were capable of producing healthy surpluses. In addition, the calamities of pestilence and war, although disastrous for trade in general, had nonetheless the positive effect that it increased the velocity of the money circulation, hence increasing the money volume for short- and long term investments. The velocity of money was furthermore increased when entrepreneurs developed and started applying new financial instruments, such as the discounting of promissory notes, which were a perfection of the bills of exchange.[114]

Generally, local governments were instrumental in mobilising big money for capital investments. To a lesser extent also entrepreneurs provided these investments. These entrepreneurs were sometimes working independently, but more often they acted in cooperation with the city governments as their agents, or even as members of their administration. Through direct taxation the city council, was able to raise considerable amounts of ready money and also by raising lump sum payments in return for encumbering future income in order to satisfy its annuity obligations. The latter became the favourite of civic long-term debt in cities all over Europe, specifically in the Republic. And as the city councils were at that time largely composed of entrepreneurs, the investments were directed towards productive goals, such as the construction of ships, exploration of the riches beyond the seas and infrastructure designed to foster production and improved communications.[115]

---

113 J.A. van Houtte, p. 49
114 Hunt & Murray, p. 204; The idea was that those entrepreneurs who had a surplus of cash bought the promissory notes at a discount, to be cashed at a later date; this provided to the other entrepreneur (the seller of the promissory note) ready cash for his business.
115 Hunt & Murray, p. 204-208

Access to and deployment of capital during economic supremacy (1580-1670)

According to De Vries & Van der Woude, three characteristics as regards the presence of minted money in the Republic can be distinguished: first, the Republic - more than any other country - had acquired a large stock of minted money. Secondly there was a very fast growth of real money volume per capita at the end of the 16th and beginning of 17th century. And thirdly, in the course of the 18th century the money volume per capita even increased, although the velocity of money fell down enormously, which indicated that the population did not spent money and that entrepreneurs invested less.[116] The first two characteristics can be explained from the enormous production of the silver mines in the Americas, of which approximately 50% went to the Netherlands. Half that quantity went to Dutch enterprises for the payments of exports of cheese, butter, grain, herring and many other products to other countries. Merchants and entrepreneurs from Spain, the north of France and the Southern Netherlands, brought in the other half, for reasons to secure their money and/or savings. In addition, the trade deficit between the Northern and Southern Netherlands during the first half of the 17th century caused a massive flow of money to the North[117]. The free exchange in precious metal, guaranteed by the Bank of Amsterdam and the free export of gold and silver in mint as well as in bars - at that time quite unique in Europe and contrary to mercantilist philosophies embraced by France and England - became one of the strongest assets of Amsterdam and a boost for Dutch economic prosperity.[118]

The free export of precious metal was also the reason why Dutch entrepreneurs could relatively easily settle in other countries, like

---

116 J. de Vries & A.M. van der Woude, p. 116
117 J. de Vries & A.M. van der Woude, p. 109
118 See also: M. Polak, Geld als water:smeerolie voor de stapelmarkt, in: *Spiegel Historiael; themanummer: Van Electron tot Euro. Geld en geldpolitiek door de eeuwen heen*, juli/augustus 1999, p. 324-333; also: W. Korthals Altes, Valuta in de wissel van de tijd; De Nederlandse gulden in het internationaal betaalverkeer vanaf de 16de eeuw, in: *Spiegel Historiael; themanummer: Van Electron tot Euro. Geld en geldpolitiek door de eeuwen heen*, juli/augustus 1999, p. 334-343

for instance Lodewijk de Geer, one of the highly respected entrepreneurs at that time. He established a commercial empire in Sweden, where he exploited the forests to fuel the blast furnaces so as to produce canons, bullets, weaponry and all other products made of copper or ore. Other entrepreneurs, such as Marcelis, Dutz and Hoeufft made large investments in Russia, France and Austria, which proved to be beneficial for both the countries in which was invested and the Republic and not in the least for the entrepreneurs themselves.[119] However, as from the middle of the 17th century, entrepreneurs in general, did no longer initiate that many new business activities for which enormous amounts of money could have been made available. The government administration during that period, for instance, did not know what to do with the repayments of the redemptions on government bonds and therefore resisted amortisation of the same. So money for investments was readily available. However, the overriding reason why entrepreneurs did not make use of the access to capital for new innovative technologies, as much as they did in the 16th and the early part of the 17th century, was mainly that the profitability of investments in new technologies, were expected to be lower than the divestment to be made of existing technologies.[120] In other words, investments in existing technologies were still that profitable, that it did not pay to transfer to completely new technologies, which would ultimately have led to higher competitiveness, but would require enormous amounts in new investments (and interest payments) with a relatively low return on investments on the short and medium term. Apart from that, the availability of raw material in the Republic (e.g. coal and ore) to design, develop and apply the newer technologies as developed in Britain, was non-existent. So, although there were ample opportunities at the start of this sub-period (1580-1670), which indeed strongly stimulated entrepreneurship and economic growth, new opportunities in the Netherlands, however, dried up around 1660.

---

119 H. Méchoulan, p. 114-116
120 J. L. van Zanden & A. van Riel, *Nederland 1780-1914; Staat, Instituties en Economische Ontwikkeling*, Utrecht 2000, p. 46

Access to and deployment of capital during the sub-period of economic stagnation and decline (1670-1815)

Apart from the above-mentioned reasons a redistribution of the surplus of taxes took place in the second part of the 17th century, primarily in favour of the regents and the relatively inefficient but highly rewarded sector of the "non-tradables". The latter consisted of small-scale artisan- and craft sector, such as bakers, millers, shoemakers, etc., which were protected because of socio-political and fiscal considerations.[121] The city governments who were administrated in the 16th and 17th century by an elite coming from the trade- and export industry, became in the course of the 17th century a secluded group, no longer directly involved in businesses. It shifted its capital investments to government bonds, rather than to businesses. Interest of these bonds to be paid by the government was financed through mainly taxation of the artisan and craft sector, which due to their numbers generated the major part of tax revenues. Therefore, the regents, holders of government bonds, were interested in maintaining the status quo of the small artisans and craft sector, thereby protecting their own interest. In addition, due to the worsened urban economy, the pressure to protect the small-scale artisans and craft sector, as providers for basic commodities in the cities, gradually increased. Consequently, an increasing part of the surplus ultimately came –through taxation - into the possession of the owners of the public debt, i.e. the regents. Subsequently, the growing group of persons living off their interest did not invest in productive activities, and in many cases, simply could not due to absence of competitive investment opportunities. This redistribution of the surplus in favour of the craft sector and the owners of public debts, caused an upwards pressure to the cost of living and wages, which took place at the expense of the manufacturing entrepreneurs, the commercial investor "*par excellence*". The redistribu-

---

121 Because of the agrarian crisis between 1650 and 1750, prices of bread decreased quite a bit, but due to action of bakers, prices of bread decreased far less than other products. Specifically in Leyden the bakers were active; the city government allowed their prices to be established at a higher level, which was a measure to protect the profits of the bakers, rather than trying to get the lowest possible price for the consumer. (See J.L. van Zanden (1991), p. 142

tion of the financial surplus to the "non-tradables" and regents, at the expense of the profit margins of manufacturing entrepreneurs, was reason for the entrepreneurs to shift from labour intensive manufacturing – textile in particular - to other activities. And that led to economic stagnation of the economy after 1650 and an absolute decline as from approximately the end of the 18th century onwards. By extracting capital from the economically productive entrepreneurs, they did no longer perceive realistic business opportunities of the variety as had been seen in the previous sub-period (1580-1670). This was primarily caused by an ever increasingly growing government debt, and the influence of disturbances in trade, due to mercantilist policies and wars with France and England as well as due to the exclusion from the French free-trade zone. The years after 1780 did not produce any more feasible commercial opportunities, which could stimulate entrepreneurial activity at all. This can be typified as "the terminal phase" in which the sick patient - the economy of the Dutch Republic - after having experienced an elongated period of crisis, came to an end.

The final blow came as from 1795, when the Dutch Republic ceased to exist and was replaced by the pro-French patriotic republic, which in fact meant a French occupation of the Netherlands. The French - although they profiled themselves as liberators of the old regime - had only one purpose in mind, i.e. to simply milk Dutch wealth. It started with - what the French euphemistically called a "contribution for liberation" - the payment of 100 million guilders. Next, the patriotic republic was obliged to join France inseparably, and finally to financially maintain an occupation force of 25.000 soldiers.[122] This led again to war with Britain, loss of colonies, and the disruption in the international trade. The economy came to a near standstill, hence low entrepreneurial activities and an enormously high national debt to France. In order to reduce that debt, the French could not think of anything else but to bring it back in 1810 to one-third, resulting indeed to an annual reduction of interest payment to one-third. Nonetheless, the French occupation totally destroyed the economy of the Netherlands effectively, hence

---

122   JL. van Zanden & A. van Riel, p. 58

reducing entrepreneurial activity to an absolute minimum. All of this swept away the foundation of the famous Amsterdam capital market in 1814, when the Kingdom of the Netherlands was about to be established.[123]

5.4. Technology

Development and application during entire period of trade capitalism (1350-1815)

In order to be competitive in the international market with many foreign competitors trying to get their share of the market, Dutch entrepreneurs had to be constantly innovative in both production techniques in developing new products and/or adaptation of existing products. To be innovative in production techniques decreased the cost price of production, leading to sharper prices for the international markets, which in many cases could not be met by other competing foreign entrepreneurs. This had an immediate effect on the market share. An indication of the magnitude of innovations may be the registration of patents by the Estate General, related to inventions made by Dutch inventors. That number rose from 60 registered patents in 1590 to 125 registered in 1620[124]. Obviously there were many more inventions and improvements made on existing technologies, which were not registered. Innovations also took place in the area of product design and/or improvement. Once an entrepreneur had successfully developed a new product, there were many other local or international entrepreneurs, who copied the product and tried to penetrate the market. Also therefore, constant innovation of the product-lines was indeed necessary to remain competitive in the market.

Entrepreneurs started to apply existing windmill technology in a new creative way for various industrial uses, which led to new technologies, resulting in higher levels of productivity. Particular-

---
123 J;. de Vries & A.M. van der Woude, p. 161
124 De Vries & Van der Woude, p. 408

ly in the shipbuilding industry the effective use of this device was at a very high level. Whereas for instance the English constructed big and cumbersome ships, merchant- as well as and war vessels, Dutch entrepreneurs/ship-owners, under the pressure of the growing market, convinced shipbuilders to abandon the weaponry from the ships and constructed a flock of smaller vessels, which were fast and could be handled by a relatively small crew. This resulted in higher productivity and competitiveness due to lower transportation rates as compared to the enterprising sector of other countries. The tremendous growth of the international market for the Dutch apparently stimulated the innovative powers of the entrepreneurs and ship-owners. One of these innovations was the famous 'fluytship', which was constructed at the end of 16th century. This ship was four to six times as long as it was wide and could therefore carry an extreme large cargo, which made the transportation of merchandise per unit even more competitive. Entrepreneurial shipbuilders, pre-eminent in designing the right type of ships, were able to improve the level of productivity in both the mode of transportation (safer water transport) and shipping capacity (unit freight cost).[125]

Another newly designed ship was a fishing boat, the so-called 'hoeker', which had small holes in the hull, so that caught fish could be kept alive in a bath of sea water until the boat's return to port. But rightly the most famous of Dutch fishing boats was the 'herring buss', which was capable of making long voyages and maintained facilities for curing and packing the catch on board. As early as the 15th century, Dutch entrepreneurs and fishermen had perfected a method of curing fish at sea, which allowed their fishing fleets to remain at sea for several weeks instead of returning to the port every night. An excellent example of an entrepreneurial quality factor input: innovation (specialised ships in combination with on-board processing techniques) as a result of entrepreneurial alertness in making use of the opportunity to supply bigger international markets. Ultimately, this led to a high productive use of resources and again increased their competitiveness. Finally, shipbuilding technology made ships far cheaper as compared to English ship-

---
125   Hunt & Murray, p. 146

builders, as there was an abundance of supply of timber and other materials available at the Amsterdam staple market. In addition, modern techniques were used, such as labour saving cranes and a certain degree of standardisation, leading to economies of scale.[126] The conclusion can only be that Dutch entrepreneurs were very much aware of the issue of what is called 'competitiveness'. With their inquisitive mind they constantly improved existing technologies, leading to higher productivity and subsequent lower cost and larger markets. By constantly applying the methodology of 'trial and error', entrepreneurs improved old and existing technologies. The energy and creativity to do so was fuelled by what Baumol has identified as the entrepreneurial drive for wealth, power and prestige. As a by-product of this drive, their success was also an instrument to survive in the country's struggle against the exploitative and the religion-suppressive Spain. The success in the sea trade generated the earnings, which – through taxation - could be allocated by the Estates General to the fight for independence from Spain.

Entrepreneurial orientation related to technical innovations came to a halt during the 18th century. As explained before, entrepreneurial investments in new technologies, as the British did (steam and coal), would not result in a higher return as compared to investments in current technologies based on wind and peat. Dutch entrepreneurs became subject to the law of "inhibitory lead" as a famous Dutch historian would have described this situation.[127]

5.5. The market

Creating new market opportunities during take off (1350-1580)

---

126 J.G. van Dillen, in Vaderlands Verleden, p. 342-3
127 One of the examples Jan Romein described in an essay in 1937 was the fact that London for such a long time used gas as street lighting. The reason was that London was one of the first cities where city lighting was widely introduced at a time that the choice of gas made sense. However, when electricity got the upper hand in other large cities on the continent, London did not directly feel to switch over to electricity from its existing and good working but out-dated technology.

Following the Black Death and the replacement of the Champagne Fairs by that of Bruges, there was a widespread growth in numbers and importance of fairs after 1350. This can be considered as a manifestation of an increasing dynamic, flexible, and growing European economy. It was caused and also stimulated by the further development of the infrastructure, improved road transport technology, together with a more intense utilisation of the Rhine as a commercial highway. In addition, it was also the local governments who were quite active in attracting fairs to their territories, for the simple reason to tax participating entrepreneurs. The Flemish count Louis of Male, for example, granted numerous fair privileges in the 1360s in an effort to weaken the monopolies of the "great" cities of Bruges, Ghent and Ypres. Similar patterns were seen in Holland.[128]

The importance of Dutch entrepreneurs as major players in international markets began modestly enough in the 15th century, when the Dutch fishing fleets in the North Sea began to undercut Hanseatic dominance of the herring trade, simply because they were far more efficient. Meanwhile entrepreneurs developed other markets. From Portugal and the Bay of Biscay, they procured salt for the fish and for distribution in northern Europe, occasionally picking up cargoes of wine from France as well. But the main market for entrepreneurs was the Baltic region, specifically for grain, timber, naval stores, flax, and hemp. Out of the 40,000 ships recorded in the Danish Sund Toll registers, as entering or leaving the Baltic between 1497 and 1660, almost 60% were Dutch vessels.[129]

As the seas became busier all the time, new market developments took place, which started in Holland. Shipbuilding as an autonomous industry came up in Zaandam and Rotterdam. Shipbuilding-entrepreneurs got orders from either the provinces/cities of the Netherlands or from wealthy merchants. This developed into one of the major industries of the delta area, which stimulated the development of other supplementary industries. Then, at a later stage there were not only trade negotiations in Amsterdam about new ships to be constructed, but the city also became an enormous

---
128 Hunt and Murray, p. 192-194
129 R. Cameron, p. 122

trading centre for second-hand ships. Subsequently, agents started to develop their brokering services, who specialised themselves in finding cargoes for ships, as well as to find shipping facilities for individual merchants or consortia of merchants. And of course there were those who were brokering in assurances as well.[130] The first cargo of Portuguese spices appeared on the Antwerp market in 1501, which was transported from Lisbon by Dutch entrepreneurs. The Spanish and Portuguese, concentrating on the exploitation of their overseas empires in Asia and the Americas, left the business of distributing imports from these colonies to other European markets to other carriers. Of these, Dutch entrepreneurs were the most aggressive in seizing this captive market.[131]

As a result of the mysterious shift of herring from the Baltic to the North Sea, Dutch entrepreneurial fishermen rapidly started the supply to domestic market, and later began exporting to France and even to Germany. Dried, smoked and salted herring was in great demand in a Europe perennially short of fresh meat.[132] Thus by the mid-15th century, entrepreneurs had developed a substantial new market and, fuelled by population growth, was to become the huge and famous herring business of the 17th century.[133] Both the fishery industry and expansion of the merchant fleet did not only stimulate the construction of ships, but provided markets to potential entrepreneurs in many related industries: construction of sawing mills, the manufacturing of sail cloth, nets, cordage and paint. These markets were flourishing since the life cycle of ships was relatively short. This was due to the dangers at sea, buccaneering, and of course the vulnerability of the material, being exposed to harsh climatic conditions at sea. From a group of 88 ships that were anchored in Zeeland in 1569, 63 (70%) were not older than 10 years.[134]

In expanding the market through the commercialisation of other products, entrepreneurs followed much the same pattern, with a rec-

---
130 F. Braudel, p. 342
131 R. Cameron, p. 122
132 R. Cameron, p. 154
133 Hunt & Murray, p. 189
134 J.A. van Houtte, p. 56

ognisably modern cast. In the beer industry for instance, the brewers first achieved the desired quality and taste of the product. Then they searched for economies of scale, first by increasing the size of each brew with larger kettles, and, subsequently, by a more intensive use of the equipment to increase the number of brews per kettle. But by to-days standards, the market expansion was pretty slow, as the technology was slow to spread and old production habits slow to change. Nearly a century elapsed between the first imports of German beer into Holland and the establishment of local breweries capable of producing a product of equivalent quality.[135] The beer market in the Netherlands was indeed of great importance. There was a tremendous demand for beer as it was considered to be a basic food commodity. The raw material, grain (in big quantities imported from the Baltic) and water was abundantly available, as was energy in the form of peat and the relatively fast transportation - over the waterways - opened up markets for the entrepreneurs and made them big exporters of this commodity.[136]

At the end of the 16th century, Amsterdam entrepreneurs developed initiatives and activities to make the city the biggest staple market in Europe. They extended the 'mother trade' (the Baltic trade) to Russia and Sweden in the north, Central Europe in the east and the Levant in the south. And to show they meant business, merchants and entrepreneurs equipped many ships for voyages to Africa, Asia and South America. This all culminated in the establishment in 1602 of the Dutch East Indian Company (VOC), which, in a couple of years, over-classed the Portuguese and the English in the trade of spices. Capturing new markets also led to initiatives of entrepreneurs to extend the range of products by developing new ones, as well as through diversification of existing ones. Hence, in addition to the trade in grain, wood, fish salt and wine, entrepreneurs started to trade in new products, such as wool, silk, linen cloth, dye, spices, jewellery, weaponry and luxury items in relatively big quantities.[137] Time and again, entrepreneurs developed new 'prod-

---

135 Hunt & Murray, p. 190-191
136 F. Egmond, p. 190-193
137 O. Gelderblom, p. 117

uct-market-combinations', which proves that they were able to find an optimum between their interests and those of their clients in different countries and even continents.

It was through trial and error that Dutch entrepreneurs probably were the first in the world to develop, albeit implicitly, a successful concise international marketing strategy. This flair for marketing (product development, competitive pricing, product promotion and distribution) as a result of their commercial attitude and industrial creativity would prove to be a remaining characteristic of Dutch entrepreneurship till about the end of the 17th century, when industrial creativity for quite a number of reasons diminished sharply.

International marketing during economic supremacy (1580-1670)

Supply and demand of goods was first concentrated to local and regional markets and once there were surpluses, these were flowing to markets of a higher order (staple market), which - in its turn - provided merchandise to other local and regional markets in which there was a shortage. Hence, 'trading' tended to develop in a hierarchical structure of markets, on top of it one general, central stock and storage -the concrete world market, which functioned as the final regulator of production and consumption. It was also on this market where prices of merchandise were fixed, based – as is the case nowadays - on supply and demand. The organisation of this world market were tuned and coordinated with a large variety of commercial functions in various fields, such as navigation, logistics, money-, credit-, bank- exchange- and insurance businesses. Ultimately, that world market was based on three fundamental functions, i.e. supply, marketing and storage of stockpile. These stocks were very important for the entrepreneurs, as they were supposed to be a buffer for the risks they ran in price fluctuations related to supply and demand. In order to reduce that risk, the entrepreneurs put much emphasis on investments in stockpile, so that these could function as a price-stabilisation in an unpredictable market (wars, protectionism, raids, etc). So, to strengthen the function of price stabilisation in these staple markets, entrepreneurs were trying to acquire a monopolistic position in these markets so as to protect the stocks against unlimited competition, in which they were quite successful.[138] Contradictory to the views of the economist Schumpeter, P.W. Klein stated that controlling the market did not weaken the staple market. Instead it was strengthened, because it stimulated the entrepreneurs who managed to limit their risks to reinvest the profits, emerging from the monopoly trade, into extending and developing new markets. However, these monopolies never had a long duration and were constantly challenged by entrepreneurs who were not part of the monopoly trade, even so with the monopolies of the VOC and WIC.[139]

Although the Dutch staple market had a global significance, European traffic and trade was still predominant in the Republic, in particular the Baltic trade of which, during the first part of the 17th century, approximately 50% of all Dutch vessels transported grain only. Next, entrepreneurs did a lot of business with Norway, Russia and Sweden. In 1578 Dutch entrepreneurs founded a factory in Archangel and - as also in the case of Sweden - were involved in the establishment and foundation of local industries. They recruited skilled labour and provided capital and entrepreneurial talents in establishing the iron- and weapon industry, shipbuilding, paper mills, etc. Among the markets of Europe, the Russian one was without any doubt among the more exotic. The delta of the North Dvina River had become a destination and a gateway to the Russian market for Dutch merchants in the late 1570s; and here, not far from the White Sea, the Tsar had founded the town of Archangel in 1584, as the sole commercial port for the Russian interior. A permanent Dutch merchant community arose there in the course of the 17th century.

---

138 P.W. Klein, De Zeventiende Eeuw, p. 100-102
139 J. de Vries & A.M. van der Woude, p 769/770. This view though has been challenged by Veluwekamp, whose research indeed confirms the existence of monopolies, however, not widespread, as Klein wants us to believe. Big entrepreneurs as the Trips and the de Geers whose business flourished on monopolies, the great majority of the entrepreneurs were never able to establish monopolies; those with monopolies were exceptions to the rule; see also Lindeblad , p. 81

By the beginning of the 18th century, this community consisted of independent businessmen trading on their own behalf, for foreign merchants abroad, and also for mutual benefit with these partners. They were commercial intermediaries between the Dutch and the Russian markets and as an outpost to the Dutch business community they maintained direct contact with the merchants of Russia.

Furthermore, since the end of the 16th century entrepreneurs had developed quite an extensive trade and navigation network in the Mediterranean to countries like Italy, Greece, Levant, Turkey, Egypt and Cyprus. But they were subject to a lot of risks because of the dangers in that area, where not only pirates were very active, but Spanish war ships as well. In addition, there was fierce competition with the French and the British, which made entrepreneurial life in that part of the world not that much easier either. In spite of the competition between Dutch and French entrepreneurs, France had probably become the largest overseas market for Dutch exports and colonial re-exports by the 1640s. Like in many other French ports, the Dutch merchant fleet was dominantly present in international trade. In Bordeaux for example in 1651, 446 Dutch entrepreneurs accounted for 70.8% of all merchandise leaving the Bordeaux port by ship[140]. Bordeaux thus established a very close link with the Amsterdam entrepôt. However, the French minister Colbert developed a policy to counter the Dutch naval and commercial supremacy in France, which he believed was out of proportion, but proved to be a double-edged blade. While the minister's initiatives aimed at protecting the French manufacturers, the 'war on tariffs' alienated 'the most powerful helping force of the Bordeaux maritime trade: the Dutch'.[141] Ultimately, this led to a gradual withdrawal from France and instead Dutch entrepreneurs started to procure their wines from Portugal and Spain.[142] Apart from the sea trade, Holland was to a

---

140   Kooijmans, p. 44
141   Kooijmans p. 46, quoting Giteau 1966, p. 459
142   Kooijmans, p. 47-48; With the outbreaks of the Dutch wars, the situation of Dutch maritime trade in France deteriorated significantly. Between 1672 and 1678 and again during the Nine Years' War (1688 to 1697), not a single Dutch vessel sailed into the port of Bordeaux, however, at the end of each war, the Dutch merchant fleet returned massively to south-western France. In 1699 and 1700, the Dutch accounted for 76% of total ship freight; by 1715 their share had declined to 65%

high extent also involved in the continental trade, the hinterland to Germany up to Hungary and Silesia. Although these markets were there before, the supply of goods increased dramatically during this period. These areas exported their products over the big rivers to the Dutch staple markets, where Dutch entrepreneurs then took over the international sea trade of these products, using the country's natural axe-connections: North-South (Baltic to Mediterranean) and East-West (Continental hinterland to Scotland, England, Eire).

The war with Spain (1568-1648) was at times a blessing in disguise, certainly as regards making use of new opportunities offered by these circumstances (weapon production) and conquering new markets. The war forced the Netherlands to start the production of weapons and in a couple of decades the country turned itself into the biggest storage place of weaponry, supplying nearly the whole of Europe with it. Waging war was for quite a number of entrepreneurs an excellent way of earning their living as suppliers to the war machine. Apart from providing a stock of weapons, the merchants also organised financial services and credit-lines for three layers of government for financing the war machine, i.e.: 1) long term loans and short term credit for the regional- and town treasurers, 2) regular payments for the national army and garrisons in the border cities, and 3) remittances of funds, subsidies and loans to ambassadors and foreign powers. Small groups of merchants cooperated also in consortia and dominated the contracts with the States General for providing advances related to the subsidies and loans, whereby the States of Holland always guaranteed the repayment of the States General.[143]

At the end of this sub-period of *Trade Capitalism,* around 1670, the grip of Dutch entrepreneurs on the international markets diminished to quite some extent, due to protective measures against the Republic and the wars, which were waged by France and Britain with the explicit purpose to curtail Dutch entrepreneurship. Their antagonism focussed on promoting entrepreneurship of their own nationals through introducing prohibitive import taxes, which hit

---

143 M. de Jong, p. 296-297

Dutch entrepreneurs right away, as was even more the case with the implementation of the Navigation Acts. These were introduced by the British to promote their own- and damage Dutch trade. These Acts included that goods entering English harbours should only be transported by either English ships or ships where the merchandise originally came from. This ultimately resulted in two wars (1652-54; 1665-67), just a couple of years after the war with Spain ended in 1648. As a result of all these wars and protective measures, markets for textiles were lost in France at the time when the Leyden textile industry was at its zenith. In addition, the French and British also hampered exports of these products to the Mediterranean as well. Furthermore, the Leyden entrepreneurs had to face an extension of the production capacity in the rural areas of England, Liege and Brabant, which could produce at lower prices than the city industries, in spite of their economies of scale. But the Leyden textile entrepreneurs reacted favourably to that competition when they were able to replace parts of their production to the rural areas, thereby restoring their competitiveness.[144] A negative side effect with far reaching consequences, though, was the end of technical innovations, which ultimately led to the loss of the market leader's position in this trade.[145]

Markets, domestic as well as international, were per definition very vulnerable. Entrepreneurs could control elements for which they were responsible themselves, such as: 1) quality production of merchandise (cheese, beer, textile, sips, fish), 2) competitive prices (applying technical innovations leading to productivity improvements), 3) mobilising capital, i.e. investments, loans and working capital, 4) developing means to transport the merchandise to any corner of the world (navigation skills, advanced shipbuilding). However, there were many elements – specifically in international markets - they could not control. These ranged from acts of war, raids, piracy and the like to protectionist measures of importing countries. In addition, these markets suffered demographic catastrophies, recessions and drop in purchasing power. Only skilled entrepreneurship would be able to handle these controllable and

---
144 JL van Zanden, 1991, p. 111/2
145 P.W. Klein, De Zeventiende Eeuw, p. 99

uncontrollable elements in such a way that - at the end of the day - there were profits.

Remarkable for entrepreneurs – not only now in the 21st century but also then in the 17th century - was to turn a disadvantage into an opportunity. So when for instance in 1592, as part of the war between Spain and the Netherlands, the Spanish authorities closed the port of Lisbon to Dutch shipping, the Dutch immediately began building new types of ships capable of the months-long voyage around Africa to the Indian Ocean. In less than ten years more than fifty ships made the round trip between the Netherlands and the Indies. And these early voyages were that much successful that, in 1602, the government of the Republic, the city of Amsterdam, and several private trading companies formed the Dutch East India Company (VOC), which legally monopolised trade between the Indies and the Netherlands. Such answers to challenges can only be given by a society that is entrepreneurial, i.e. first, a government (to a large extent consisting of entrepreneurs), which create an enabling environment for entrepreneurs (security, reasonable taxation, education and a good portion of tolerance). Secondly, investors who were ready to share the risks with the entrepreneur and thirdly, there was a society in which entrepreneurship had a relatively high status.

At balance though, wars were costing the Republic more than it could gain through the delivery of weaponry to warring parties. French and Algerian pirates hijacked many hundreds of Dutch ships, but likewise ignited the development of a new market for Dutch entrepreneurs, i.e. piracy. As long as merchants were able to earn their living in trade without direct danger of invasions and the like, there was not that much interest in piracy as a commercial activity. This changed, however, in the course of the 17th century, when piracy became indeed profitable and an instrument for commercial warfare for both the government and the private sector, as proved to be true with the legendary capture of the Spanish silver fleet by Piet Heyn in 1628.[146]

---

146 I.J. van Loo, Kaapvaart, handel en staatsbelang. Het gebruik van kaapvaart als maritiem machtsmiddel en vorm van ondernemerschap tijdens de Nederlands Opstand,

Decline of international markets (1670-1815)

In this sub-period, the domestic/regional market for entrepreneurial activity in the Netherlands developed in such a way that at the end of the 18th century three concentric circles of regional markets could be distinguished. The first was the "Randstad Holland", which formed the core of the economy. In this strongly urbanised western part of the country, an approximate number of 80% of the population was active in manufacturing and the service sector. Agriculture was a subordinate source of employment[147]. The second domestic market circle was a centre that was surrounding an area, which was highly productive and specialised. This area consisted of the provinces of Groningen, Friesland, Zeeland and North-west Brabant, as well as the area between the big rivers. Their mainly agricultural activities were, via urban entrepreneurs, also directed towards the international market. The third domestic market area consisted of the regions, which were situated in the higher part of the Netherlands - the provinces of Drente, Overijssel, Gelderland, Noord-Brabant and Limburg. Their main economic activity was agriculture.

For the entrepreneurs, these domestic markets were complementary to the international markets, such as the Dutch settlements in the Mediterranean, Archangel, etc., which were part of the Dutch trading system. Dutch entrepreneurs abroad purchased export commodities from foreign local merchants and producers and sent these to their principles and business partners in the Dutch Republic and elsewhere. Conversely, these entrepreneurs sold imported commodities, which they received from their suppliers in the Republic and from elsewhere, to foreign local merchants and consumers. Initially in the late 16th century and the first half of the 17th century, these merchant settlements had been instrumental in the expansion of the Dutch staple trade. Via the settlements, Dutch entrepreneurs spread international supply, demand and commerce across Europe and the world and drew new regions into the circle of the international market place. When, subsequently, during the second part of the 17th centu-

---

1568-1648, p. 367/8
147 JL van Zanden & A. van Riel, p. 72-73

ry, entrepreneurs lost international markets, Dutch merchants in the settlements abroad again found and developed different markets, now for the purchase of raw materials and the sale of finished products on behalf of the Dutch export industry. However, these settlements gradually lost their function in the first decades of the 18th century, when foreign competition crushed Dutch industry and industry-related trade.[148] The decline of the Dutch Mediterranean settlements can be attributed to two structural developments. First, entrepreneurs in the Dutch industry-based trade suffered heavily under French competition (Mercantilism), particularly in the cloth manufacturing, whereas there was no alternative business, which could compensate for the loss. Secondly, Dutch entrepreneurs lost their primacy in Mediterranean commerce - especially the Italian and Spanish trade - as these became routine and accessible by local entrepreneurs from these countries.

In spite of the gradual loss of merchant settlements in Europe, Dutch entrepreneurs in transport services became in the course of the 18th century the most important carrying traders, handling the bulk of the transportation in north-western Europe. In time of peace, revenues in transportation were relatively low, but changed as soon as war broke out. Then there was scarcity of cargo space, of which skippers of a neutral country could benefit a lot. Best earnings for the Dutch transportation sector, was during the Seven Years War between France and England (1756-63) and the American Revolt (1775-80). However, the latter resulted in a war with England (1780-1784) as the British did not consider these Dutch entrepreneurs neutral anymore. Apart from these political considerations, the shipping market was also for other reasons, not an easy one for entrepreneurs. It was a risky business. In research carried out on this issue, it proved that the average profitability of 34 ships between 1780 and 1814 was approximately 6%. However, behind this figure there were many differences, ranging from a loss of 50% (pirate-trade) to a profit in that market segment of 64%, specifically for ships, carrying the "flag of convenience", sometimes under Danish-, Russian-[149], and later during the war situation with France also under Prussian flag.

---
148 J.W. Veluwekamp (1996), p. 164
149 JL. van Zanden & A. van Riel, p. 91

The war with Napoleonic France since 1795 completed the degradation of the Netherlands from the centre of international trade to the periphery of a closed-off continent. Obviously, this also had a devastating influence on trade, manufacturing and agriculture. The connection with the colonial empire (East- and West Indies, South Africa, Ceylon, etc.) got completely lost and was fully incorporated by warring parties of the French and British. This forced entrepreneurs to a complete stand still of the manufacturing of ships in the Zaan region, near Amsterdam. However, they managed to continue the important export trade of dairy products from the provinces of Holland and Frisia to England, making use of all sorts of contraband trading activities. Nearly all colonial products were also imported into the country in the same way. The barriers in sea-trade also had a couple of advantages. It stimulated, entrepreneurs to search for replacing products, such as for instance sugar beet for the no longer available cane sugar. Also land-trade increased, in particular with the increasingly important German market. So when British merchandise could not reach the country in the usual way, it was shipped to Hamburg, Bremen and Emden and from there, entrepreneurs transported these goods to the Netherlands.[150] Trade with France was at a low ebb as well. Although the "Bataafse" Republic was an ally of the French, France kept on continuing their national protectionist policies vis-à-vis Dutch entrepreneurs, hence import duties of Dutch agricultural products remained high when exporting to France. In addition, Dutch manufactured products were completely banned from import in France. Only after the complete incorporation of the Netherlands into the French empire (1810), these protectionist measures disappeared, although slowly. So when in 1812 a program of complete economic integration started, it was too late for Dutch entrepreneurial activities in trade and manufacturing to restore their previous trading position and benefit from the large French market, the more so as Napoleon was about to be defeated (1813), leaving the empire - including the Netherlands and its entrepreneurs - in complete disarray.

---

150 H.J.F.M., van den Eerenbeemt, p. 180

6. INSTITUTION DEVELOPMENT

As has been elaborated in chapter three, institutions - the rules of the game in a society (constitutions, laws, conventions) - is affecting the performance of the economies, hence the performance of the entrepreneur. It shapes the interaction between human beings and reduces the uncertainties of everyday life. It can influence opportunity conditions, related to capital, labour, raw materials and the market. In addition, it may also influence socio-cultural factors, which are supposedly significant for the emergence of entrepreneurship. The governmental role has been described as being one of three possible types, i.e.: *protective, promotional and corrective*. Obviously, the government's role in institution development is a top-down process. But there are also bottom-up processes taking place in institution development. For the purpose of serving their own interest entrepreneurs are establishing private sector institutions, which are able – among others - to lower transactional cost when doing business. Below follows an analysis of the issue of 'institution development' as has been developed by both the government and the private sector in the three periods during *Trade Capitalism,* i.e. the period of economic take off (1350-1580), then follows the period of economic supremacy (1580-1670) and finally the period of stagnation and economic decline (1670-1815)

6.1. The period of economic take off (1350-1580)

Government initiatives in institution development

To guarantee 'law and order', is one of the main functions of a government. Not only to protect the people and country falling within its jurisdiction, but also to create institutions (legal framework and enforcement of the same) that will enable (business) organisations, to carry out their activities safely, orderly and cost-effectively (low transactional costs). During the Middle Age there had been a very loose governmental structure between the various regions in the delta as well as in the Holy Roman Empire of the German Nation of which the delta area was official part. Initially, there was hardly any emperor showing interest in the Low Countries, which gave ample room to the local nobility to control and/or extend their territory and thus to fight their own wars which, obviously, severely hampered business- and entrepreneurship development. One of these very damaging wars, which lasted even more than one hundred years of civil strife, broke out in 1350. In fact, it was nothing more but a confrontation between two groups of the nobility. The one group (Hooks) were more or less representatives of the old feudal order, whereas the other (Cods) represented the powers of the future monarchical authority of the Dukes and the bourgeois of the cities in the delta area. Entrepreneurs in cities like Dordrecht (at that time becoming an important staple market for merchants from the Hanse) and also in Leyden and Amsterdam were very active in developing their businesses, but their enterprising sector suffered time and again when fights revived. Transportation of merchandise to markets in other cities was unsafe, which hampered the production and in other cases increased the cost price of the merchandise. Entrepreneurial risks ran high and continuity in businesses was to a high extent absent. However, the end of the 15th century marked an important period in the economic development of the Netherlands, as the party struggles between Hooks and Cods diminished and finally faded away.

Important for the business community were both the era of peace that followed and the reforms of central administration, which had already started in 1477 and was completed by Hapsburg Emperor Charles V in 1531. It changed the medieval personalised way of running an administration into an un-personalised bureaucratic administration of an emerging modern nation state. Next, a so-called Great Council was established in the city of Mechelen, which was supposedly the highest court for the entire Netherlands. In addition, each Province had a Provincial Court. In each of the Provinces, 'Stadholders' both in charge of the army and as representatives of Charles V, were appointed for life.[151] These functionaries were recruited from the highest nobility. Obviously, these administrative innovations were important foundations for the development of the economy, as these provided some sort of a legal structure to entrepreneurs, necessary to reduce risks in establishing and running their businesses. And as we have seen in the study of North and Thomas[152], property rights and the enforcement of it, are of great importance in developing entrepreneurship, as it safeguards the benefits in return of 'socially desirable' activities.

However, things turned out differently. Prior to the War of Independence with Spain (1568-1648), the merchants of Antwerp were already the fiercest adversaries of Spanish rule, when, without any success they had pointed out to Philips II (successor of Charles V), that the Inquisition caused a great deal of damage to trade and freedom of the city. Moreover, heavier taxes were imposed and this again stirred unrest under the population, in particular the entrepreneurs, and their frustration found a way out in the 'Iconoclastic Fury' of 1566[153]. The only answer Philips II could think of was to send an army to suppress the revolt, but that again was costing money, which resulted in even heavier taxation of the businesses. It meant a 10% levy on all trade transactions and a 5% levy on transferring real estate. There were many protests against these measures, 'as it would affect trade and industry adversely, apart from the fact that it would stimulate the departure of skilled labour to countries like

---

151 H.P.H. Jansen, p. 245-246
152 D.C. North & R.P. Thomas, The rise of the Western World; A New Economic History, Cambridge, 1973, p. 2-3. Individuals must be lured by incentives to undertake the socially desirable activities. Some mechanism must be devised to bring social and private rates of return into closer parity (...) A discrepancy between private and social benefits or costs means that some third party or parties, without their consent, will receive some of the benefits or incur some of the costs. Such a difference occurs whenever property right are poorly defined or are not enforced. If the private costs exceed the private benefits, individuals ordinarily will not be willing to undertake the activity though it is socially profitable. See also: De Soto, H., The Mystery of Capital; why capitalism triumphs in the West and fails everywhere else, London 2001
153 This was in fact a merger of two separate developments against Spain, i.e. the heavy taxation, initially due to centralisation efforts of the administration of Philips II and the emergence of Protestantism (Calvinism), which was apart from ideological conviction, also a clear position against Spain, being the protector of Roman Catholicism (Inquisition).

England'[154]. The war, or in the words of the French historian Henry Méchoulan 'the first modern revolution'[155], had started and obviously disrupted trade and industry to a high extent. Quite a number of cities were still adamant as regards which party to support, either Spain, or the Dutch revolutionaries. Amsterdam e.g. was in favour of Spanish rule as entrepreneurs, in particular the merchants wanted peace in order to do their business without all sorts of disrupting events. But finally, in 1578, Amsterdam had to surrender to William of Orange, the Stadholder and army commander of the revolting Dutch provinces. A new local government was installed, which was Calvinistic in nature, however, was to reconcile to the requirements of the merchant class and therefore religious fanaticism was out of the question. A year later, though, a number of the Southern Provinces of the Netherlands decided to a breach with the rebelling Dutch army and concluded peace with Philips II. As a reaction, the Northern Provinces decided in the same year (1579) to found in Utrecht the first republic in Europe, the Republic of the Seven United Provinces and to continue their war of independence with Spain. The 'founding document' of the Republic, however, was mainly a document on how to put a defence system in place, rather than a constitution.

In these provinces there were 58 cities that had voting power in the Provincial States. These functioned as the building blocks of the sovereignty of the United Provinces. They allowed to be taxed, albeit through a decentralised tax systems. This was very much to the liking of the entrepreneurial class, which was strongly represented in the city councils and were in the position to monitor taxation for the enterprising sector, i.e. the height and allocation of the tax money. Thus, in order to finance the war against Spain, the province of Holland for instance - in addition to current taxes - introduced in 1585 a war tax on the sale of wine, beer, meat, peat, salt, soap, rye, cloth, spirits and the utilisation of the weighhouse, which was readily accepted by the private business sector.

---

154 Méchoulan, H. p. 33
155 Méchoulan, H., Amsterdam ten tijde van Spinoza: Geld en Vrijheid (J. Noorman trans. Amsterdam au temps de Spinoza), Amsterdam 1992, p. 19

Interestingly, the government structure was very decentralised and connected entrepreneurs to local governments. The entrepreneurs were therefore in the position to influence the enactment of legislation, which served their (and others') business interests. This form of 'self-government' proved to be an essential element in the commercial success of the Republic. The new Republic, although completely new in Europe as an institution, was in fact a continuation of the strong particularism of the cities dating back from the Middle Ages, which gave ample room for the entrepreneurial class to operate successfully in that environment. This was totally different as compared to other nations (Spain, France, England) where at that time there were many efforts to strengthen central- rather than local governments. In quite some cases centralisation proved to be 'exploitative' rather than supportive to business development and, to some extent, hampered the free development of entrepreneurship. This difference was exactly where Dutch entrepreneurship had a winning edge over their foreign competitors in the period of *Trade Capitalism*.[156]

On the other hand, though, local governments in their shortsightedness did not always protect the interests of the entrepreneurial community effectively, as is shown in the case of for instance Bruges. The city government forced 'nations', groups of foreign merchants, to move from Bruges to Antwerp, in order to protect their own local entrepreneurs. And that has been one of the reasons why Antwerp, as a trade metropolis, took over from Bruges. It is a sad example of over-protection of the rights of local entrepreneurs, which resulted in the move of the all-important English drape-trade from Bruges to Antwerp where it met far more sympathy.[157] Another example of local unproductive government intervention, at the explicit request of the entrepreneurs in 1531, was the enactment to prohibit the manufacturing of textile in the rural areas of Holland, as it meant too much competition for their urban based manufacturing. But

---

[156] However, it was also one of the important reason for the decline of the Republic in the 18th century, when the centrally governed powers (France and England) defeated the ineffective and often indecisive amalgamation of the strongly decentralised Republic.

[157] H.P.H. Jansen, p. 229

also local governments often lacked enforcement of laws and directives, so this measure never had any effect.[158]

As was common practice in the late Middle Ages, city councils kept on continuing to set rules and regulations for entrepreneurs and by doing so supported them in running their business in an organised manner. These included, among others, regulations related to opening hours, the specific place of the market booths, quality guarantees, price formation, competition, admission of 'foreign' merchants, mischievous trading practices, and so on. Similarly there were also detailed worked out regulations for the transport sector, such as e.g. tariff structures, arrival and departure times, berth, discharging-berth, regulations concerning who, where and when somebody had its turn, ethical standards, penalties, and so on. The same was applicable for the manufacturing sector, where the authorities set rules, such as the size of the enterprise, organisation of labour, standards for education/training, production means, production volume, quality requirements and standardisation, wages and prices. Finally, regulations also existed for the finance sector, such as initiating new exchange banks, lending facilities and insurance facilities.[159] But local governments had of course to be paid for their services and the way this was done had also its roots in the late Middle Ages, where income was generated from the region under their jurisdiction. In the city of Breda, for example, which was the territory of the Prince of Orange, entrepreneurs who needed an 'octrooi' (a licence to which in many cases a number of monopolistic clauses were attached), could not do without the 'limited liability company Oranje-Nassau'. It stands to reason, that 'Oranje Nassau' enjoyed financial income by providing these licences.

In their dealings entrepreneurs could experience problems from another centrally led institution, i.e. Justice. On the one hand Roman (written) Justice was practised in the Republic, though in the rural areas common law was practised up until the 17th century. Although the greater part of Roman Justice was not codified, it

---

158 H.P.H. Jansen, p. 253
159 C. Lesger & L. Noordegraaf, Ondernemers & Bestuur, p. 31-32

did not affect its validity.¹⁶⁰ Apparently, it was worth the trouble to appeal for justice, since a legally founded state apparatus in combination with an effective monopoly of violence was the best guarantee for entrepreneurs to realise their targets, even if enforcement of the law and regulations was not always optimal. Altogether, promoting the establishment of a legal framework was of great importance to the entrepreneur, as it had the potential to limit business risks.

In promoting businesses, city governments played a dominant role in establishing - what we would nowadays call - an industrial policy. They tried to promote branches of industry in their cities, by luring entrepreneurs from other cities into theirs, offering better conditions for establishing their businesses. This included, among others, to charge low- or even freedom of rents for empty churches or convents where their products were promoted. These churches had been confiscated as a result of the Reformation. Entrepreneurs applying to city magistrates to get support in starting a new enterprise or even a totally new industry, received some form of assistance, such as bounties, patents, monopolies, cheap loans, tax exemptions, exemptions from civic duties, free use of city owned equipment, or special arrangements for the provision of labour. Local governments also tried to limit competition of the rural areas in favour of entrepreneurs active in industry and retail trade. Indeed, it looked like as if the Republic consisted of a number of part-economies with their own particularism, their own mint and their own tax-system. But 'this tempering of civic particularism with a much greater measure of provincial collaboration than pertained in any of the South Netherlands provinces (under Spanish rule) was to prove an abiding pillar of strength to the future Dutch world entrepôt'¹⁶¹. In general, local government was quite active in promoting the general business interest, in particular once it saw the advantages of tax-income as a result of a thriving business community. It became not only active in promoting the industry, but also in establishing strict quality

---
160 A.C.M. Kappelhof, p. 317-318
161 J. Israel p..24, as quoted in J. de Vries & A.M. van der Woude, p 217; See also: C. Davids, Staple Market, p. 167)

control standards and ensuring access to adequate sources of good raw material, for instance, water in the case of beer production.[162] Obviously, the tax revenues were to quite some extent allocated to the development of the infrastructure, particularly waterways. This was important for the entrepreneurs as domestic commercial navigation served three important purposes. First, to distribute in a cost-effective manner raw materials and semi-finished products to other harbours for further distribution to processing- and production centres or for export. Secondly, to supply products for the urban areas throughout the country, such as food, construction material, peat and all other products, which were needed for daily life in the cities and for opening up markets. Finally, it was important for them to transport both, all sorts of domestically produced products and imports between the various harbours in order to supply the domestic markets and the hinterland.[163] Also local governments of the coastal cities were very active in promoting local businesses and made tax revenues available for investments in the new 'herring busses' and big nets for the fishing industry.[164]

Apart from *promotional* activities, government authorities also took *corrective* actions. Quality performance was regularly checked in order to combat unacceptable levels of quality in the production of, for instance, beer, textiles, etc. If not done, it could - in their eyes - be very harmful for both the consumer and the export business. To that end local governments in e.g. Leyden, Amsterdam, Haarlem, Delft and Gouda established 'halls' where the quality of the produced merchandise was certified by sworn-in government authorities, which approved the quality with a seal or any other type of certification. The measure was implemented and enforced in order to correct badly produced products and by doing so it protected the serious entrepreneurs in their drive to export quality merchandise, as international competition was always luring around the corner. These quality control 'halls' were places to trade the merchandise, and simultaneously incorporated in some instances local banks

---

162 Hunt & Murray, p. 190-191
163 J. de Vries & A.M. van der Woude, p. 229
164 Hunt & Murray, p. 189

where entrepreneurs could put unsold merchandise in pawn. These services were specifically provided to support the micro entrepreneurs, who had a very modest production and needed government assistance to get their business off the ground, or at least stay in business. At the end of the market day, the entrepreneurs could put their merchandise (cloth, pipes, or else) in pawn at a small interest fee; in 1672, Leyden, for example, charged only 3.6% interest.[165]

Private sector initiatives in institution development

One of the most important private sector institutions during the entire era of trade capitalism were the guilds. Between 1400 and 1820 there were as many as 1900 guilds in the Netherlands. Depending on time and location, they exercised much influence in the areas of justice, military, religion, social and politics. Between 1400 and 1800 the guilds in Dordrecht influenced the composition of the city council. In Utrecht the magistrates of the city between 1304 and 1528 (more than two centuries!) were, although indirectly, chosen by the guilds. Moreover, the guilds exercised the right of petition, a means to force the local government to develop the right legislation for their own goods. In addition, they were allowed to solve disputes within the guild proper, hence without interference of the official legal powers in the city.[166] Finally, their most important reason for existence was the economic function they exercised.

Guilds were 'organisations in which professionals of the same trade, with the permission of the local government, united with the specific purpose to promote together their economic interests, taken into consideration the general interest'.[167] They were monopolists of the labour market and actually some sort of business cartel. They regulated competition among their member-entrepreneurs by introducing all sorts of measures to limit the production. These included, among others, in raising thresholds for new entrants into the profession, fixing the maximum scale of enterprises, the number of workers per each business and fixing the minimum quality stand-

---

165 C. Davids, Kapitaal, p 101; See also :.J.A. van Houtte, p. 66
166 J.A. van Houtte, p. 64
167 Quoted by E.J. Fischer (1999), p.12

ard of the produced products or services rendered. In quite some cases the guilds also procured raw material for their members, which had a beneficial effect on both the price level and the availability. Finally, by regulating the production volume they also safeguarded sales and profits.[168] Jewish entrepreneurs and others who, according to the guilds 'exercised heresy' were usually not allowed to become a full member of the guilds. In Amsterdam, for example, they were excluded from the membership with the exception of the brokers- printers- and the surgeon guilds; but even in theses guilds jewish businessmen were nonetheless subjected to certain limitations.[169]

Specifically in the Netherlands the guilds, or entrepreneurial branch association, as they also might be called, were a guarantee for their member-entrepreneurs and workers that there was always work, whatever the number of foreigners and immigrants that came into the country. These foreigners came to the Republic as both political/religious and economic refugees, as the conditions - especially wages - for the latter were far more favourable than in the country they came from. But also to the consumers the guilds were a wanted entity, as in their view 'the uncertainty (…) about the quality of the products was the basic reason for the formation of the guild organisation'. And because of the fact that the guilds could offer a solution to that quality problem, entrepreneurs in the urban economies were capable to acquire a monopolistic position and to retain that for centuries.[170]

Also other forms of entrepreneurial cooperation took place. In the fishery business, for instance, consortia of ship-owners (partenreders) made relevant investments, which were financed by financiers, entrepreneurs and the skippers themselves.[171] Consortia of entrepreneurs were also established in procuring raw material for the textile industry, which were then supplied to the management of the workshops where the drapes and cloth were manufactured. Also the sales of the finished product was mostly organised by official group journeys of entrepreneurs to markets in Deventer, Frankfurt and

---

168 E.J. Fischer, 1999, p 12; See also : Hunt & Murray, p. 35-37
169 E.J. Fischer, 1999, p. 14
170 C. Davids, Kapitaal, p. 99
171 J.A. van Houtte, p. 62

elsewhere, under supervision of a chief, thereby reducing the cost of transportation and competition in the sales of the merchandise.[172] Clearly, in furthering the economic interest there was often no alternative for the entrepreneur – in spite of their individualistic attitude - but to work together with colleagues. For transactions they had done for other entrepreneurs, they charged a small percentage. This was a form of rendering mutual services, rather than providing services as part of a partnership. Forms of the latter were the so-called 'participation partnership', in which certain ventures were carried out at the mutual benefit of those who participated in the deal. The institutional form of cooperation among entrepreneurs was the partnership, which was usually formalised by written contracts, specifying the rights and obligations of each partner. By means of correspondence, among widely separated partners or agents, they kept abreast of developments, political as well as economic.[173] After the deal had been concluded, each of the collaborating entrepreneurs went their own way again. Whatever the form of cooperation and loyalty, reliability and personal trust were important aspects of commercial life among entrepreneurs. That type of solidarity among merchants and entrepreneurs was not so much a form of class-solidarity. As a matter of fact, entrepreneurs were all too often individualistic orientated, who – nonetheless - tried to limit their risks by selected patterns of cooperation among them. Competition and business rivalry, though, were usually rife.

Another form of institution development by the private sector was the organisation of the various levels of retailing for the distribution of goods. Next to the general type of markets where all sorts of merchandise and food stuffs were traded, entrepreneurs tended to specialise in certain product groups to be marketed in special places of the towns, for instance, the goose market, cheese market, bread markets, fish markets, etc. In fact, trading was done at any place that lent itself to it, even on ice, when the big rivers got frozen over. Local governments regulated the establishment and operations of the markets, specifically as regards the supply of merchandise. In

---
172 R. van Uytven, p. 42
173 R. Cameron, p. 125

order to protect the production of small local manufacturers, similar merchandise from elsewhere was then banned. In a number of cases in the 16th century, the local governments, financially assisted by rich entrepreneurs, started to build here and there halls, places which were roofed and where traders could market their products, irrespective the condition of the weather.[174] Next to the highly regulate markets, different other types of markets emerged, such as e.g. the so-called 'private markets'. These were market places, which were developed to circumvent the strictly regulated 'open markets'. A variation on that was 'the local inn', where entrepreneurs and merchants came together to do business, as well as to provide loans at usury rates.

A first serious competitor to the markets was the emergence of shops. Entrepreneurs, often before stallholders at the market, established small shops, which proved to be a strong stimulus for trade in general. The big difference of course was that markets were held with intervals, whereas the shops were always there at a fixed location. The first entrepreneurs who started a shop were artisans, who used their place as a workshop and sales-outlet simultaneously. The real shop owners came a little later. These entrepreneurs penetrated in between the artisan and the consumer and limited their activity to the procurement of merchandise and the sale of it only, without manufacturing the merchandise themselves. Entrepreneurs gradually specialised their shops in different types of activities. There were shops who started to sell merchandise per weight, such as grocers, or per the seize, such as textile retailers, but also shops for hardware, furniture, clothes, pharmacy, money changer, banker. And there was also the innkeeper, who often functioned as an intermediate for road transportation, shoemaker, and so on. In conclusion, there were three main reasons, which attracted entrepreneurs to become a retailer. First, the growth of the population and positive economic development required a change in methods of the distribution of goods. Secondly, a fixed selling place and longer opening hours coupled with promotion and bargains, was an attractive venture for potential customers. And thirdly, the retailer was able to get

---

174 F. Braudel, p. 23-32

credits from his supplier, the wholesale merchant, as well as was he able to provide short-term credit to his customers. In many cases a retailer was an entrepreneur who lived among those to whom he owed money and those who owed money to him. In fact he was constantly living on the brink of bankruptcy.

Entrepreneurs who were active as hawkers completed this whole distribution network. These travelled with merchandise on their backs from hamlet to hamlet. In quite some cases the hawkers opened up markets in the villages for retailers, creating markets for them, or to establish a new shop. Also for the wholesaling entrepreneurs, the hawkers were a 'god-sent' as they were instrumental in selling unsold stock lying idle in their warehouses.[175] With the further increase of the population and the economic activity, the wholesale business came up strongly. Entrepreneurs, who had been successful in the regional and/or year markets, tended to switch over to entrepôts. These were bonded warehouses to store their merchandise, which was either sold through domestic trade by retailers, hawkers, market vendors, or exported to other regions or even countries.

A private sector institution of a very special kind was the staple market, which could be considered as some sort of world market, being the follow-up of the local and regional markets. Supply and demand was first concentrated on local markets. Surpluses flowed to inter-local and, subsequently, to regional markets. In this way there arose a hierarchical market structure and on top of it one central storage facility of goods - the staple market. A first trial in the Netherlands as regards the institutional set-up of such a staple market was in Dordrecht, which came up strongly around 1380, but declined in the 1420s. But the real world famous Dutch staple market in Amsterdam came into existence in the 16th and 17th century and established itself as the international trade market. Clearly, entrepreneurs had made the Amsterdam staple market to function as the international major collection and storage point and as a centre of distribution. In addition, it became the focal point of business information and communication and as the final

---
175 F. Braudel, p. 67

regulator of production and consumption. Here the price of the commodities and products were fixed. Peripheral to the staple market, albeit of extreme importance to the total success of the national economy, were additional and complementary entrepreneurial activities. These included development of services in the field of the money- and credit markets, establishment of banks, set-up of the bourse, newsgathering, information provision and the founding of insurance companies.[176]

6.2. Institution development during economic supremacy (1580-1670)

Government initiatives in institution development

The economic policies of the nation-states in the period of T*rade Capitalism* had a dual purpose, i.e. building up economic power to strengthen the state, and to use the power of the state to promote economic growth and enrich the nation. Profits and power were two sides of the same coin. The state sought to obtain revenues to maintain their greatly expanded military forces, however, this led them frequently to enact policies that were indeed detrimental to truly productive activities. According to Adam Smith, this then led in many countries to forms of Mercantilism, which in his view was perverse, because they interfered with the 'natural liberty' of individuals and resulted in what modern economists call a misallocation of resources. In its innermost core, Mercantilism was in fact 'state-making' and 'national-economy-making' at the same time. Adam Smith, however, held that policies were devised by merchants and imposed these on rulers and statesmen, who were ignorant of economic affairs. Just as merchants are enriched to the degree that their income exceeds their expenditures, nations would also enrich themselves to the extent that they sold more to foreigners than they purchased abroad, taking the difference, or the 'balance of trade' in gold and silver. The strongly decentralised Republic, more or less governed by the wealthy merchants, could only follow a more

---
176 P. Klein, as quoted by de Jong & Paridon, p. 25

open economic policy. Living principally by international trade, the Republic simply could not afford the restrictive, protectionist policies as adopted by their larger neighbours. They established free trade at home, welcoming to their ports and market the merchants and entrepreneurs of all nations. And that policy ultimately led to European dominance of Dutch entrepreneurs. According to Colbert, the principle French minister of Louis XIV, 20,000 ships, more than three-fourth of which belonged to the Dutch, carried all the trade of Europe[177]. Colbert reasoned that France could increase its share only by decreasing that of the Dutch, an objective he was prepared for to go for war. That is why he promulgated in 1664 a comprehensive system of protective tariffs and when this failed to improve the trade balance, he resorted in 1667 to still higher, virtually prohibitive tariffs. Dutch entrepreneurs, who carried a large portion of French commerce, retaliated through their government with discriminatory measures on their own. Such measures of commercial warfare contributed to the outbreak of the actual war in 1672, which ended in a stalemate. In the peace that followed, France was obliged to restore the tariff of 1664.[178] And with Britain, the situation was not that much different. Two wars had broken out with England as a result of the British Navigation Acts, a trade protective measure to curtail Dutch trade supremacy.

Recent studies on entrepreneurship show a direct relation between the level of entrepreneurial activity and economic growth, although in some cases, high economic growth was not directly related to high levels of entrepreneurial activity.[179] In the case of the mercantilist attitude of France and Britain, it was not entrepreneurship that was promoted, as a result of which economic growth was realised. In these countries it were primarily protective measures, backed up by power politics (wars) that produced economic growth. The open market approach of the Dutch was in fact a very modern one, which is nowadays fully embraced by the greater part of the world. However, in those days (around 1650/1660), countries like France,

---

177   R. Cameron, p. 134
178   R. Cameron, p. 152
179   P.D. Reynolds, p. 45

England and Spain were far more interested in centralised nation building, which needed economic prosperity (taxes). Although it had probably the right commercial attitude, the Republic was simply too small in terms of human resources to wage effectively wars against these big countries[180]. If ever, there had been a "World Trade Organisation" at that time, things would have been developed so differently; however, 'ifs' do not exist in history writing!

Indeed, Dutch entrepreneurs got a different type of support from central, provincial and city governments in optimising their international trade position. This got its momentum when the supply of spices to northern Europe till the 1590s, which was taken care of by the Portuguese, South Germans, Italians and some Spaniards, stagnated due to wars.[181] Hence, entrepreneurs from the north of Europe saw their chance to collect the spices directly from the supply sources in Asia. First the English tried to take over the trade, immediately followed by the entrepreneurs from the provinces of Holland and Zealand. After a few failed attempts, among them the running aground of Willem Barentsz at Nova Zembla, the first ships loaded with spices returned from the East in Amsterdam. This great success led to other expeditions initiated by other towns of the Republic and a 'company' to bring all forces together, was erected. Nonetheless, competition of other 'companies' from various other Dutch towns was the order of the day. It was the political leader of the Republic, Johan van Oldenbarneveldt, who supported the idea of establishing one united company so as to combine forces and to compete effectively with similar enterprises of other nations. Van Oldenbarneveldt succeeded in convincing the various competing towns, such as Rotterdam, Delft, Hoorn, Enkhuizen and Middelburg in working together with Amsterdam in the establishment of the United East Indian Company (VOC) in 1602.

---

180 According to Wennekes, France, at that time, had 20 million inhabitants, England 6 million, whereas the Republic under 2 million inhabitants. See: Wennekes W., Gouden Handel, p. 394

181 The closure of the Lisbon Harbour was mainly the result of the temporarily amalgamation of Spain and Portugal between 1580 and 1640 (Personal Union), and as Spain was in war with the rebellious Republic, harbours which they controlled were closed for the Dutch.

An important issue of fundamental significance was the fact that the Estates General, as well as the local governments of the cities, wholeheartedly promoted the idea of free competition. Free competition had always been at the core of the Republic's success in attracting international business. Moreover, the strong autonomy of the cities, the building blocks of the Republic, stimulated competition to a very high extent. However, there were three major exceptions to that principle, i.e. the VOC, the Nordic Company and the West Indian Company (WIC), primarily for creating an optimum condition to guarantee positive financial returns for the heavy investments to be made in these trades.[182] The same was applicable for the whale fisheries in Spitsbergen. Because of the hostile attitude of the British, the Estates General erected the Nordic Company, who was given the monopoly till 1642 of fishing whales in the area of Spitsbergen.[183] As the English ambassador to the Netherlands truly stated in 1663, '*It is mare liberum in the British Seas but mare clausum on ye coast of Africa and in ye East Indies*', and he could have added 'Spitsbergen' as well. In contrast to Spain and Portugal, in which trade with the overseas empire was regarded as a royal monopoly, the Estates General of the Netherlands turned over both the control of trade and powers to privately owned joint-stock companies, i.e. the VOC for the Indian Ocean and Indonesia, and the WIC for the west coast of Africa and North and South America. Although chartered initially as purely commercial ventures, the companies soon discovered that to succeed in commercial competing with Portuguese, Spanish, English, and French rivals, they needed to establish territorial control. In becoming successful, these companies became 'states within the state'. Monopoly of trade, with respect to both own nationals and competitors of other nations, naturally followed.

---

182 This was very different though with the British, who had established the Muscovy Company (1555), the Spanish Company (1557), the Eastland Company (1579), the Levant Company (1583) and finally the East India Company (1600). Each of these companies also received monopolies granted by the crown, however proved to be an obstruction to the development of the commercial expansion of London, as there were too many entrepreneurs, the so-called interlopers, excluded from doing business in the areas where monopolies ruled the waves. Amsterdam was in that respect far more accessible by whatever entrepreneur, which created competition. And this led to lower prices and a greater diversification of products.

183 P.W. Klein in Stuyvenberg, p. 95

Another exception to free trade was the government-sanctioned 'College of the Fisheries', which regulated the herring fisheries. The ships of only five cities were permitted to take part in the 'Great Fishery' (as opposed to the local fresh herring fisheries for domestic consumption). The College licensed vessels to control quantity and also imposed strict quality controls to maintain the reputation of the Dutch herring. These restrictive policies paid handsomely as long as the Dutch maintained their commercial dominance in the European market, but as other nations gradually adopted Dutch technology the policies contributed to stagnation. The eventual decline of the herring trade was - according to Cameron - in part a cause of the decline of the Dutch economy as a whole.[184]

From the above it follows, that the VOC and WIC were important policy instruments to achieve the objective of primacy in world trade. Territorial expansion outside Europe seemed an imperative requirement. In 1624 the WIC attempted to conquer the Portuguese colonies in Brazil and occupied the territory till approximately 1650. The Dutch governor, Johan Maurits, tried to bind the local Portuguese entrepreneurs in Brazil to the WIC by allowing them a freer form of trade as compared to the trade system the Portuguese had introduced before. Although things looked quite settled, there still remained all sorts of objections from the local Portuguese business community. Many of them had big debts as a result of the advances from Dutch entrepreneurs, which they got for their future sugar production, to be used for the purchase of new and far more expensive slaves. Finally, revolts broke out and due to wars in Europe with England the Republic was no longer capable to defend the territory effectively. A similar development took place with the founding of New Netherlands and New Amsterdam on the isle of Manhattan around 1625. The Republic laid claim to the entire Hudson valley and surrounding areas. In present day Albany, fort Orange was constructed and land was given out under the 'patron system' of ownership to such entrepreneurial families as the Renselaers and Roosevelts. However, as in the case of Brazil there were not that many Dutch entrepreneurial colonists, who were prepared to settle in these areas. During the second war with

---
184 R. Cameron, p. 156

England (1665-1667) this territory was exchanged with that of Surinam. Given the territorial expansions in the East and West Indies, both the Estates General and the Dutch entrepreneurial sector had probably over-extended their capabilities, taken into consideration the absolute small size of the Dutch population - which at that time not more that 2 million. This was approximately 8% of the population of competing states like England and France together[185]. Nonetheless, the policy of the Estates General was to protect the business community as much as it could.

The continuing wars and fierce competition with Spain, England and France, apart from piracy, made entrepreneurial activity in the Mediterranean not that easy. In order to cope with the situation, weaponry at the ships were made heavier and, in addition, the government established in the Mediterranean between 1610 and 1625 a number of 20 posts for consuls and diplomats, in order to protect the commercial interests of the Dutch business community. Finally, in 1625 entrepreneurs and government authorities founded in Amsterdam the 'Directorate of the Levant Trade', a legal public/private body, which supervised the regulations as regards the weaponry on ships, which were trading in the Levant and this example was followed by other cities as well.[186]

But also in the Netherlands proper, there was sufficient support and government protection for entrepreneurs carrying out their business. As from 1609, for example, the staple market trade got increasingly regulated. In addition, the Amsterdam local government of whom many were entrepreneurs took a number of measures to regulate the flow of money and goods. The Bank of Amsterdam (1609) and the Exchange (1612) were the most significant initiatives in this field. Other measures included the adaptation of the brokers' fees and those of other agents, the extension of the 'Waag' (for official weighing and calibrating produce) and the perfection of the system of inland commercial shipping between towns in- and outside the Republic. Obviously, there was a strong bond between the business community and the government and the attitude the

---

185 Around 1650 France's population counted 20 million; England at that time 6 million.
186 P.W. Klein, De Zeventiende Eeuw, p. 104/5

government took was that of supporting the business, rather than conducting it. As long as there was international free trade, the attitude of the government of the Republic was advantageous for the economy, however, changed drastically when all sorts of trade restrictions from the other countries were imposed, often violently enforced, as during the wars with the French and the British. As mentioned before, the Dutch were no match to the big powers, as the Dutch delta was a relatively small area with a small population and army. In addition, the highly decentralised government was not the type of government for fast decision-making in effectively opposing these powers.

Apart from the *protective-*, also the *promotional* function of the government towards entrepreneurs was quite impressive and, by to-days standards, sounds even modern. In the late medieval period we can observe city governments in the delta region, who initiated a tradition of supporting new ventures in industry. Apparently, they understood the importance of a thriving economy in their cities as a mean to ascertain security (through taxation) and prosperity. Entrepreneurs applying to city magistrates for assistance in starting a new enterprise or even an entire new industry could receive some form of support, such as bounties, patents, monopolies, cheap loans, tax exemptions, exemptions from civic duties, freedom from rent, free use of city owned equipment, or special arrangements for the provision of labour. The Dutch Revolt (as from 1586) did not interrupt in this established practice of municipal sponsorship for starting entrepreneurs. City governments in the Republic continued to encourage starting entrepreneurs, in order to combat poverty, create employment for the growing urban population and increased the possibility of levying taxes. The city councils remained the sole public institutions, which were actively involved in the promotion of new ventures in industry.[187] Likewise, local governments often contracted selected entrepreneurs in order to promote the growth of new businesses and branches of industry with the objective to

---
187   C. Davids, The Staple Market, p. 167. When the Republic eventually *did* see the rise of an alternative source of support for beginning entrepreneurs, it was a private, not a public body which supplemented the role of town governments: the Economic Branch of the *Hollandse Maatschappij der Wetenschappen*, founded in 1777.

substitute imports and to profile their city as a centre of trade, industry and shipping. The majority of these new industrial ventures arose in the textile production and glass manufacturing. In return for the heightened profile these entrepreneurs gave to these cities, they expected local governments to provide them with cheap capital and labour and a certain protection of their market position. New industrial ventures that received support from a city government were as a rule allowed to develop their business outside the prevailing corporate system, in particular that of the guild system, with their many restrictive regulations.[188] Likewise did the government of Haarlem offer the support to new entrepreneurs in shipbuilding in 1666 and 1678/79. Reviving the local shipbuilding industry was a declared aim of the policy in Haarlem from the 1630s onwards, if not before. Previous attempts to attract entrants into the industry had not been successful. The arrival of four shipbuilders specialising in ships for inland navigation, and the simultaneous establishment of mast makers' and canvas weavers' shops, was therefore a most welcome event. The shipbuilders and mast-makers not only received gifts of money and plots of land to practise their trade, but also secured the city's promise that the members of the local skippers guild would not be allowed to have their vessels or masts constructed anywhere else except in Haarlem. Other industries also benefited from the perks offered by local governments. Glass manufacturers typically obtained a local monopoly for the production of certain kinds of glass, free use of buildings, interest free loans or exemptions of excises on fuel and beer. The first sugar refiners in Dordrecht obtained an exemption from excise as well as freedom from interference of members of the transporters' guild, and pioneering entrepreneurs in Alkmaar received a full local monopoly for twenty-five years.[189]

Although spontaneous applications for support in the textile industry were not uncommon, the usual course of events was that city governments themselves tried to lure textile manufacturers to their towns by offering them attractive conditions for settlement. These

---

188   C. Davids, The Staple Market, p. 177
189   C. Davids, The Staple Market. P. 169-170

manufacturers might be part of an existing 'floating' population of textile entrepreneurs (Flemish or Huguenots refugees), or entrepreneurs already establish in other towns in the Dutch Republic. Apart from free housing, free building, looms and spinning wheels owned by the city government and/or cheap loans and subsidies for the transportation of equipment, the entrepreneurs in textile manufacturing also could obtain reduction of labour cost. Contracts between city authorities and starting entrepreneurs in textile production often included the kind of arrangement concerning the provision of cheap labour. In this respect an agreement was concluded in 1631 between the town of Delft and a company of cloth manufacturers from Amsterdam, whereby the city magistrates would supply the entrepreneurs with a workforce of 125 orphans of ten years and older, who during their six year period of service would earn little or no wages at all. The practice itself was already known in Delft for over 30 years. The textile industry in Leyden had been using children on a regular basis since 1582. The cost of feeding and clothing the children was usually borne by the town. This particular form of 'forced child labour' was just another device for entrepreneurs to reduce labour cost.[190] The contracts between the local government and contracting entrepreneur also stipulated that if entrepreneurs did not achieve a certain level of production or to bring a certain number of looms into operation before a certain dead-line, they would be liable to penalties.

In addition, municipalities could also arrange for starting entrepreneurs to let them work outside the corporate guild system, however, in that case they were subject to other municipal regulations. These regulations were enforced either directly by the municipal authorities, or by newly created institutions called "*neringen*", which were working next to the existing guilds. 'The first "*nering*" supervising the making of *bays (baai-nering)*, was probably founded in Leyden in 1578, in the wake of the first influx of Flemish entrepreneurs. A *nering* was a corporation created by a town government for the purpose of supervising an entire branch of industry according to more or less detailed rules as laid down by the municipal author-

---
190 C. Davids, The Staple Market, p. 169-171

ities. In contrast with a guild, a *'nering'*, by definition, comprised all persons involved in the production process in a given branch of industry. Appointees of the municipal government, and representatives of principle producers', governed these *'neringen'* jointly.[191] The superintendents and governors kept a close watch on every stage of the production process, to ensure that all goods produced met a given standard of quality, held to be the hallmark of the industry concerned and could take *corrective actions* if and when required. For this purpose they were not only authorised to inspect production on site, but also to compel all producers to present their wares for inspection and registration at the central meeting place of the *'nering'*, which was the hall. The governors of a *'nering'* also supervised the implementation of wage regulations, kept a register of employers and employees, and administered justice in disputes between *'nering'*-members and in cases of breach of *'nering'*-laws.[192]

Actually, central and local governments exercised their *corrective* function vis-à-vis the entrepreneurs in three ways. First, there was the variant where the government left the guilds or crafts in charge of supervising themselves the production, quality and labour conditions of the various trades. Secondly, the variant in which delegates of local governments were fully in charge of exercising control without any interference from the guilds. In that case a college appointed by the magistrate supervised all stages of the production process, administered justice in cases of disagreements and rendered advice to the city governments regarding new rules and regulations to be introduced. A third variant was the *'nering'* as discussed above. It was some sort of public/private business association consisting of representatives of the government and the entrepreneurs. An exam-

---

191 In nowadays terminology we would call them "clusters"; this is a catchword for small and medium-sized businesses who are working together in order to be more attractive to the market, in terms of quality performance, innovations and pricing; in that way the clusters try to make their joint production more attractive to the market, as well as do they promote the region in which they are active. The latter is reason why regional government authorities often provide support to these clusters, e.g. in adequate infrastructural facilities. Contrary to the *neringen,* clusters are fully managed by the business community itself, without any interference of government authorities. See also C. Davids (1995), p. 170

192 K. Davids, The Staple Market, p. 173

ple of the latter is the case where in the cloth industry of Gouda, where there was no guild, the city desperately wanted to support the small entrepreneurs in their efforts to improve their businesses. In these cases, halls, *'neringen'* and the guilds could function as part of the 'small commodity production' and in that way could offer an acceptable alternative for a capitalistic mode of production. By doing so the local governments were often at bay with the early modern capitalistic entrepreneurs such as, for example, Pieter de la Court, who in his publication *'Welvaren van Leiden'* of 1660, made a fool of all these institutions, with their governors, superintendents and the like who, in his view, were mere barriers to conduct sound business. In spite of these views, it would not be correct to see these institutions as organisations to raise barriers for the development of capitalism.[193] Obviously, as in present-day western economies, local governments at that time understood their responsibilities and the importance of creating an enabling environment for the (starting) entrepreneur.[194]

There were local governments who *promoted* their local industry and employment by making available equipment for those who were not able to purchase these. Since the mid-17th century the city government of Delft had a large number of spinning wheels and different other pieces of textile equipment in store, where many generations of entrepreneurs and artisans made use of. The administration for borrowing these pieces of equipment was maintained until 1800. In 1671 the mayors of Gouda decided to assist entrepreneurs in another way by providing them a loan, at an annual interest rate of 3% for allowing them to buy raw material for the production of cloth in the city. And it also happened that city governments bought the produced merchandise of the entrepreneurs, in lean times when business was low. In the 1630s

---

193 C. Davids, Kapitaal, p. 112-115
194 According to Davids, P.W. Klein concluded from his studies that the Republic was dualistic as regards the rules and regulations it enacted: there were no regulations as regards free competition for the wholesale trade, whereas there was quite strict regulation related to the local manufacturing sector, supplying the wholesale business and the distribution of the same. Also Klein was of the opinion that government regulations did not exclude free entrepreneurship. See Davids in Kapitaal, p. 20-28

in the local government of Delft decided to buy all unsold stock of cloth from the local markets and sold these through intermediates to either peddlers or other market places.[195] But also smaller towns outside the province of Holland were quite active in attracting new businesses. The local government of Zwolle, for example, tried to attract the bigger industries, in order to cope with the pressure of unemployment and to reduce the monies required for taking care of the poor. In 1609 an Amsterdam manufacturer, Herman Rotgers, got permission from the town of Zwolle to establish a soap manufacturing company and gradually the town increased the number of other manufacturing companies, albeit small scale business units (weaving of stocking, paper mills, silk factory, etc.). This meant an extension of the early modern capitalistic relationship between entrepreneur - the owner - and the wage earners. The town with an estimated population of 7.700 of which an approximate number of 10% were entrepreneur (artisan, manufacturer, merchant) also had a pawnbroker's shop, which provided micro credits to those in need. In case larger amounts for investments were needed, loans could be obtained from rich individuals, mostly merchants. In addition the city government of this little town was also active in promoting infrastructure for their business community. After the Peace of Munster in 1648, the local government of Zwolle took part in the construction of a road system to the German cities by granting a subsidy to a local construction company.[196]

Historical research, related to support measures of eight cities in Holland between 1575 and 1795, indicates that local governments were indeed quite active in promoting commercial activities in their towns. In addition to what we have seen above, these measures included a large range of agreements, such as: granting citizenship free of charge, subsidies, monopolies and patents, tax holidays and exemption of paying rent, making cheap labour available by putting orphans at the disposal of those interested. These promotional activities of the city council was also meant to prevent social unrest of

---
195 C. Davids, Kapitaal, p. 103
196 J.C. Streng, p. 72

the city population, which might take place as a result of unemployment, which happened for instance in Utrecht. Both, the resulting economic development and the government policies formed the basis of the emergence of the enterprising manufacturing sector.

The producer/owner as a capitalistic entrepreneur became since 1650 increasingly important. These entrepreneurs often were no longer member of the guilds and therefore not bound to rules and regulations of these organisations. Instead they only received general type of directives from the city government, related to, for example, fire prevention and fire fighting. However, it goes too far to assert that there existed complete free climate for exercising entrepreneurship. By way of granting monopolies here and there and even because of cartel formation, competition was in quite some cases kept outside.[197] However, it should be a misunderstanding to suggest that that the majority of entrepreneurs solicited for government support. Between 1575 and 1700, entrepreneurs in other branches than textile, glass and shipbuilding, hardly applied for municipal support. At present, their range of options is insufficiently known, but it may be that opportunities to attract capital and labour in other ways were still so abundant and the market so large, that government support was normally deemed unnecessary.[198] Recent studies of entrepreneurship in 21 developed economies from all over the world have indeed revealed that the best possible government support is not so much the development of 'push support measures', which may create a 'safety-net' mentality, but rather should the government's emphasis be on creating incentives ('pull-measures') to stimulate high entrepreneurial activity.[199]

Institution development in the banking business was strongly *promoted* by the government as well. Initially, banks were mostly private initiatives, which included many merchant firms, who carried on a banking business as a side-line activity, until the famous "*Wisselbank*", or Amsterdam Exchange Bank, was founded in 1609. This was a public-owned bank as it was founded under the auspices

---

197 R. Rommers, p. 459-464
198 C. Davids, Staple Market, p. 174/175
199 P.D. Reynolds, p. 45-47

of the city itself. It was an exchange bank rather than a bank of issue and discount. Funds could be deposited here and transferred from one account to another in the books; but the bank did not issue banknotes or made loans to merchants by discounting commercial papers. Its principal function, which it performed so well, was to provide the city and all the Dutch and foreign merchants with a stable and reliable mean of payment.[200] It was indeed created as an instrument to facilitate payments in Amsterdam's rapidly growing foreign trade, in fact a clearinghouse for world trade. But its success in persuading merchants both at home and abroad to make payments in bills drawn on the bank, depended crucially on its identification as a public rather than a private institution. In this respect, its impersonality and its corporate status were in sharp contrast to the private banks of the Venetian Rialto or the dynastic court banks of Genoa and Augsburg. In addition, the number of international trade transactions and the reliability of the same were strongly promoted as a result of the quality of justice spoken at the Dutch 'trade courts', as well as by the integrity of the public notaries.[201] 'Amsterdam (the Exchange Bank) was in fact a citadel of right-dealing humanism: adjudicating and conserving, its viability tied up with the integrity of the ministry itself'.[202] Its primary concern was to keep the agio - the difference between bank money quotations and that for account specie - as high as possible, if necessary by calling on syndicates to make deposits at times when withdrawals were anticipated. For all the global ramifications of the bank's payments, even by the end of the 17th century, it had only two thousand depositors. And since business was exclusively a matter of transfer between accounts, there could never be any question of the bank being caught short on withdrawals unmatched by proper reserves. Although it was against the regulations, the Bank also lent money, albeit to two clients only, the VOC and the city of Amsterdam.[203] 'It was this sacred dependability which made Amsterdam bank money so desirable a form of settlement of business, even though it actually cost

---

200   R. Cameron, p. 128
201   Hunt & Murry, p. 116
202   S. Schama, p. 345
203   J. De Vries en A.M. Van der Woude, p. 167

depositors to have accounts, rather then paying them interest'.[204] The Amsterdam Exchange Bank was even able to survive the storm of 1672 when, during the war with France and England, it was able to pay 90% of all their outstanding debts.

Contrary to the Amsterdam Exchange Bank, the Amsterdam Bourse was its moral antithesis. It was as hazardous as the bank was secure.[205] If the bank was the bastion of prudent conservatism, the bourse was a playground for unrestrained passion and reckless enthusiasms. 'The bank was the church of Dutch capitalism; the bourse was its circus'.[206] The line between casual betting and organised trading in stock was often blurred. While those, who had subscribed to a particular business venture had a real interest in the return of a cargo, those who traded in paper were gambling less on the actual profitable outcome of a voyage, than on short-term price fluctuations on the exchange. 'All this was regarded with spurious piety by the city fathers. They considered the Bourse a sink of wickedness but understood well enough that it was indispensable to the operations of the city's trade'.[207] The outlandish operations was more or less controlled and *corrected* by the city government, in that the Bourse was licensed to be the only place where these dealings were allowed. Also opening and closing time were strictly regulated. This could nonetheless prevent the gambling practices at the Bourse, as was the case in the so-called 'tulpmania', in which ultimately the government took the required *corrective* action and brought it to an end. The tulip, an imported luxury from Turkey, could easily be transplanted and horticulturally reproduced *ad infinitum* through the splitting of outgrowths. The growers themselves tried to produce different varieties by experimenting with these outgrowths. The market for this product expanded greatly. In the late 1620s early 1630s and due to its limited trading of these outgrowths (between the lifting in June and the planting in October) a lively trade developed, which increased the price of the bulbs. This led to a situation in

---

204 S. Shama, p. 345
205 Schama, S. P. 347
206 Schama, S. p. 347
207 Schama, S. p. 348

which merchants bought the bulbs from the growers in winter for future delivery in June. These 'futures', then, could be sold by means of a negotiable piece of paper with a notional delivery date upon it, like some very doubtful bill of exchange. The closer the delivery date that the deal was made, the higher the risk of the buyer having to settle with the grower, but the more dazzling the possibility of realising a profit from prices that by the day and by the hour fluctuated. 'At this point, the craze had gone into orbit on its own thrust, and it took an act of intervention from a public authority to bring it sharply back down to earth -with a tremendous crash.'[208] Altogether it is quite remarkable that the trade in futures as is currently seen in the 20th and 21st centuries started already in the 17th century as a negative by-product of capitalism.

Private sector initiatives in institution development (1580-1670)

As shown in figure 5 on next page, there were three forms of enterprises, which entrepreneurs gradually developed, prior and during this period. This became more or less common during the later period of *Trade Capitalism*. In the first form, 'artisan micro enterprises' primarily exercised manufacturing in a pre-industrial setting. These independent micro entrepreneurs, with or without some workmen and apprentices worked nearly exclusively for the nearby market. These micro entrepreneurs, such as shoemakers, weavers, tailors, bakers, blacksmiths, etc. were spread over the entire Republic and were mainly organised in guilds. In most cases they took care for retailing of their own products, although also peddlers, hawkers and market folks were involved in distributing their products.

A second form of the enterprising sector in which entrepreneurs were active was the small commodity production, some sort of cottage/house industry. In both the rural and urban areas, where wage earners at home (in rural areas) often with their family members, worked for capitalistic merchants ("*Verlegers*" or wholesale entrepreneurs), who provided the raw material for further production. They sometimes

---
208 Schama, S. p. 350-362

also financed tools and took the responsibility of marketing the final product.[209] Contrary to the rural areas, the small commodity producers in the cities were less dependent in their working relationship on the wholesale entrepreneurs. This form of enterprise was more or less the bridge between the small commodity production and the international purchasing and sales markets (raw material in quite a number of instances imported; the final product than often exported). This form became specifically conducive for somewhat complicated production techniques with various stages of production and/or processing of the goods, which was predominantly made with foreign raw material. Obviously, this required close supervision of the operations. The cloth manufacturing in Leyden was an example in this type of operations.[210]

A third category of industrial enterprises was the one where entrepreneurs established concentrations of industries, producing for a larger regional or international market. These consisted of the so-called '*trafieken*'. These were refining and processing industries that were primarily supplying the semi-finished products to both trading firms for the staple market and large industrial enterprising sectors, such as e.g. the ship building industry, whose final production was predominantly exported. This type of business form was a non-mechanised way of manufacturing, in which some tens of labourers worked: an early business model of capitalistic employer-employee relationship. Entrepreneurs had been developing this type of enterprise because of concentrated supply of raw material and energy-related needs (peat); moreover, it had been grown under a regime of far-reaching economic freedom.

Apparently, entrepreneurs understood that international trade would never get any scope if not a strong service sector would be developed. Hence, through entrepreneurs' initiatives, adequate institutional development took place by regulating the transport-, harbour- and transhipment sectors. Brokerage, notary services, towing-cranes, do-

---

209 Obviously, there was quite a lot of competition between the rural and urban cottage/house industry, as in the case of the Haarlem linen weaving mills, one of the greatest centres in the Republic, who lost a lot of business around 1750 to the rural areas of Brabant and Twente with their lower wages. In spite of heavy competition from Scotland, Ireland and Silesia, as well as the emergence of cotton as a substitution for linen, it was also the start of Twente to become the all important textile centre in The Netherlands till far into the 20th century. See Faber in Stuyvenberg, p. 142-143

210 Faber in Stuyvenberg, p. 140-141

mestic transport, mail-services, docking and storage services and the like, were developed. These were subject to strict regulations of the local government authorities. Of great importance of course was also 'the exchange', where goods were traded and as a consequence also functioned as information centres for entrepreneurs and merchants regarding the movements of prices, surplus of or scarcity in commodities. The growth and organisation of the bank and credit institutions was closely linked to that. The entrepreneurial merchants developed new financial instruments, which made it easier and also safer for the entrepreneur to do business with overseas partners.

Generally, the merchant performed the function of bankers and it was, indeed, these merchants who started in the 1620s with the service to supply credits to foreign buyers, taking their stockpile as collateral. That was also the start of a growing increase in capital export from which, ultimately, the emission companies developed. All of this created chaos in the production and use of mints. One of the functions of the Amsterdam Exchange Bank was to provide a contribution in settling the chaos in the production and use of mints. This was highly necessary, as the increase in trade and manufacturing required transparency in finance.

The Bank, in addition, provided loans against species, which increased the trade in gold and silver considerably, and although it was officially not allowed, it also provided credit lines to the city of Amsterdam and the VOC. In 1650 the Bank had approximately 2000 accounts and stockpile of gold and silver of as much as 10 million guilders (equivalent to 700m Euros/2005)[211] and continued to be an important financial centre for Europe till far in the 18th century.[212]

---

211 Calculation is based on methodology as worked out by: Zandvliet, K., De 250 rijksten van de Gouden Eeuw, Amsterdam, 2006, p. XIII
212 See also J. de Vries & A..M. van der Woude, p. 107-197

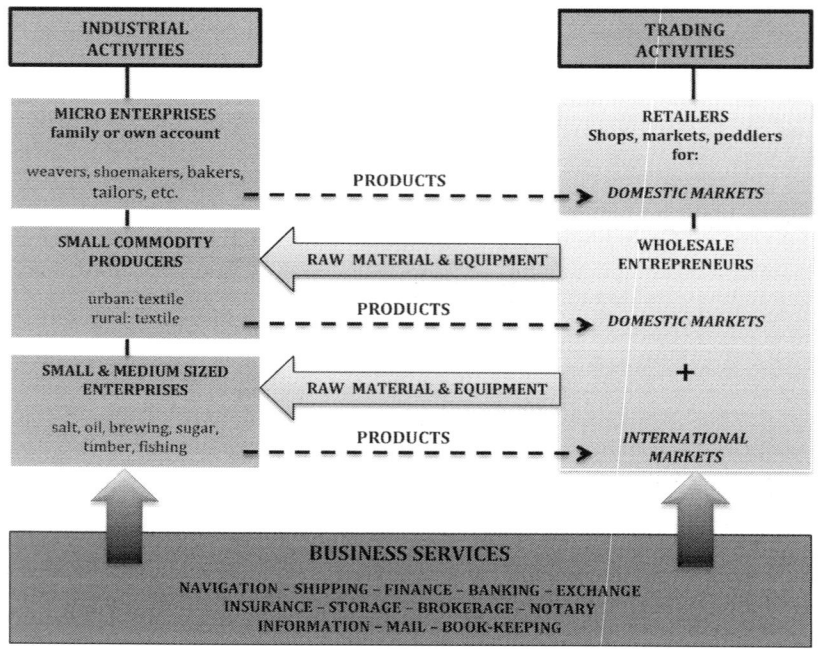

Figure 5: Simplified entrepreneurial relationships

The development of new financial instruments and/or improvement of existing ones were extremely important for accelerating the business. It gave the entrepreneurs the possibility to provide credits to the supplier of the raw material or final product, which were shipped to the Amsterdam staple market. First, there was the 'Letter of Exchange', which provided the funds to the prospective supplier. And that document was again linked to the products in the staple market. These funds were provided at relatively low interest rates and added to the absolute lower cost of the merchandise, which was an advantage that other nations at that time did not have. It gave a leading edge in international competitiveness. The development of these financial instruments led to even more sophisticated financial products, such as the emergence of commission trade and acceptance credit, which were specifically used during the last period of Trade Capitalism (18th century). But already during this period there were trading agents who carried out orders of entrepreneurs by trying to find buyers for their merchandise, hence established trade agreements between seller and buyer, for which the trade agents got a certain percentage as a remuneration for the service they provided. Obviously this trend diminished the need for immediate (suppliers) credits through the 'Exchange Letter', but instead promoted the use of acceptance credit, which was provided by financial firms, which were specialised in accepting and discounting foreign 'Exchange letters'. This meant that the financial firm authorised a client to submit an exchange letter, with the guarantee that the financial firm would be paying if need be. Subsequently, Dutch trade capital was then utilised for the international trade, including trade of merchandise that never came into the country.[213]

The more competitive the business climate became, the more entrepreneurs understood that accurate and fast information could affect their business considerably. Timely information about backloads could decrease cost of transportation, but also could change the price of commodities in stock if, for instance, harvests of these products had been successful or not. Also in case of hostilities between countries, it was important for entrepreneurs to know where these occurred, as well as the intensity of the conflict. The entrepreneur could then assess what effect that might have on the safety of ships, as well as on the availability of certain raw materials or finished products. The collection and analysis of information had two sides: on the one hand there was the rational analysis of data, which were both stored in archives and available to civil servants. On the other hand the dissemination of tips and rumours were often leading to breeding a certain atmosphere at the exchange. All of that was applicable to areas related to the question of creditworthiness of enterprises or governments and to expected supply, changes in the demand, information about wars, epidemics and stocks; in short, all information directly related to price movements. So, the central position of Amsterdam in the world's staple market attracted lots of merchants from all over the world, who had both foreign and local representatives in many trading parts all over the world, from Russia to the Levant and from Asia to South America. This

---

213 J. de Vries en A.M. van der Woude, p. 770

again added to the central position of Amsterdam in collecting and analysing information from anywhere.²¹⁴ The great importance of business information for entrepreneurs is specifically proven by the fact that already in 1585 printed journals were in circulation, which included information about merchandise offered for sale and a 'daily' pricelist of 205 permanently obtainable products.²¹⁵ The central position that Amsterdam took as regards the collection, analysis and publication of information also had an important positive side effect. In the 1620s the regular newspapers appeared with advertisements, focussing primarily on works of art, engravings, and books, which were for sale. In this respect the Republic was advancing other countries with almost one century. The number of books printed in the 17ᵗʰ century, exceeded those printed in all European countries together. Contrary to nearly everywhere in Europe where books for political or religious reasons were burnt, Amsterdam entrepreneurs were printing, selling and exporting large quantities.²¹⁶

Another form of private business services, as developed by innovative entrepreneurs, included the renting of cargo space for export. In case an entrepreneur wanted to sell merchandise abroad and did not have his own ship to transport the load, he could charter a ship or space for his load from a skipper or ship-owner. This was to be confirmed by a public notary, who described all details, such as the route, destination, the price and other particulars related to the logistic arrangement.²¹⁷ And in order to provide for security during these trips, entrepreneurial organisations were established to protect these against attacks from others. So, for ships travelling, for instance, to the Levant, twenty-two Amsterdam entrepreneurs established in 1625 the Directorate for the Levant Trade. These supervised the armoury equipment of the ships sailing to the Levant, in order to protect them from attacks of Spanish war vessels and pirates from Bulgaria.²¹⁸

---

214 J. de Vries en A.M. van der Woude, p. 185
215 H. Mechoulan, p. 194
216 H. Mechoulan, p. 195/6
217 O. Gelderblom, p. 155
218 O.Gelderbloem, p. 237, see also P.W. Klein, De Zeventiende Eeuw, p. 104/105

A form of 'unwritten' institution development, in a number of cases among entrepreneurs during this period, were mutually informal arrangements made as regards cooperating in specific business ventures. They tried to make 'gentlemen agreements' as regards the division of specific markets and trade in products. In 1618, for example, Hendrick Broen and his brothers in law Jacques and Marcus van Uffelen (all three originating from the Southern Netherlands) concluded an agreement with another entrepreneur from the province of Holland, Albert Reynersen, to purchase during two years the total harvest of cumin and aniseed from Malta and to split it half-half. The same happened with five traders on Russia, who made a common deal to share the production of the fishing of salmon in the rivers near Kola and when one of them decided after one year to abandon the deal, he promised not to interfere during the remaining period of the concluded gentlemen agreement. Several of these deals took place, which confirms that entrepreneurs tried to form small cartels and monopolies in order to safeguard or increase their profits. However, if and when cartels and monopolies with considerable interests were officially initiated, the Estates General was very hesitant to grant a charter. This was for instance the case when in 1608 it refused the charter to seventeen entrepreneurs for the establishment of a company with the monopoly for trade in Russia along the lines of the British Muscovy Company. The Estate General was afraid that such a company would limit too much the freedom of other entrepreneurs to do business. The same reaction was recorded during scarcity of grain due to wars in the Baltic Sea. The Russian Grain Company (consisting of a number of grain dealers) requested the Estate General to grant them monopoly for the grain business on Russia. And again this request was turned down, as one feared that this might result in only one supplier of grain to the Republic, capable of fully controlling the sales price of that commodity. The same was also applicable in the case with a planned establishment of a compulsory insurance company for ships travelling within Europe. The idea was that with the income from insurance premiums, together with private capital, a company would be erected for doing exclusive business to the Levant, as was the case with the British Levant Company. There was outright resistance to that plan from both the government and the large majority of the entrepreneurial community. Neither the Estate General nor the Amsterdam local government wanted to limit competition in Europe, which was a completely different stand as compared to trade outside Europe with the establishment of VOC (1602), the Nordic Company (1614) and the WIC (1621).[219] The monopolies granted to the VOC and the Nordic company were indeed inspired to fight the British in their endeavour to control all businesses in these areas. The monopoly granted to WIC, though, was unnecessary and the majority of Dutch entrepreneurs, who refused to invest in the Company, properly understood that; it took two years before the first ships sailed to the West Indies. And it took only a few years thereafter, before the WIC got its final blow.[220]

The institutional setting in the fishery industry also changed over time. The ships that went to sea operated along the lines of a "*partenrederij*", some sort of business association, in which also the crew could financially participate. The required capital was brought together by a limited number of entrepreneurs. At the end of the 16th century, this changed in a capitalistic way, in which the participation of the limited number of ship-owners changed into an 'open' financial participation of any ship-owner and merchant firm with sufficient capital. In its institutional setting, this 'open' mode of financial participation looked alike the later developed 'limited liability company'[221] This is a clear example of what D.C. North would call the evolution of an institution that would create 'an hospitable environment for cooperative solutions to complex exchange' providing economic growth.[222] Obviously, these types of institutional

---

219 O. Gelderblom, p. 238-241
220 The loss of Brazil in 1645 to the Portuguese meant to be a disaster for the WIC, due to the inability to recuperate from the debt position it had built up. So the shareholders, primarily entrepreneurs, experienced massive losses, however, they tried to save whatever could be saved with quite some inventiveness. They opened up new territories for growth, rather than behave as belligerent crusaders. Curacao became one of the most important slave markets; in fact they shifted primarily to trade, i.e. slave trade, as suppliers of merchandise manufactured in Europe and as the transporters of raw sugar to be processed in Amsterdam. See also J. de Vries en A.M. van der Woude, p. 468
221 P.W. Klein in Stuyvenberg, p. 94
222 D.C. North, p. vii

development were quite necessary in order to facilitate the capital inflow for new fishing businesses to be established or to finance the heavy investments to be made. The whale fishery was a case in point. Whale fishery became a big hype as from 1612, when the Amsterdam merchant Lambert van Tweenhuysen – following the British - equipped two ships for fishing on whales in Spitsbergen. Because of the hostile attitude of the British, the General Estates erected the Nordic Company, who was given the monopoly of fishing whales in the area of Spitsbergen. This Nordic Company, actually, was a cartel, to which independent companies became a party. Under their auspices, an approximate number of 20 ships annually were equipped for coastal fishing, after which the whales moved to open sea.[223] In this way the company was granted a monopoly. However, internal competition within the company occurred soon, as some entrepreneurial fishermen who were members of the Delft Chamber had discovered new hunting grounds and then started to hunt whales for the benefit of their own and outside the newly formed company. Their party was then called the 'Small Nordic Company'. However, when entrepreneurs of Amsterdam and Alkmaar discovered the same hunting grounds in the same year, they claimed the exclusive hunting rights. Ultimately, the feud had to be dealt with by the Estates General. In 1622 the 'Small Nordic Company' merged into the 'Nordic company'. Dutch whaling, which produced the necessary fat and oils, had become very important, since the production of vegetable oils and fats enormously stagnated at that time.

6.3. Institution development during the decline of the economy (1670-1815)

Government initiatives

As from the start of *Trade Capitalism,* municipalities actively *promoted* entrepreneurs to start new businesses in their cities. Contrary to state support to entrepreneurs in other European countries, the Dutch Republic's municipal councils were the sole public institu-

---
223 P.W. Klein in Stuyvenberg p. 95

tions, which were actively involved in the promotion of new ventures in industry. In so far as provincial governments of the Estates General concerned themselves with the promotion of industry, this never included support to individually starting or emerging entrepreneurs.

Additional support to the city councils was provided by a private initiative, i.e. the 'Economic Branch' of the '*Hollandse Maatschappij der Wetenschappen (Dutch Society of Science)*, founded in 1777.[224] This initiative stimulated the city authorities of Amsterdam to extra *promote* entrepreneurial activities by making available floating schemes, established in 1782 by a municipal loan office (*stadsleenkamer*). This loan office provided cheap loans for entrepreneurs who were temporarily short of cash, on security of goods, stocks or bonds. The working capital of the loan office - amounting to 2 million guilders - was procured by the municipal *Wisselbank* (the Amsterdam Exchange Bank) through the city treasury.[225] In the field of institution development for promoting entrepreneurial activities, it was only city governments that took action. The centrally operating Estates General did not take initiative in this area, apart from the establishment of the Chambers of Commerce during the French occupation in 1813, in Amsterdam, Rotterdam, Dordrecht, Middleburgh and Flussing.[226]

In as far as taking *corrective action* by government authorities in this sub-period, its interventions were not really impressive. The economic decline of the Republic was, to a high degree, caused by institutional incapacitation. The decentralised structure of the Republic closed off the most fundamental financial support to military-political needs, reason why the state increasingly became weaker (both relatively and absolutely) and in the longer term was not even capable to defend itself. The Fourth British-Dutch War (1780-84) led to a crisis whereby the gap between the regents and the entrepreneurs was manifestly shown. This crisis then was the start of the ultimate decline of the Netherlands when the French troops in 1795 came to 'liberate' the country.[227] That decline had already been accelerated, when just a few years before, the govern-

---
224 C.A. Davids (1995), p. 167-177
225 C.A. Davids (1995), p. 175
226 H.F.J.M. van den Eerenbeemt, p. 181
227 JL van Zanden & A. van Riel, p. 107-108

ment was not able to take any *corrective* action when the Amsterdam Exchange Bank, loaded with capital, lent large sums of money to unreliable European states, ending up with many bad debts. The bankruptcy of France in 1789, as a result of the French Revolution, was indeed a final devastating blow to the Bank.[228] From an institutional point of view, the French period produced only one positive result; it broke up the congealed Dutch society with its regents and guilds. The period proved to be a hinge between the old regime of the Netherlands and the new Kingdom that became established in 1815 and provided the basis for a modern society.

Private sector initiatives in institution development (1670-1815)

Apart from the city exchange banks and the cashiers, a third financial institution i.e. the privately owned merchant banks, emerged as from the 1660s. These developed strongly in the fist part of the 18th century. Entrepreneurs, who before worked in the trade-connected money business, founded new types of financial institutions. Because of increasing international competition, these entrepreneurs, specifically those who were active in investments in England, decided for reasons of profitability to invest their capital in a different way and to switch over from direct trade to the business of providing acceptance credit. Their capital consisted of their private wealth filled up with loans on collateral from private persons. One of them was the merchant banker Hope en Co[229]. Archibald Hope was a Dutch businessman from English descent who traded in 1664 in Rotterdam with England and Ireland. He possessed a couple of ships with which he imported raw material from England for the distillery of gin in the city of Schiedam. Two of his eight sons went into the business of their father and even one of them became in 1751 the financial adviser of Stadholder William IV, to assist him in drafting the so-called 'Proposition of 1751', which entailed the introduction of an entire free trade harbour system, in order to revitalise Dutch trade. Ten years later the transfer of the firm from trading to fully-fledged

---

228 F. Braudel, p. 370
229 In 2005 this bank went bankrupt

merchant banking was completed.[230] Hope and many other merchant bankers kept on developing new financial instruments. An important one was the emission business, which included issuance of long-term loans to foreign powers. Although the Dutch economy was around 1780 no longer sound, the country was still quite rich. Population was decreasing and de-urbanisation was taking place. Furthermore, a decline became manifest in the labour intensive manufacturing centres and, finally, a fundamentally changed function of the staple market had resulted in decreasing profitability. Therefore, much of the capital wealth got invested in foreign business ventures abroad, since the return thereof was much higher as compared to investments in domestic commercial ventures. In 1780 interest earnings from foreign investments amounted to 15 million guilders, which increased to 30 million in 1790[231]. It has been suggested that a form of venture capital or a loan guarantee fund, which could make finance available for risky business ventures in times of crisis, was lacking in the Dutch financial sector at that time.[232] However, taken into consideration the absence of new business opportunities as a result of emerging new technologies abroad (steam, coal) which were extremely competitive for Dutch industries and manufacturers, it must be concluded that, in accordance with good business practices, entrepreneurs looked for the highest return of investments and these were no longer offered in the Netherlands. Furthermore, at the end of the 18th century, also the Dutch financial sector got increasingly in danger and made heavy losses as a result of both lendings to unreliable foreign governments with bad repayments ethics (or none at all), and the financial difficulties in the aftermath of the French Revolution.

As already mentioned before, one of the private sector initiatives was the establishment of the '*Hollandse Maatschappij der Wetenschappen*' (Dutch Society for Sciences), which had an 'Economic Branch' that was closely modelled on the Society for the Encouragement of Arts, Manufacture and Commerce in London. Its objective was to promote the general welfare of the Dutch nation and its

---

230   J. de Vries & A.M. van der Woude, p. 174-175
231   J. de Vries en A.M. van der Woude p. 785-786
232   J. de Vries & A.M. van der Woude, p. 785-786

colonies by diffusion of useful knowledge in every branch of economic life. Its main instrument was the granting of awards and premiums for promising inventions and initiatives, paid from a fund established by its members. Although the Economic Branch did not grant every request for financial aid, the total number of premiums and awards granted between 1778 and 1787 amounted to 282. In the following decade it fell to just over 90. Another private sector initiative was the erection in 1777 of a half philanthropic, half commercial institution, called "*Vaderlandse Maatschappij van Reederij en Koophandel*" (National Society of Shipping and Commerce), by the inspirational preacher Cornelis Ris in Hoorn. That institution was devoted to activities related to shipping, trade and industry. It equipped a ship for whale fishing and started a trading company and a business in wallpaper (imported from China). Children of the poor were trained in spinning in order to make them ready for the society and to escape poverty. The objective was to revive prosperity and so there were other initiatives as well, for instance in Enkhuizen, where they started in 1780 a so-called Economic Workhouse, as a share-holding company.[233] But all these private initiatives did not really alter the sorry state in which the Netherlands got caught.

In the area of international trading it was not that much better either! At the end of the 18th century the VOC became heavily lossmaking and finally got bankrupt. Various historians have criticized the irrational character of the entrepreneurship of the VOC management, the bookkeeping system and its legal structure. In addition, stories about rampant corruption were manifold. Previous historical analysis of the entrepreneurship of the Governors of the VOC assessing that 'the idea that the VOC was a strict rational organisation which coupled efficient management to a cunning commercial strategy still leaves to be desired'[234] The analysis of the historian Van Zanden is that the pricing policy of the monopoly products was not optimal, caused by the fact that shareholders were more interested in short-term profitability, rather than in continuity of the business. By trying to increase the profitability, thus increasing the difference between

---

[233] J.G. van Dillen, p. 353-354
[234] J.L. van Zanden (1996), p. 422

cost- and selling price, which could easily be done with a monopoly product, prices were driven that high that the demand decreased, with the result that the overall profitability decreased. The management of the VOC also made a tragic error in the dividend policy. In the 17th century the dividend was determined by the heights of the profits made in that specific year, which of course fluctuated from year to year. In order to establish the disbursements of dividends, the management introduced in the beginning of the 18th century a change in that policy by bringing the dividend on a constant level, which was too high when the VOC's business declined. This, subsequently, led to a disharmony between profits made and disbursed to shareholders. This ultimately resulted in an increase of debs to such a level, which could no longer be controlled. By bringing the dividend on a constant level, irrespective the business result, it disconnected business achievements with the rewards (dividends), which in goods business practices is an anomaly. Obviously, the level of reward of a certain year is always a strong stimulus for taking *corrective* or *promotional* actions, which in the case of the VOC was absent. This regulation shows a form of recklessness, or a naïve belief in static business practices, something that can only be expected from non-entrepreneurs, the so- called Governors, who had become too remote from doing down-to-earth business. The collapse of the VOC was also attributable to the rigidity of its institutional structure. It included six different independent companies, the Chambers of Amsterdam, Rotterdam, Delft, Zeeland, Hoorn and Enkhuizen. The management of these Chambers was in the hands of trustees, who were appointed by the mayors of each of the cities. From these, the so-called Heren XVII (Governors) were appointed and these formed the top management of the VOC. Such structure was not really appropriate for a vigorous and flexible execution of commercial management and entrepreneurial tasks of the VOC, as each of the Chambers had their (hidden) agenda, not to mention the Governors personally. The fundamental problem was that the widened gap between the political elite and the entrepreneurs. In addition they insulated themselves from newcomers from outside, which was reason why the quality of the VOC top management, who only was recruited from the political elite, deteriorated considerably. It was no longer able to recruit experienced merchants/entrepreneurs any more.[235] After the fourth Anglo-Dutch trade war, which reduced the VOC fleet by half and the continuing Napoleonic wars, the Company was indeed a financial wreck. It was nationalised in 1796 by the new Batavian Republic, which finally allowed the charter to expire on 31 December 1800.

During this period (1670-1815) international competition had become increasingly stronger. Other countries had copied Dutch navigation techniques and their protectionism as a result of the mercantilist policies, specifically of France and Britain, had out-competed Dutch entrepreneurs. Nonetheless, the commission trade, which came up during this period mitigated the decline considerably. The core of the commission trade was that the commissionaires did not invest in the merchandise proper, but in services which were related to the logistics of merchandise, such as credit, storage, insurance, etc. Because of these services entrepreneurs were able to spend more money for purchasing raw materials and/or finished products, which increased the trading volumes of the merchandise. This is the reason why international trade in 1770 was even 25% higher than in 1720 as is shown in the table on next page.

The more the commission trade specialised itself in business services, the more direct contacts took place between international vendors and buyers, thereby bypassing the Amsterdam staple market. This became the start of a new type of business, namely the trading houses, of which a few are still in existence under their own name in the 21st century.[236] The big change between the old merchant family firm and the newly emerging trade houses was in particular the sustainability of the latter. These were in business for centuries long to come, whereas the merchant family firm was – with some exception - only active during one, or at the most, two generations.

---

235 JL van Zanden & A. van Riel, p. 99
236 Insinger & Co and Van Eeghen & Co; see: Jonker J. and K. Sluyterman, *Thuis op de wereldmarkt; Nederlandse handelshuizen door de eeuwen heen*, The Hague, 2000, p. 86-89

TRADE	1720 at million guilders	1770 at million guilders
European sea trade	151	167
Land trade with Belgium and Germany	16	30
Intercontinental trade	31	46
TOTALS	**198**	**243**

Table 2: Dutch international trade flow comparison 1720-1770. Source: *Thuis op de Wereldmarkt*, p.81

Also other forms of business specialisation took place, such as firms of ship-owners who were active in administering and hiring out ships. Another specialised function was that of the ship brokers, who was a great help to entrepreneurs. These agents were intermediaries between suppliers of cargo space and those of cargo that should be shipped. They also took care of the transfer or storage of merchandise and did all the paperwork related to arrivals or departures of ships. In fact shipbrokers speeded up business between harbour and ship and by doing so reduced transactional cost considerably. This took a sharp turn when the French invaded and occupied the country: in 1806 there were still 1500 foreign ships coming to Amsterdam; in 1807 it went down to 200 and in 1808 there were none foreign ships coming to the city.

7. SOCIO-CULTURAL ASPECTS AFFECTING ENTREPRENEURSHIP

Below follows an analysis of socio-cultural aspects affecting entrepreneurs by identifying various elements that make up the socio-cultural environment in which entrepreneurs exercised their businesses. As elaborated at length in chapter three, these aspects include: *cultural legitimacy, security and social mobility of entrepreneurship, the integration of foreign entrepreneurs*, but also aspects related to ideology and need-achievement. All these aspects will be looked upon during three periods of *Trade Capitalism,* i.e. economic takeoff (1350-1580), economic supremacy (1580-1670) and, finally, stagnation and economic decline (1670-1815)

7.1. Socio-cultural developments during economic takeoff (1350-1580)

What, from a socio-cultural point of view, distinguished the delta area around 1500 most with other parts in Europe, was probably the absence in the Netherlands of the feudal system in the way it was existing and exercised elsewhere, resulting in a relatively classless society. The lack of the feudal system emphasized in a way the individual dimension of society, rather than the collective dimension, which became less developed. And, it was that individual dimension, which provided chances for individual entrepreneurship, personal inventiveness, own responsibility and a relatively high appreciation for political, economic and personal freedom. In concrete terms it meant for the Republic a specific constellation of society, which had its effect not only on landownership and land utilisation, but also on the absence or relatively weak position of the guilds. Next, it had its influence on the relation between urban and rural areas, the structure of the households, family life (the cornerstone of society) and the flexible individual changes of profession between, for example, farmer, seaman and fisherman. It was a plural ecclesiastic society, which could emerge thanks to a relatively large degree of tolerance and room for personal freedom. There existed a the strong appreciation of independence and the anxious defence of acquired political rights. In short, it was an open, modern resembling civic society. Contrary to other parts of Western Europe, the farmers formed a free class in society. Their only collective 'duty' was the fight against natural elements, i.e. the water. Both nature and the market were the only aspects that really mattered them. And the combination of both of these led to the emergence of an agriculture, in which finally specialisation in cultivation and animal husbandry became the dominant features in a relatively strongly emerging money economy. Quite significant was the market-orientation and free entrepreneurship. The guild system was indeed present in the delta, however it was not that strong as in other countries. Actually, the guilds were fitted into the cities' particularism and in fact became an instrument in the hands of the city governments, who heavily focused on the general interest of the civic society in general, rather than on the particular interest of the guilds.[237]

In addition, two important developments, affecting the interest of entrepreneurs, had taken place at the transition from the Middle Ages to the pre-modern time. Because of the victory of the Reformation (around 1560) the clergy, as a political power, had been eliminated so that only the bourgeois and nobility filled up the political bodies of these days. From these remaining classes the nobility was already in quite a weak position and in many cases poor, as a result of the long social and internal frictions of the 15th century. With the arrival of the Reformation though, the nobility had to make new choices, i.e. pro or anti the Spanish ruler, Philips II, and the Catholic Church. Many of them could, for social or ideological reasons, not break their loyalty, thus placed themselves outside government institutions when the "new order" triumphed.[238] This resulted in a very strong position of the bourgeois in political bodies, among them predominantly entrepreneurs. And these entrepreneurs could then influence government measures, rules and regulations, which were in their own business interest.

---

237   J. de Vries & A.M. van der Woude, p. 199-202
238   J. de Vries & A.M. van der Woude, p. 585

No doubt, legitimacy of entrepreneurship in the Netherlands during this era was quite high, not in the least as many of the ruling elite were either entrepreneurs or, in one way or another, related to the business community. An important aspect taken into consideration when assessing entrepreneurial legitimacy was the new thinking that came up in the wake of the emergence of calvinism. The new concept of earthly life that it brought - in particular the idea to serve God by developing and unfolding personal talents and to try to resist the temptations of earthly life by ascetic discipline - gave legitimacy not only to the existence of the Republic as a state, but also to entrepreneurship. And this also justified the close inter-linkage between government and entrepreneurs.[239] As a matter of fact, nearly everything had to give way to exercising entrepreneurship. The importance of it was extremely well portrayed at the event of the 'Alteration of Amsterdam' (1578), when the city transferred from Spanish to Dutch rule. Contrary to the political and religious importance of this event, the new protestant regents of the city did not want the Amsterdam trade to be disturbed by either religious fanaticism, or fiscal pressure and political tutelage.[240] This gave ample room for anyone, who wanted to exercise entrepreneurship. Together with the freedom of religion, the high level of legitimacy of entrepreneurship attracted a host of foreign immigrants with much business experiences, among them: catholics, lutherans, mennonites and jews. With hardly any problem were they fully accepted in the Dutch business communities, as long as they contributed to the economic well-being of the Republic and did not confess their creed overtly. Legitimacy of entrepreneurship in circles of the nobility was, on the contrary, absolutely low. The nobility was supposed to refrain from artisan-type of work, production and/or commercial entrepreneurship, as it would bring loss of status. However, even in that class of society there were some borderline exceptions of entrepreneurial activity they did undertake. In the rural areas, for example at the Veluwe-region, some families of the gentry possessed the water right of some brooks. These provided the driving force to a number of paper- and copper mills, for which the mill operators

---

239 J. de Vries & A.M. van der Woude, p. 209
240 O. Gelderblom, p. 87

had to pay a fee to the gentry. But these were exceptions and could hardly be counted as an entrepreneurial activity.[241]

In this strongly expanding economy, social mobility was relatively high. Particularly the many large cities offered opportunities to rise to the status of the big merchant and, in addition, even to become member of important city councils. Hence, many of the already existing merchant communities in these cities were completed with entrepreneurs coming from the river regions from outside Holland, following the re-orientation of trade. Quite a number of entrepreneurs from Zeeland and Holland had initially for business purposes first settled in Antwerp, but later returned when the centre of gravity of trade started to move to the north.[242] A famous example of these entrepreneurs was Elias Trip from the city of Zaltbommel, who became one of most influential entrepreneurs in Amsterdam. But also quite a number of early immigrants from Flanders, starting in Holland as peddlers, moved very quickly to positions in the wholesale business in the bigger cities. 'Merit' was indeed the keyword and, undoubtedly, the relatively strong economic growth in the delta gave ample opportunity for those with the right type of capabilities to move on the social ladder, irrespective their descent.

Looking at the marginal groups in Dutch society till approximately 1580, most of their members were active in some form of business, as to them this was the surest way for survival. Given the high legitimacy of entrepreneurship in the Republic, different ethnical, cultural or religious groups - although at that time (1580) not yet that numerous - were fully accepted in business activities. In a strongly expanding economy with freedom for all, it was very attractive for immigrants who fled for political and religious reasons, to join Dutch entrepreneurs and to enjoy the high legitimacy of that profession. To indigenous Dutch entrepreneurs, the marginal groups - jews and Southern Netherlanders - were a blessing rather than a threat, as they contributed to the then already flourishing economy in the north with new and/or expanded market knowledge. There

---
241   J. de Vries & A.M. van der Woude, p. 619-620
242   O. Gelderblom, p. 108

was ample room for both starting entrepreneurs and professionals of high calibre in that growing economy. In 1579 nearly 25 entrepreneurs from the Southern Netherlands came to Amsterdam and their number grew steadily to 120 in 1585 and 214 in 1589.[243] These 214 entrepreneurs consisted of 47 merchants, 61 wholesalers, 11 peddlers and of 10 in service-type of activities (of the remaining 85 no profession was known).[244] Academic research over this period has not shown that social integration of the few marginalized groups posed a serious problem, although the early immigrants strongly tended to stick together to their own community. Apart from emotional security reasons (moving to another country with different cultures and norms), this sticking together was also stimulated by business practices, as running a business was in many cases a matter of trust and confidence, which was better guaranteed by their in-group, the family or kinship. Therefore, entrepreneurs of expanding businesses, run by members of marginalized groups, recruited their additional staff from either their own family, or ethnic and/or religious community they came from. And the same was applicable for marriages, which were primarily concluded with members of their own community, bringing in quite a number of cases different businesses together.[245]

Running a business was indeed risky for any entrepreneur. Not only when travelling by land, but not in the least, also at sea, particularly for those who were involved in the sea-fishing business. And although state government and coastal city governments, gave protection to the fishing fleet, this did not prevent entrepreneurs from considerable losses of their assets, due to piracy or acts of war. Instead of getting discouraged, and to withdraw from the profession, entrepreneurs kept on searching for new ways to diminish their risks, realizing though that it was impossible to avoid uncertainties, whilst doing business. As described earlier they founded partner-

---

243 O. Gelderblom, p. 87
244 O. Gelderblom, p.88, figure 3.1, p.100, table 3.3
245 In a study on the 250 richest people in the Republic during the 17th century, it proved that nearly all –in one way or another- are connected through marriages. See: Zandvliet, K., (ed), De 250 rijksten van de Gouden Eeuw, Amsterdam, 2006, the section on family trees, p. 417-433

ships, consortia and insurance companies in order to share the risks, which prevented many of them to discontinue the business in case of a catastrophe. Generally, local and state government never posed a threat to entrepreneurs, as it was well understood that a thriving entrepreneurial class was the basis of and guarantee for freedom from Spanish rule; ultimately, it generated the tax income required to defend the Republic.

In order to cope with business risks and uncertainties, which easily could affect their personal life as well, entrepreneurs - through their calvinistic religion - had quite a supportive ideology, which perhaps unintentionally encouraged individuals to behave entrepreneurial. In order to understand the mind of the entrepreneur, it may be appropriate to shed some light on the way the calvinistic ideology was generally perceived. The breach with Spain, ignited by tax payment and aggravated by religious differences caused, in the words of the historian Simon Schama war with the 'tyrant Spain', which had a parallel with the defence against the 'tyrant sea'. In the minds of those who fought this battle on two fronts, these 'tyrants' were causally connected.[246] It was all laden with scriptural significance. *'The making of new land belongs to God alone'*, wrote the great 16th century hydraulic engineer Andries Vierlingh, *'for He gives to some people the wit and the strength to do it'.*[247] In other words, the special favour of the Almighty had delegated to the Dutch a kind of license in the act of territorial creation. As a consequence they held a sacred title to their land that precluded intervening allegiance to temporal lords or emperors. They found themselves as reincarnations of the biblical Children of Israel.[248] There was the view that the Dutch had an eternal *covenant* between God and his children below, the 'Nederkinderen'[249] (Nether-kids). Nonetheless, the Calvinistic Church generally took a passive stand as regards economic policies and dealings and, therefore, it is not likely that protestantism as such really had much influence in the emergence of the capitalistic mentality

---

246 S. Schama, p. 42
247 Citation from Joh van der Veen, quoted in Shama, S.,The Embarrassment of Riches, New York 1987, p..35
248 S. Schama, p. 35
249 S. Schama, p. 45

of the entrepreneur. The Reformation did put the door wide ajar to a mercantile-oriented society, where rational actions and dealings were dominant. But according to the Dutch historians, De Vries & Van der Woude, that door was already far ajar.[250] Actually, in as far as one can speak of the capitalistic mentality, it had already been formed during the late Middle Ages with the emergence of the ever-increasing money economy.[251] The moderate view of the Calvinistic Church tallied quite well with the practical interest of the autonomous cities in the Republic, as they wanted to create and maintain a favourable climate for the entrepreneurs allowing them to do business. This led to much instigation on moderation of ecclesiastic-moral questions and to demand subordination of the ecclesiastic to the secular authorities. Obviously, there were of course a number of calvinistic die-hards, even among entrepreneurs, but in general the religious climate was moderate. In fact, the fundamental state of mind was closer to the moderate Christian Humanism of Erasmus, than to that of the reformer Calvin.[252] This socio-cultural aspect stimulated and led to psychological need to achieve the entrepreneurial objectives - according to Baumol - wealth, prestige and power. And quite a number of them must have been seriously working at achieving that level, as seen from the many images Dutch painters made from their 16th and 17th century entrepreneurial countryman, which overtly manifest their worldly achievements.[253]

7.2. Socio-cultural developments during economic supremacy (1580-1670)

By 1600, the medieval hierarchy, in which the merchants held a relative modest position, no longer corresponded with the social reality. The fact that in some regions entrepreneurs had earned so much that they had surpassed the nobility in wealth, had consequences

---
250 J. de Vries & A.m. van der Woude, p. 213
251 J. de Vries & A.M. van der Woude, p. 207
252 J. de Vries & A.M. van der Woude, p. 208
253 J. Leymarie, *Die Hollaendische Malerei, Genf,* 1956, p. 122 and 133 in particular. See also: Zandvliet, K., (ed), *De 250 rijksten van de Gouden Eeuw,* Amsterdam, 2006

for the division of power and the legitimacy of entrepreneurship. In the Netherlands the leading merchants saw themselves as an elite that in many respects was a match for the nobility. And in some way they also behaved like that. They realised that a mitigated form of external pomp was of quite some importance for the reputation of the entrepreneur. Provided that it was not shown with exaggeration, it confirmed the reliability and creditworthiness of the merchant. Legitimacy of entrepreneurship in the Republic, their acceptance as full members of society - in contradiction to many other countries - never left much to be desired.

But the class of entrepreneurs was not a homogeneous class; there were stratifications and status differences among them. As shown in figure 5 a distinction in entrepreneurship is made between industrial- and trading activities. Industrial activities were carried out by roughly three main groups of entrepreneurs, i.e. those who owned micro enterprises (family- or own account worker), small commodity producers (mainly in textile) and entrepreneurs active in small- and medium sized businesses (mainly involved in processing and manufacturing of salt, beer, sugar, timber, etc.). Trading activities, though, were carried out by retailers (shop owners, marketers and peddlers) and wholesalers. In quite a number of cases, though, the wholesale entrepreneur was also directly involved in processing and manufacturing of products to be traded mainly abroad by their own company. The famous Trip family was an example of such a 'wholesale entrepreneur'. The type of companies, which the Trip family managed, diversified their business and by doing so was spreading their risks. Moving from consortia to consortia and from monopoly to monopoly, they were in an ever increasing scale involved in the trade of weapons, tar, wood, copper and powder. In addition, they also participated in transactions of the VOC and even supplied a number of governors/directors to this phenomenal organisation. They possessed ships, foundries and other industrial enterprises, as well as had important interests in Sweden together with another well-known wholesale entrepreneur, Louis de Geer. Finally, 'the family' traded with West Africa, the East Indies and

North America.[254] Based on research of the tax registry in that period, it appeared that the richest inhabitants of Amsterdam were indeed the wholesalers, people with a very high status in society. More than two-thirds of all entrepreneurs in the city, among them nearly all wholesalers, possessed a capital of over 50.000 guilders (3.5 million Euros/2005)[255] and their tax payments represented 56% of the total tax revenues.[256]

Another example of high *social mobility*, related to entrepreneurship, is shown in the example of Hans Bontemantel, who lived during the period of Spinoza in Amsterdam. He descended from his mother's side from the famous 'Geuzen', who strongly rebelled against the Spaniards. His father was a well-to-do merchant and married the daughter of the General Treasurer of Holland. Hans Bontemantel got his education at the Latin School, where he was acquainted with the Classics. That school, 'Atheneum Illustre' was founded in 1632, with a focus on providing liberal education to students in competition with the more strict theological high school of Leyden. From the inaugural speeches made by the humanists Vossius and Barlaeus, it became clear that the school not only wanted to teach Latin but to create a new specie of man: the '*mercator sapiens*, the learned merchant. This school provided the possibilities for the merchant and entrepreneur to be educated not only in philosophy, languages and physical geography, but also in moral values in trade, such as 'desire' and the indispensable limitation of the same.[257] Anyway, in 1644 Hans Bontemantel travelled to Denmark and Sweden for a business trip and was also able to visit the courts of the kings as he was in the possession of a letter of recommendation obtained from Andries Bicker, the mayor of Amsterdam who impressed him a lot. In 1646 he married the daughter of a medical doctor of the VOC, who actually was not in the position to help him to obtain a higher position in society. But that was already secured through the intervention of a distant family member (Frans Banningh Cocq) and in 1653 he finally became member of the Amsterdam Senate.

---

254 F. Braudel, p. 357
255 K. Zandvliet p. XIII
256 O. Gelderblom, p. 232
257 H. Méchoulan, p. 255

In return Bontemantel voted for Banningh Cocq in his drive to become the mayor of Amsterdam.[258]

Legitimacy also existed for women entrepreneurs. In a study on women entrepreneurship between 1580 and 1815, it was concluded that the share of women at various food markets in the Republic was as high as 75-100%, whereas in shop keeping they accounted for 10-60%. However, among merchants, women were least represented, i.e. to a maximum of 25%.[259] In the majority of case women worked together with their husband's business. Social status, though, played indeed an important role, as women of high social status were not involved in these trade-related activities with the exception of providing financial services, specifically when continuing their husband's business as a widow.[260] The higher one climbed on the social ladder, the heavier the cultural norm weighed, resulting in far less women as entrepreneurs.

The Dutch Republic was an open society with a high degree of *social mobility*, for those who had qualities, as is also proven by a certain Jan Poppen, a German immigrant from Holstein who, as quite a number of other Germans did, came to the Republic. Around 1568 he started as a simple servant in the house of Hans Simonsz de Oude, who lived and worked as a grain merchant in Amsterdam. He managed to marry into the family and approximately 10 years later he established himself as merchant in Amsterdam, active in the long distance trade to the Baltic, Portugal and Spain and when in 1602 the VOC was established, he was one of the biggest investors in the venture. At a later stage he was one of the initiators for trade to the White Sea area. The career of his son Jacob (1576-1624) went even a step further. He married at the age of 27 years the daughter of a member of the Council of Amsterdam and became lieutenant of the Civil Guard. Three years later he was one of the regents of an orphanage and at the age of 33 he acceded the Council and finally became mayor of the city of Amsterdam in 1621, 1622 and 1624.

---
258 H. Méchoulan, p. 68-69
259 Heuvel, D. van den, Women & Entrepreneurship; Female traders in the Northern Netherlands, Amsterdam, 2007, p. 268
260 Ibid. p. 271

Another person, the above-mentioned Frans Banningh Cocq, was the son of a pharmacist from Bremen who married the daughter of a notable, which provided him a chance to visit the university and to engage in a rich marriage. Very soon he also acceded the Council, became four times mayor of the city of Amsterdam, and was elevated to the peerage by the king of France. And the same applied to Nicolaas Tulp, the son of a cloth manufacturer, who had been member of the Council for half a century and also became four times mayor of the city. Hence, it was not descent, but quality and being part of a network could bring second-generation immigrants to the highest position in Amsterdam, probably the biggest metropolis of the world at that time.[261]

The personal advantages of the entrepreneur to take part in local government were in the beginning of the formation of the Republic not that clear. At the start of the new political reality, it was indeed possible to combine entrepreneurship with some public function, such as member of the city council. In the city council of Leyden, around 1600 when also all nobility had disappeared, one could already find 4 brewers, 2 cloth-dealers, 2 merchants in grain, one notary, a textile dyer, a shoemaker, and a baker. And in Rotterdam in 1610, 10 out of 24 city council members came from the transportation sector. After 1610 a new generation emerged who never had any part in the hostilities and the freedom fight from the Spanish Hapsburgs. They started to enjoy the economic advantages, which the previous generation had produced. This was the start of the development of an administrative urban elite, the 'patricians'. During the time of Stadholder Frederik Hendrik (1625-1547) it became customary for the urban 'patricians' (former entrepreneurs) to send their sons to universities and thereafter, by way of completing their education, to send them on the 'Grand Tour', i.e. a long cultural journey to France and Italy. Their wives and daughters used to dress themselves wealthier and with increasing finery. The habit started to construct beautiful mansions, with beautiful gardens. A carriage with a couple of horses became the standard as one of their status symbols. Obviously, they had discovered the public functions, fi-

---

261 C. Lesger, in Kapitaal p. 56 and H. Mechoulan, p. 240

nancially as well as from the point of view of status. However, during this period, the regents-patricians never isolated themselves from other groups in society, in spite of the fact that through co-option they distributed the public functions among themselves. In Amsterdam and other cities there were quite a number of entrepreneurs, who could afford a more or less same life style as these regents and who maintained a lively contact with them, vice versa.[262] The symbiosis between the public and privates sector, or in other words the cooperation between the entrepreneurs and the regents, was in part an expression of the realisation of a fine-meshed structure of *'licenten'* (safe conducts), which allowed merchants to do business with the enemy. In this way they acquired Spanish silver that was indispensable for trading in the Levant, the Baltic Sea and Asia. Next, the revenues of the *'licenten'* served as a basic income for the Board of Admirals, using these funds for waging wars.

A prominent argument, which is presented by many scholars, is that individuals or groups at the periphery of a given social system, specifically in situations in which entrepreneurial legitimacy is low, often promote entrepreneurship. Clearly, during this period there was a great influx of immigrants into the Northern Netherlands. And many of these religious, cultural and ethnic minority groups indeed embraced in many cases entrepreneurship, however, never because they were forced into it as a result of perceived *marginality* or alleged low legitimacy of entrepreneurship in the Netherlands. Not only were push factors (e.g. religious prosecution or economic hardship in the country) at play for minority groups to establish themselves in the Netherlands. There were certainly also pull factors playing a role, whereby the Dutch government had pretty well recognised that economic growth was the result of skilful entrepreneurship. A case in point was the fact that as early as 1581, 1588 and 1592, the Estates General drew up *'sauvegardes'* for the Portuguese Nation[263] in order to be connected to existing trade. These documents allowed Portuguese merchants living in the Republic and elsewhere the right

---
262 J. de Vries en A.M. van der Woude, p. 681
263 The word "Nation" refers to business settlements of foreigners in a given country, with the purpose to do import and export business mainly between their country of origin and the country where their settlement (Nation) was established.

to trade freely by way of the Netherlands. In this respect they were treated similarly as Dutch merchants. As a matter of fact, quite a number came from Antwerp and had already established ties with the jewish community in Amsterdam. Their settlement brought about the transfer of their rich trades, such as the diamond business and trade in tobacco, silk and sugar in particular[264]. The trade in sugar, in that respect, proved to be so important, that the number of refineries in Amsterdam in 25 years increased from three to twenty-five, manufacturing for export as well.[265] The economic supremacy in the first half of the 17th century was not determined by the value of the products of the staple market, but instead was brought about by the trade in colonial products, which was controlled by the East India Company (VOC) and by the companies of Portuguese jewish merchants.[266] From the two- to three thousand jewish entrepreneurs in Amsterdam in the 17th century[267], there was only a small close-knit group who, after 1600, came straight from Portugal instead of Antwerp. They were the ones who had access to a very high quality of precious stones and pearls from the East- and West Indies. They were strongly involved in that business, particularly as the market for these products was growing as a result of the increase of purchasing power of the population and, not in the least, of the purchasing power of the entrepreneurial class, as can be seen from the many paintings of that period. But it was not only the Portuguese minority who, as a marginal group, adopted entrepreneurship voluntarily in their new political, social and cultural environment. The same was applicable to the refugees from Flanders and France.

The history of the Antwerp staple market clarifies the background of the Flemish entrepreneurs who came to Amsterdam after 1578.

---

264 Nearly all of the immigrants, also those coming from the Southern Netherlands were dealing in luxury goods; mass merchandise (staple market business) was generally carried out by the indigenous Dutch entrepreneurs (Gelderblom p.63) and as such this immigrants' business orientation was a welcome addition to the Dutch economy.

265 O.Vlessing, p. 231; this again proves the direct relationship between the level of entrepreneurial activity and economic growth (see also P.D. Reynolds in Global Entrepreneurship Monitor)

266 O.Vlessing, p. 223-243

267 The estimated Jewish population around 1650 in the entire Republic was approximately eight thousand, which also includes Jews from eastern Europe (Ashkenazim)

They belonged to the indigenous entrepreneurial community, which had emerged from the 1530s onwards in Antwerp. The presence of foreign missions in Antwerp (the English Merchant Adventurers, the German Hanze, Portuguese, Italian) offered the indigenous Antwerp traders an excellent opportunity to learn new trading techniques, to develop new products and explore new markets. More importantly for the development of the indigenous entrepreneurs, was the growth of the manufacturing sector, which was focussed on export trade in both Antwerp and its surrounding area.

Approximately one third of all immigrants coming from the south came from the Antwerp hinterland and it is not likely that these immigrants belonged to the entrepreneurial elite of the Southern Netherlands. Also immigrants coming from the city of Antwerp, with the exception of a few tens, were not from that entrepreneurial class either. According to the historian Gelderblom who did research after immigrants from the Southern Netherlands, a large number of them came with hardly any capital and could not even be reckoned to the class of wholesale entrepreneur. Approximately 50% of them who arrived in 1585 was younger than 25 years[268]. The majority of immigrants did not only establish themselves in the Republic in order to evade poverty or to exercise their protestant religion, but also to build up or extend the business they had already started down south. They were very successful and their importance for the Dutch economy is clear, taken into consideration that 32% of the 764 entrepreneurs who founded the Bank of Amsterdam were from South Netherlands origin[269]. Interestingly in this respect is the research that Gelderblom carried out on Hans Thijs, who grew up in Antwerp, but left the city in 1584 to marry the daughter of Augustijn Boel, who had already migrated to Amsterdam before. Between 1585 and 1611 he lived and worked in Elbing, Danzig and Amsterdam. Like his father, he was also in the jewellery business, but later extended his business activities in hides, skins and leather together with his father-in-law who also lived in Danzig but moved back to Amsterdam in 1593. During the period when Thijs lived in Danzig, he was travelling extensively to Warsaw and Krakow to do

---

268   O. Gelderblom, p. 164
269   O. Gelderblom, p. 123

business with the gentry, as well as to Lübeck, Kiel, Copenhagen, Leipzig, Stockholm, Regensburg, Vienna and Rome. Thijs and Boel also bought in 1589 and 1590 four ship-parts, which gave an average annual interest of 12%, being higher than the interest on regular Dutch lendings. Thijs extended his business then with chamois, and through his father-in-law, living then in Amsterdam, he sent this product also to his brother Matheus who lived and worked in La Rochelle, France. After he moved from Danzig to Amsterdam in 1594 he extended his jewellery business not only in Amsterdam and surroundings, but also sent precious stones and the like to another brother in La Rochelle, Paul Thijs, for the marketing of this commodity in Bordeaux, Rouen, Paris, Lyon and even Montpeliers. Next, he also went into the salt- and wine business, again together with his father-in-law. After Hans Thijs made investments in 1602 in the VOC[270], initially with 12.000 guilders to be increased to 26.000 guilders soon thereafter, he disposed of the leather business and concentrated primarily on the jewellery business. The profits he made were reinvested in VOC shares he bought in 1610 and 1611 and when he died in 1611, the value of his possessions was as high as 255.000 guilders (18 million Euros/2005)[271] of which 60% was invested in shares and fixed assets, whereas the remaining 40% represented the balance of his direct business activities.[272] Another example raised by Gelderblom is Dirck van Os, a son of a carpet weaver who had moved in the 1550 from Den Bosch to Antwerp and left the city after the Fall of Antwerp to Middleburgh, at the age of 28 years. In 1588 he moved to Amsterdam where he married an Antwerp girl. As an entrepreneur he traded in grain, leather, oil, salt and precious stones. Together with Pieter van Pullen and Isaac Lemaire (also from Antwerp) he traded extensively with Russia. In addition, he was active as an insurer, ship-owner, provided loans and was one of the financiers of the reclamation of the Beemster Lake. Finally, he became known because of his involvement with

---

[270] Obviously, immigrants from Portugal and the Southern Netherlands were not the only ones. There were numerous individual foreigners who were attracted by employment opportunities in the Netherlands, such as with the VOC, which recruited many people from Denmark, Norway and Germany (H. Mechoulan p. 244)
[271] K. Zandvliet, p. XIII
[272] O. Gelder blom, p. 127-148

the East Indies trade. He was one of the directors of the earlier erected Companies and when the VOC was established he participated heavily - together with his brother - to the tune of 47.000 guilders.

From these and other similar research a couple of conclusions can be drawn. First and foremost, minority or marginal groups in the Netherlands were never forced to go into entrepreneurship, as the theory of marginal groups goes. As a matter of fact, members of these marginal groups just continued their earlier activity, as entrepreneur in the country they fled from. The overriding reason was that there were ample opportunities in the Dutch Republic for entrepreneurial activity, without getting into conflict with indigenous Dutch entrepreneurs. These indigenous entrepreneurs were much more focused on mass merchandising with the Baltic, whereas the Portuguese and Flemish entrepreneurs were largely involved in trading Asian and South American products and luxury goods. Their business activities were complementary to that of the Dutch entrepreneurs. The Second conclusion may be that the immigrant entrepreneur could make use of the well-developed business infrastructure in the Republic, such as the availability of ship-holds, low transactional cost and an efficiently working market. And this was an important push factor to stick to their original profession as entrepreneur. A Third conclusion is that the Dutch government apparently understood the significance of promoting, attracting and facilitating foreign minority groups into the mainstream of entrepreneurial activities, as a vehicle for economic growth. In order to finance the war against Spain, that economic growth was indeed highly needed.

The above gives already some insight into the *social integration* of minority groups who were involved in entrepreneurial activities. As elaborated before, integration into Dutch society came even to a point in which they could become mayor of the most important city at that time in Europe, Amsterdam. Generally, there was indeed a relatively high level of social integration into society, in particular as regards the trading section of society. Amsterdam, for instance, counted in 1585 30.000 people; in 1622 150.000 and in around

1670 the population was as large as 200.000. The increase was to a high extent attributable to the arrival of many ethnic minorities who went in trade or services. These minorities could integrate into Dutch society quite easily. A stay of some years in a town, the payment of 50 guilders or a marriage with a local person, were sufficient to obtain the '*poorterschap*', the civil right that was required to exercise a profession and/or to become a member of the guild. Creed did not matter. Freedom and tolerance were in fact commercial imperatives of the municipalities in the Dutch Republic.[273] The Netherlands, and in particular Amsterdam, had many different ethnical groups and denominations of various belief systems within its borders. And although in many other places in Europe where this led to strife and conflict, the situation in the Republic was different. Social integration was, in the words of the French historian Méchoulan, due to the fact that strife and conflict did not pay off in a society, which was oriented towards trade. Individual economic activities required a rational approach in attitudes and behaviour, which were contrary to emotional utterances as a consequence of differences in creed. And although commercial activities had strong competitive characteristics, they also produced a climate of mutual dependency. And this mutual dependency, caused by economic self-interest was the cement of social integration. Rembrandt nicely illustrated this, when he painted six burghers charged with supervision of the measures and weights, showing them beyond the limitation of their religion. Three persons - a calvinist, a mennonite and a catholic – in that painting were standing there as one man for the principle of trade: the indisputable, universally unshakable measures and weights.[274] However, this was in some cases different with regard to jews and other denominations, who in the view of some, exercised 'heresy'. These were usually not allowed to become a member of the guilds. In Amsterdam they were excluded from the membership with the exception of brokers-, printers- and surgeon guilds; but even in theses guilds the jews were subjected to certain limitations. Jews were not allowed to run shops. Therefore, they concentrated on trade activities and professions in which no guilds

---

273 H. Méchoulan, p. 57
274 H. Méchoulan, p. 125-126

were practising, such as in the silk-, diamond-, tobacco- and sugar industries. German jews, or Ashkenazim, who for the greater part only spoke Yiddish, often belonging to the city proletariat were mainly active as peddlers or street hawkers.[275] Generally, there was also a strong orientation among immigrants to their own ethnic group exercizing the same reliogion. Immigrants erected the Refugees Church in Amsterdam and in 1579 they founded also the so-called Walloon Church, of which the administration was for the greater part in the hands of entrepreneurs of South Netherlands origin. This was, to even a higher extent, the case with the Lutheran Church. However, for the greater part, immigrants became members of the official Calvinistic Church.

Looking at the issue of risk and uncertainty it is safe to state that the course of life of a person in the Republic was very difficult to predict and uncertain. Actually, that was true for anyone living in Europe, although in a different nature. A small farmer in France or Germany never knew whether or not he would survive the next harvest, but whatever happened - also in the case of a very rich harvest - he knew he would remain farmer, as well as his sons would continue live on the same soil in the same village. In a study about people of 'small funds' in the Golden Age, the historian Van Deursen concluded that a working relationship in that period, particularly in the province of Holland, could be characterised as very unstable and uncertain. His research revealed that, a Hollander was handling *insecurity* of life in a different manner as compared to elsewhere in Europe; he never knew when and in what profession he would end his life, leave alone would he know his son's profession. Contrary to nearly everywhere else in Europe, where a change in career would provide a lot of insecurity and be seen as a loss of status, the Hollander was actively looking for *mobility* and because of that was often rewarded with a higher life style.[276]

Another important socio-cultural aspect in determining entrepreneurship is *security*. With security in here is meant essentially the

---
275 E.J. Fischer, (1999), p. 14
276 A.Th. van Deursen, p. 353-354

protection of entrepreneurs against uncertainties, want, social disapproval and political interference. Henry Méchoulan describes this important aspect through two intertwined elements, i.e. money and freedom[277], both subject to uncertainty and insecurity. He reminds us that freedom in this respect depends for the greater part on the duties and obligations one chooses. According to his analysis the freedom that the Republic enjoyed consisted of the desire for independency, freedom of consciousness, freedom of mobility, entrepreneurial freedom and tolerance concerning people from other countries and of all walks of life, as long as these contributed to the economic power of the city or country. As Spinoza said: 'a nation is independent as to its ability to take care for its own prosperity. And certainly, people are better able to watch over their own security the more powerful they are, which comes as a result of their wealth'[278]. Both, Amsterdam and the Republic understood the relationship between money and freedom, as observed in the words of William Temple, the British Ambassador to the Republic at that time: 'Greed is indeed making many victims, but altogether far less than war. If people are just working to satisfy their wealth, nobody will cut somebody's else throat because of superstition and is no blood-shedding taking place unless it serves a clear interest'[279]. And that clear interest of the English and the French was obviously shown in their wars against the Dutch Republic.

The ideology of 'freedom and money' as a mean to assure security, however, could also turn into the thirst for immediate gain and profits, which then became a danger for freedom and money itself. This happened, for example, when the *Heren XVII* - the directorate of the VOC - in 1644 declared that 'the establishments and fortresses which we have conquered in the East Indies, may not be considered as national territory, but as the property of the merchants, who have the right to sell these to any one they want, even to the king of Spain or any other enemy of the Seven United Provinces'![280] In another

---

277 Méchoulan, H., Amsterdam ten tijde van Spinoza; Geld en Vrijheid (J. Noorman trans. Amsterdam au temps de Spinoza), Amsterdam 1992, p. 14
278 Tractatus Politicus, cap. V, 12 and cap. VII, 16. (English translation made by author)
279 Méchoulan, H. p. 17
280 Quotation from C.R. Boxter, *The Dutch Seaborn Empire, op.cit.* p. 45-46 in H. Méchoulan, p. 60

instance, Amsterdam merchants tried to accumulate quick money when they went even that far as to co-finance the reconstruction of the in 1666 burnt down city of London, being the fiercest competitor of Amsterdam. And a final example to show that freedom and money also had its reverse was when France was preparing an invasion in the Republic in 1672. At that time there were even some Dutch entrepreneurs supplying the French war machine. De Witt, the political leader of the Republic at that time, tried in vain to convince the *Heren XVII* to strengthen the army. But the merchants were not really ready to finance the army and to protect their own freedom and independence. Their pursuit of profits apparently had made them blind.[281] Entrepreneurship and government were too much of the same breed. Hence, government representatives were reluctant in taking measures, which were not wanted by entrepreneurs. But that is exactly what government should have done; it should have had an eye for long-term consequences of certain actions and should have taken corrective measures to contain entrepreneurial short-term advantages or the 'quick buck'.

In sprite of this short-sightedness the entrepreneur in the Republic was portrayed as being close to a heroic figure. Many paintings from the 17th century made by famous Dutch artists like Rembrandt, Mierevelt, ter Borch and many others, show their status and importance.[282] But not only painters, also poets gave brilliance to entrepreneurs. Famous Dutch play-writers like Vondel and Bredero wrote about the economic expansion of the Republic, which – according to them - was due to innovative entrepreneurship. They wrote lyrically about the Bourse, the trade in the West-Indies and Mediterranean, the business partnerships, the shareholders meeting, entrepreneurs who were fast in arithmetic an calculating prices, the trade in shares, share prices, etc. Entrepreneurs were indeed the pillars of the Dutch economy and culture and because of the wealth they created and the taxes they paid, they were highly instrumental in the liberation of the Republic from Spanish Habsburg rule.

---

281   H. Méchoulan, p. 260-262
282   K. Zandvliet

7.3. Socio-cultural developments during economic decline (1670-1815)

Legitimacy of entrepreneurship during this sub-period of economic decline remained very high. Research on this issue[283], indicate that at the end of the 18th century, the entrepreneur was traditionally still seen as the most prominent Dutch citizen and trade was regarded, since time immemorial, as the basis for economic welfare of the country. *Social mobility*, on the other hand, had been in decline as the regents, originally emerging from the class of entrepreneurs, segregated themselves from society. The regents became a class in itself in a society that became increasingly congealed. They were also the ones with big capital and owners of government bonds, who ultimately were paid by the taxes, which were levied from mainly the large number of micro and small enterprises. Quite a number of these businesses were run by *marginal groups* such as the jews, whom could be found in entrepreneurial activities as haberdashery, kosher butchery, porcelain retailing, inn-keeping, silver- and goldsmith activities and even cheese making. Jewish entrepreneurs were also disproportionably represented in high-risk areas of the economy, such as illicit speculation in commodity futures, or the infamous 'trading in the wind' on doubtfully generated stock issue[284]. Another marginal group that came into the country during this sub-period was the wealthy Huguenot immigrants from France, who fled their country in 1685 as a result of the Revocation of the Edict of Nantes. In the Netherlands they continued their entrepreneurial activities in luxury industry and therefore were strongly protected by city governments for their perceived contribution in increasing the economic growth of the city. A very important consideration for a positive *social integration* into society of these marginal groups was that also the Huguenot entrepreneurs brought many business contacts with them from France. Although they had to fly their country, it did not mean that all contacts with former associates hade been frustrated. In line with the thinking of Baumol also the

---

283 JL. van Zanden & A. van Riel, p. 79
284 S.Schama, p. 590

huguenot Gabriel Ardent[285] was of the opinion that the entrepreneur *"pur sang"*, does not have affection for his fellow man; he is only interested in other economic forces and contacts, such as buyers, sellers, creditors, money-lenders, etc. He wants to increase his status, power and wealth and that implies keeping in contact with those who can be instrumental in achieving these entrepreneurial objectives. And that was exactly what the huguenots did.

Also in this period, the highly protective business association - the guilds - was present in many branches of economic life and in a way protected the interests of the specific business sectors they were active in. On the one hand it gave *security* to those belonging to the guilds. On the other hand it also banned competition, which frustrated new innovative entrepreneurs in many of their activities, since they were hampered in making use of new opportunities. But that type of protection, providing *security* to entrepreneurs, came to an end. After the disastrous war with the Dutch rival, England (1780-84), a strong movement of the Patriots came up in the Netherlands in 1787. This movement was strongly influenced by the Enlightment, which later in 1789 would become the source of the French Revolution. These Patriots were against the lot of the squeezed middle class of small and micro entrepreneurs, artisans and traders. Their view, seen from the production side of economic life, demanded a government that should do away with the current particularism, in which the regents and their dependents had nestled in a complacent position of power. Although the movement was frustrated by Prussian troops, the French as a consequence invaded the country in 1795, abolished the guild system and hopes revived for a drastic change in line with that of the French Revolution. But ultimately the French did not have much more to offer but a complete destruction of the Dutch economy. And all of that brought the level of security for the majority of entrepreneurs at a very low ebb.

The going *business ideology*, also throughout this sub-period or - even stronger - specifically during this period, was 'entrepreneurial liberty', which meant to do trade without an restriction and in all

---
285 F. Braudel, p. 148-151

freedom with any country they wanted. This was even the case with countries in which the Dutch Republic was in war, which was tacitly accepted by the government.[286] Being inhabitants of a geographically small country without large armies, the 'freedom philosophy' in trading was their strength and economic survival. As has been discussed in this study before, the decline of the Dutch economy was in large measure attributable to the mercantilist trade policies of the larger countries, which were even prepared to wage wars to reach their goals. Generally speaking the cities, run by merchant oligarchs - the regents - followed free international trade policies. No tariffs encumbered exports or imports of raw material or semi-finished goods, which were to be processed and re-exported; tariffs and taxes on consumer goods were for revenue, not for protection of domestic industries. The trade in precious metals, in particular, was entirely free, in striking contrast to the policies of other nations. Amsterdam with its international 'Bank of Exchange', and favourable balance of payments, still was till far in the 18th century the world emporium for gold and silver. The entrepreneurial concern for freedom and toleration was real, particularly with respect to freedom of the seas. As a small maritime nation, surrounded by vastly more populous and powerful neighbours, Dutch entrepreneurs resisted the pretensions of Spain to control the western Atlantic and the Pacific Ocean, of Portugal to the South Atlantic and Indian Ocean and to Britain to their so-called 'British Seas', including the Channel. The Dutch jurist Hugo de Groot (Grotius) wrote during this period his famous treatise, *Mare Liberum* (Freedom of the Seas), destined to become ultimately one of the foundations of current international law. Although favourable to Dutch entrepreneurs, this was not accepted by countries like England and France, which had adopted a mercantilist policy, meaning to fight trade wars for the benefit of their own nations and entrepreneurs.

---

286 R. Cameron, p. 155-156

8. ENTREPRENEURIAL CHARACTERISTICS

In this section three main characteristics will be examined, i.e. first, the *identity* of the entrepreneur. This includes aspects such as a) individuality vs. collectivity, b) whether or not the entrepreneurs belong to the mainstream or may be outsider-entrepreneurs, c) whether or not the entrepreneurs belong to the family firm and also what their religious orientation is. A second main characteristic will be *the entrepreneurs' orientation* and drive towards expansion and innovation. The third characteristic to look for during this period will be what specific *entrepreneurial traits* can be found, such as: risk-taking, their positive or negative self concept, their level of initiative and independence, their problem solving capabilities and creativity, their search for business opportunities and, finally, also their specific psychological need to achieve something in life. Some of these traits have been dealt with in the previous chapter, albeit in another context when describing the social-cultural environment of the entrepreneurs. In here, an effort is made to describe specifically the individual entrepreneurial trait, rather than the socio-cultural environment in which he performs. The three main characteristics will be examined per three sub-periods of Trade Capitalism, i.e. during economic take-of (1350-1580), the economic supremacy (1580-1760) and, finally, during economic stagnation and decline (1670-1815)

8.1. Identity of entrepreneurs

During economic take-off (1350-1580)

Before elaborating on entrepreneurial characteristics, it may be helpful to present a somewhat rough stratification of the world of the entrepreneur. Merchants at the beginning of this period (around 1400) - specifically those that were connected to the hanseatic trade - could be categorised as follows. On top was the big merchant who was nearly exclusively involved in wholesale businesses in various geographical areas and different business sectors, related to long distance trade. Their wealth did not only come from trade activities, but was the result of lending practices, shares in ship companies, or rent from real estate. These very rich merchants were in many cases members of the regent's class. Below them we find a middle layer of entrepreneurs, doing business primarily with one single country or region. They were in many cases not only wholesalers but were involved in retail as well. These entrepreneurs carried out professions such as ship-owners, weavers and brewers. At the bottom of the class of entrepreneurs we find the small merchants who could be subdivided into two groups, i.e. the shop-owners, retailers and peddlers, who were for their business very much dependent on the bigger merchants and the wholesalers with some more money. These were able to buy in bigger quantities and to supply the small retailers for their shops or booths.[287] Also small artisans were living at the level of the class of entrepreneurs at the bottom. Their micro businesses gave a wider outlook to the world as compared to their wage-earning employees, but materially they hardly differed. A large number of guild masters – specifically those active in small community production - could not even permit to recruit employees; in 1581 in Leyden there was only one wage-earning employee at every five or six artisans. Not any of the more than 50 pin making manufacturers in the city of Gorichem in 1597 were rich enough to do independently business with foreign markets. Micro entrepreneurs had to live by the day and to buy new raw materials with the profits they obtained during the past week, as they did not have any financial reserves at their disposal.[288]

As has been discussed before, the historical lack of a strong feudal operating system in the Netherlands contributed to the fact that the collective dimension of society, and thus also of entrepreneurs, was developed to a lesser extent than the individual dimension. In

---
287 P. Dollinger, p. 199-200
288 A.Th. van Deursen, p.14; a solution to the lack of financial reserves was the 'putting-out' or 'Verlag' system, whereby merchants/entrepreneurs in the cities often provided raw material and/or advances for wages, so as to guarantee production for their trade (see also: C.A. Davids in: Kapitaal, p. 97)

addition, the calvinistic ideology - so very important for the identity of the nation and people's independence - emphasised the individual responsibility of men. And entrepreneurs acted accordingly. However, in cases of purely commercial reasons or to evade risks, collective behaviour was never absent, as was the case for example in the fishing business in the 16th century. In spite of the fact that financial enterprises were a significant phenomenon in the Dutch economy, there were groups of ten or fifteen small entrepreneurs who - in their desire for profits and risk-sharing with their modest funds - invested also in more or less lucrative undertakings. In Rotterdam in 1591, for example, the entire herring fisheries were in the hands of micro- and small entrepreneurs *('backers, cuypers, lijndrayers, blaeckers, schoenmaekers, visschers, strieluyden, suyvelcopers ende andre diergelijcke luyden, die meestal van seer cleyn vermogen zijn'*[289]) They formed combinations of ten, fifteen or more participants, who financed together the cost of the trip of one certain herring buss.[290]

In carrying out the entrepreneurial function, there was initially a handsome division of labour between the indigenous 'mainstream entrepreneurs' and the immigrant 'outsider entrepreneurs', in that the mainstream businessman was predominantly involved in mass merchandising (grain, timber, beer, etc.) and dairy export, whereas the outsider entrepreneur was - given his previous business experiences - mainly involved in the luxury trade (spices, diamond). Conventional wisdom holds, that an 'outsider entrepreneur' has to take larger risks in running the business than the 'insider/indigenous entrepreneur', leaving the riskier business to the 'outsider'. The study of relevant literature does not support that view, although the nature of the risk, attached to the type of products they traded in, was obviously different. So if there were differences in entrepreneurial risk-taking it had more to do with the nature of the products and markets, rather than with the notion 'insider-outsider'.

---

[289] Bylsma, p. 41, quoted in A.Th van Deursen, p. 31-32. (...all sorts of small entrepreneurs, such as e.g. bakers, shoemakers, dairy buyers, fishermen, etc., businessmen with a very small capital only)

[290] A.Th van Deursen p. 31-32

Already in this period of trade capitalism a striking phenomenon can be observed in that trading houses were primarily staffed with family members and with those that came into the family through marriage. That was not only the case with the 'outsider' entrepreneur, the immigrant, who had a natural inclination to stick to the family for reasons of psychological security. This was also the case with the mainstream entrepreneur, albeit for different reasons. Also in here the argument ran that business was a matter of trust and confidence and these could best be found within the circle of the family. This did not automatically lead to non-innovative or non-expansive behaviour as is often seen when family members join the business. On the contrary, we see in quite a number of cases that expansion of the business took place, just because of using family members, for instance, as representatives of their father's or brother's businesses overseas, which in the 17th century became even common practice. In addition, young family members became thoroughly trained through apprenticeship in related family businesses and then became entrepreneurs in the business of their fathers, or married into another befriended business family.[291] Then innovation and expansion of the business usually took place, up until the second generation, after which there are examples of assumed decline in entrepreneurship as argued by quite a number of researchers. However, recent historical research has indicated that this is a gross over-simplification. Entrepreneurs, who later became financiers, instead of continuing in production or trading, did so because - due to increased international competition and trade wars - there was hardly any better alternative for the high returns they could otherwise get[292].

The origin of proto-industrial entrepreneurs in the Netherlands was related to those who had been trading as a merchant before and, subsequently, had build up wide knowledge of markets, prices, quality requirements, logistics, as well as with the supply side, such as raw material providers and processors of finished or semi-finished products. They were also the ones who were familiar with

---

291 P. Dollinger, p. 223
292 J.L. van Luiten & A. van Riel, p. 41-48

the 'putting out' (*Verlag*) system and had capital means at their disposal, either generated through their own work as wholesalers, or through contacts they had with money lenders or banks. But also artisans found themselves in favourable opportunity conditions and transformed themselves into 'industrial' entrepreneurs. In their contacts with the merchants, they saw chances, particularly in the textile industry, to start industrial entrepreneurship, given the expanding domestic and foreign markets for which they produced. In conclusion, it can safely be stated that the socio-economic origin of industrial entrepreneurs was rooted in entrepreneurs who before had been working at a less complicated business level. They grew together with their business to a higher – commercially and intellectually more demanding - level of entrepreneurship, which was required in an increasingly sophisticated economy with more and differentiated markets, products and logistical means.

The *religious orientation* of the entrepreneurs was definitely calvinistic. However, they were keen enough to understand that part of the economic growth of the Republic in which they flourished so well, was to quite some extent dependent on entrepreneurs with a different orientation (catholics, mennonites, jews). Therefore, they did not allow their calvinistic orientation to become a political or religious 'pressure-cooker'. They realised that 'freedom' was needed to strengthen the individual, which in its turn guaranteed a maximum of economic opportunities, from which each entrepreneur ultimately benefited. However, this relaxed stand does not negate the notion that the calvinistic orientation indeed strengthened the no-nonsense mentality that entrepreneurs had already in their genes as from the late Middle Ages. The fact that the Reformation was so successful in the Netherlands may be caused by the fact that the calvinistic belief-system coincided so well with already existing norms and values in society. Calvinism, at best, may have strengthened existing entrepreneurial attitudes and virtues, but was never the cause of it.[293]

There have been some suggestions that old entrepreneurs, those with relatively many years of entrepreneurship, may be somewhat

---
293 J. de Vries & A.M. van der Woude, p. 207

less expansive and innovative as compared to those, who are new in their entrepreneurial role. Any such view was not found in the socio-economic research related to this sub-period 1350-1580. What can be said though, is that many young family members went abroad to Russia, Poland, France, Germany, etc. in order to represent their father's firm or to conclude separate business deals, which indeed are forms of market innovation and expansion. The driving force behind these foreign missions was the patriarch of the family, the principle 'seasoned' entrepreneur, who was eager in expanding the business. In that sense he was probably more innovative and expansive then was the younger generation in the business, although he left much of the physical activity to the younger members of the family. In summary, 'age' was not the determining factor of innovativeness; it was rather a state of mind, a matter of the level of inquisitiveness.

Identity of entrepreneurs during economic supremacy (1580-1670)

'Holland is a country where the earth is better than the air; and profit more in request than honour; where there is more sense than wit, more good nature than good humour, and more wealth than pleasure; where a man would choose rather to travel than to live, shall find more things to observe than desire, and more persons to esteem than to love'.[294] It was the British Ambassador to the Republic in 1673 who painted this picture, in his account about the population of Holland. A more in-depth analysis of the identity of the Dutch entrepreneur is given below, using various different angles such as individuality verses collectiveness, their religious orientation, the orientation towards their own family members and those outside the family when it comes to business.

Instead of a *collective orientation*, entrepreneurs, in general, had a strong tendency towards *individuality*. The overall idea was that it was the activity of the individual entrepreneur (applying skills,

---

[294] Quote from Willem Frijhoff in Hollands identiteit in de vroegmoderne tijd, in: *Spiegel Historiael*, January 2000, p. 36

making investments, exploit expertise) that would lead to success or failure. Nonetheless, as in the previous period, collective traits could be found, as there were many reasons why entrepreneurs at that time worked together in close partnership with other colleagues. Reasons for it were to spread the risks of doing business, or because business ventures were, or became, financially too large to be financed by one individual, specifically in international trade with its long distances. A nice example is that of skippers of tow-boats, who were organised in guilds and whose income consisted of a fixed amount per trip plus a share in the profits of their collective enterprise. Obviously, there were fluctuations in the income of the skippers; sometimes they earned the salary of unskilled labour, whereas in other years they earned three times as much. The guild invested the saved money in bonds, but also provided credits to their members, in order to allow them to keep the basic income at a reasonable level. There was also the collective system of entrepreneurs who ran ships or mills by taking participations of various values and through a commissioner collected the revenue or profits (dividend). This reduced the risks of the investors or entrepreneurs considerably. [295]

Finally, there could be the psychological reason of 'togetherness' with its own ethnical group. This was the case with Dutch business communities abroad (in Archangel, for instance), as well as with the various refugees who came to the Republic, such as the Flemish merchants and the jewish entrepreneurs from Portugal and Spain, who were also very much sticking together. That 'togetherness' or 'social capital' was indeed important, since anyone who became ill, lost his job, or got into financial trouble, was dependent on the willingness of others to help; hence, it was necessary to ensure oneself of that willingness and trust. The best way to do so was to render personal services. The exchange of services was determined by the principle of reciprocity: anyone who did someone a service could expect one in return.[296] Although there was no segregation of immigrant entrepreneurs from the Southern Netherlands, there was nonetheless strong preference – as we have already seen - for cooperation with family members. Entrepreneurs focused on continuing their business by

---

295 J. de Vries en A.M. van der Woude, p. 173
296 L. Kooijmans, p. 30

applying five general traits, which determined the social- and commercial strategy. These were: 1) transferring the business to the next generation within the family, 2) specialisation, 3) maintaining established relationship with suppliers and buyers, 4) cooperation with family members and, finally, 5) the inclination to marry persons who were active within their specific business sector.[297] Their bent for *collectively* doing business with their own group is in conformity with the finding that entrepreneurs also wanted to secure their markets and products for possible competition by the formation of outside cartels and monopolies.[298] Only in the course of the 17th century a good number of them, in particular the children of the initial immigrants, married into Dutch entrepreneurial families.

As mentioned in the previous section of this study, it has been suggested that *'outsider'*-entrepreneurs will be more willing to take risks because of their marginal situation, as compared to *'mainstream'* entrepreneurs. The minority groups or immigrants living in the Netherlands, usually, did not find themselves in a marginal situation. Just like indigenous entrepreneurs, they perceived opportunities by going into business. Generally, they became successful business people. From the 320 biggest accounts of the *Amsterdam Wisselbank* (Bank of Exchange) in 1609, 50% originated from entrepreneurs originally coming from the South. However, their financial position should not be overestimated either, as their input in Dutch trade did not lead to the rapid expansion of the Dutch staple market. As a matter of fact, Amsterdam had already a strong position in the Baltic trade in the 15th century, far before emigrants arrived in the Northern Netherlands.[299] 'The arrival of the great merchants with their wealth in money and expertise, undoubtedly added an important extra dimension to the economic life of the fiercely young Republic, but at that time the economic situation had already matured'[300]. Amsterdam enjoyed already a leading role in the Baltic and North Sea, so that immigrant en indigenous entrepreneurs, who

---
297 Veluwekamp, J.W., *Handel op Archangel; Nederlandse ondernemers in Rusland in de 17e eeuw*, in: Spiegel Historiael, nr. 3, jaargang 36, p. 127-132
298 O. Gelderblom, p. 22
299 O. Gelderblom, p. 12
300 J. De Vries & van der Woude, *Nederland 1500-1815*, p. 767

settled in the city, could benefit from an elastic supply of holds, low transactional cost and an efficient operating market. The emergence of Amsterdam was furthermore activated due to the crisis that Antwerp experienced in the mid 16th century, forty to fifty years before the 'Fall of Antwerp', which caused a relatively strong migration wave to the northern Netherlands.[301] Ultimately, the Netherlands received likely as many as 150.000[302] refugees from the South[303], approximately 10% of the population at that time. That great migration initially engendered some friction in the host cities, where the perceived sin of the southerners was their immoderation - they were too rich or too poor, too lawless or even too fanatical in their calvinism. But their integration into the northern society - and one should add, their enrichment of it, both materially and culturally - was only a matter of time. If immigrants received rough treatment in Dutch towns, it was less because of their foreign origin than their indigence or, in the case of the Scandinavian and German seamen, who kept showing up in taverns and street brawls. The same was applicable to other ethnic groups. If the jewish presence was easily absorbed, it was not because it was so ubiquitous and indispensable to the metropolitan economy, but because it was so discreet and so marginal. In 1672, three years before the opening of the great synagogue in Amsterdam, there were 7.500 jews of the nearly 200.000 in habitants living in Amsterdam or just 3.75% of the population.

---

301 As a matter of fact, the Antwerp staple market was different from Amsterdam in that the former was –according to De Vries & Van der Woude- primarily a meeting place for foreign entrepreneurs, who were focussed on transporting their merchandise over land and were dependent on favours of the Habsburgs. Therefore the two cities differed that much that the Antwerp immigrants had to change their mode of trade operations. The merchants who migrated to Amsterdam brought capital, expertise and contacts, but they used these potentialities differently than before, since they were confronted with new possibilities, institutions and challenges.

302 There are various estimates as regards the number of immigrants form the south: Van Schelven arrives at 60.000, Van Houtte at 80.000 and Briels at 150.000. Briels arrived at his estimate after extensive research of qualitative sources and the "Poorterboeken", official registers of the municipality. However, his extrapolations based on the "Poorterboeken" are controversial. (See O. Gelderblom, *Zuid-Nederlandse Kooplieden en de opkomst van de Amsterdamse stapelmarkt (1578-1630)*, p. 17, footnote 46

303 The population in the Republic at that time hovered around 1.5 to 2 million. Percentage wise, the immigrants represented 10% of the indigenous population. This percentage disregards immigrants from Spain and Portugal (Jews), north-western Germany and Scandinavia.

It is true that they were disproportionately represented in sectors of the economy - constituting for example 13% of the depositors of the Amsterdam Bank. But they were still very much on the fringe of the great trading staples like Baltic grain, Muscovy furs or Swedish iron and copper. Flemish diamond polishers, which had brought the craft from Antwerp, mounted a campaign to restrict jewish encroachment and largely succeeded in curtailing their share until the very end of the 17th century[304]. Sugar refiners were similarly hostile, preventing the Portuguese house of Preira and Pina by legal intervention from directly marketing their products. Tobacco processing was the one area where the jewish 'Brazilian connection' (through Portuguese family ties) helped establish them in a profitable and secure economic niche. Exclusion from the guild membership was only gradually lifted and, as we have seen before, in some trades exclusion existed not at all.[305]

As discussed in the previous section, the 'family firm' was relatively strong embedded in the Dutch way of doing business at that time. Making use of 'trust' and 'social capital' was the answer to the many uncertainties in doing business, specifically in international trade. In addition, many of the then newly arrived immigrant groups who were sticking together for reasons of 'togetherness', culture, religion, as well as also to cope effectively with uncertainties in business. More important than the question of religious doctrine was the question of loyalty and trust, the question whether someone was 'one of us' or belonged to the others'. The historian Kooijmans illustrates this with the case of Andries van der Meulen, an entrepreneur from Antwerp who migrated to Amsterdam, and did not want to marry his daughter to *those who did not agree with us in religious matters, because I would fear that God would revenge himself on me and my house*'. Van der Meulen also thought that a marriage with someone who was not a zealous protestant would cause discord in the family, which was to be avoided at all cost.[306] Loss of reputation meant loss

---

[304] At some later stage, though, the Jewish entrepreneurs were able to control the supply of pearls and diamonds, obviously in competition with the immigrants from Antwerp.(See O.Gelderblom, p. 22)
[305] S. Schama, p. 590
[306] L. Kooijmans, p. 27

of credit, so an entrepreneur had to be very careful to protect his good name. Everybody was very touchy on this point. A person's reputation was closely linked to the name of his ancestors and his family.[307] Hagen's assumption that the 'family firm' inherits the danger of negative entrepreneurial orientation, due to failure of talent or lack of interest in entrepreneurship, is not valid - at the least not for this period. Family ties were the result of intermarriage and of the sons' succession to their fathers' businesses. These were aspects of a strategy aimed at reducing risks as well as the commercial and social survival of the family.

As regards the socio-economic origin of the entrepreneurs, a distinction has to be made between the indigenous Dutch entrepreneurs and the immigrants. The roots of the indigenous Dutch entrepreneurs are lying in the centuries prior to this period of global entrepreneurial dominance. This particularly so in terms of knowledge and expertise concerning everything related to logistics. The geographical position of the delta at the crossroads between East- West and North-South had made the Dutch entrepreneur familiar with both, all known sea routes and shipbuilding. This was reason why they could make an efficient use of these sea routes and, as a consequence, became familiar with all forms of international trade. This in itself stimulated manufacturing in food processing, such as dairy products and beer, as well as the manufacturing of the shipbuilding-related products, such as paint, cordage, textile, etc. The basis of Dutch entrepreneurship was the drive for economic survival, which could be achieved by doing interregional- and later international trade. The socio-economic origin of the immigrant entrepreneur was different in that they had their roots in the already existing trading metropolis such as Antwerp, and Bruges, as well as from trading communities in Portugal and Spain. A number of them came to Northern Netherlands with market knowledge (the far East, Brazil), expertise in the production of certain commodities (textile, diamonds, tobacco) and general trading experience. Above all, as refugees per definition avail of a lot of vitality and character, these characteristics

---
307 L. Kooijmans, p. 30

were of importance in their performance to become a successful entrepreneur in their new country.

Religion, evidently, kept on playing an important role in the lives of many entrepreneurs. Kooijmans illustrates this handsomely through the earlier mentioned study he made of Andries Van der Meulen, the immigrant from Flanders, who was convinced that God directed his life and was thankful for all that God had given him. But, according to Van der Meulen, this did not mean that one could be dependent on God alone. He assessed a fellow entrepreneur who expected God to solve his financial problems, as very naive: '*for someone who has debts to hope that he will soon be rich and able to pay off his debts is very silly, displaying more fantasy than faith*'[308]. Van der Meulen also advised his colleagues – in case of financial difficulties - to inform his creditors of this situation, because if he waited any longer, people might say he was unreliable and rightly so. One could not make devout statements and meanwhile keep on borrowing money while one was bankrupt. It was a question of faith, of conscience, of reputation. Those were essential values in trade. A merchant was dependent on others and it was often difficult to know whether a person was trustworthy. One had to go by reputation. Indeed, much stress was laid on the sense of duty. There was room for the pursuit of happiness, but one's duties came first. Among these were the christian duties of being devout and charitable. Fulfilling these duties was largely a question of participating in public rituals: devoutness was expressed by going to church. One was expected to go to church to communicate, to be charitable. Failing to fulfil these obligations damaged your reputation. Honour and respect were, next to reputation and reliability, the essentials, certainly for people in business. 'Honour' and 'respect' were terms that were used with great frequency in the 17th and 18th centuries.[309]

Being a mennonite in the first half of the 17th century was both a support and a hindrance to entrepreneurial success. Because mennonites eschewed an aristocratic life-style and were only

---

308 L. Kooijmans, p. 27
309 L. Kooijmans, p. 31

rarely involved in politics, 'the whole shrewd and conscientious rationality of Baptist/ Mennonite conduct was thus forced into non-political callings'[310]. In some ways, according to Weber, mennonites were even more suited to capitalist success than calvinists. However, while in theory, at least, mennonite beliefs could have discouraged an entrepreneurial spirit[311], many mennonites nevertheless became active in trade and indeed prospered from it. While they probably constituted no more than 4% of the city of Amsterdam, preliminary research suggests that mennonites may have accounted for more than 7% of the merchants who had accounts at the Amsterdam Exchange Bank and were over-represented in merchant circles[312]. Certainly, the influx of anabaptist immigrants from Flanders helped to boost mennonite involvement in trade and the textile industry. Anabaptist ethics against excessive consumption and their close-knit community may - according to Weber's theory - have helped early accumulation of capital. The fact that mennonites were shut out of political office for both theological reasons and legal restraints helps to explain why only few mennonites were members of the economic elite in Amsterdam. An additional explanation is their failure to participate fully in the more risky, yet more profitable East- and West Indies trade. But that changed in the 17th century. Mennonite restrictions against the use of armed ships loosened, as many of them began to abandon pacifism, which was part of their religious belief. This opened the way for increased involvement in the United East India Company (VOC). The close social- and familial ties, formed within a dissenter church, helped the mennonite elite to amass comfortably large fortunes, especially by the 18th century. Capital continued to consolidate within a more exclusive and wealthier circle of merchants and manufacturing families, specifically when the religious and social distinctiveness

---

310 M. Sprunger, p. 213

311 Mennonites, especially the Waterlander branch, seem to have been influenced by Coornhert's emphasis on the "rechtvaardige koopman" (the righteous merchant). Business was inherently neither good nor bad –the value depended on the social relevance and proper conduct of the enterprise and the use of profits. So long as one's business contributed to society and one gave generously to the poor, then commerce was compatible with the Mennonite faith. (see also M. Sprunger, p. 216)

312 M. Sprunger p. 214

of the mennonites began to wane[313]. Although calvinist fanatics occasionally sought to impose new religious orthodoxy, the merchant oligarchs succeeded in maintaining religious- as well as economic freedom, for catholics and jews and lutherns. The calvinistic voice, denouncing the inequities of the world and the profanities of money, could be heard thundering from pulpits through the length and breath of the Republic. But to what end, and to what effect? As Simon Schama wrote: 'it warned, but it seemed helpless to restrain. And if it could not restrain, did it then, as Weber also argued, sanction the increase of riches as an outward sign of salvation?'[314]

Identity of entrepreneurs during economic decline (1670-1815)

In addition to the arrival of Flemish immigrants and Portuguese jews around the 1600s and the French Huguenots in 1685, who fled to Holland as a result of religious prosecution, approximately 27.000 German[315] guest labourers from the north western part of Germany came for purely economic reasons. The Flemish, jews and huguenots, however, were very active in entrepreneurial activities as was described at length in the previous sections of this study. The Germans were active as handymen in various sectors in the Republic, such as in the peat exploitation, textile mills, whale hunting and tile- and brick manufacturing. This "*Hollandgängerei*" diminished in the second part of the 18th century due to better economic conditions in Germany. Similarly as with the Flemish and jewish immigrant in the 17th century, the huguenots and Germans coming in the 18th century were not conceived as being *outsiders versus mainstream* inhabitants. They were all expected to contribute to Dutch economic growth and as a matter of fact indigenous Dutch entrepreneurs and city governments were

---

313 Quite in contrast with Menno, Jacob Pietersz., a Flemish Mennonite preacher working in the industrial Zaan region, believed that the drive to make money was not only divine, but also natural; there was nothing divine about poverty. However, he also warned entrepreneurs to reject unbridled capitalist competition. See M. Sprunger, p. 215-216
314 S. Schama, p. 323
315 J.A. Faber, p. 149

very much in favour of their inclusion into their business society. In particular so, as they usually brought with them a wealth of business contacts and often very well developed artisan skills. In the case of the Germans, they too were wanted, in order to fill the vacancies in various economic activities, which was equally important from the point of view of economic growth. Although the Flemish immigrants, after three to four generations, had already quite well integrated into genuine Dutch society, jews, huguenots and Germans remained very much on their own as ethnical groups. Indeed, many of the jews were here as long as the Flemish were, but their religion kept them pretty closely knit together, although in business practices entrepreneurs from all rank and file, mixed according to economic principles. The French huguenots, around this time, were first generation immigrants and obviously they remained together for reasons of security and possibly also because of their cultural identity, including language. The Germans and Scandinavians were guest labourers, temporarily in Holland to earn money for their families back home, and their intention was not so much to build up a living in a new country; obviously they were not that much interested to get integrated into Dutch society.

8.2. Orientation of entrepreneurship: expansion and innovation

Expansion and innovation during economic take-off (1350-1580)

According to Joseph Schumpeter, entrepreneurs further economic development by introducing 'new combinations' or innovations. Schumpeter identified five types of innovation, of which three are related to innovations that strongly came up in this period. These three are: first, the opening or penetration of a new market; secondly, the introduction of a new production process; and third 'the introduction of a new good - that is one with which the customers are not yet familiar - or of a new quality of a good.'[316] On the basis of these three types of innovative characteristics, entrepreneurs thoroughly transformed Dutch proto- industrial activities between 1500 and 1580. The beer brewing industry is a case in point. Daily beer consumption in the Netherlands was in comparison to other countries very high. Numerous breweries were spread out all over the delta, in particular in the cities, as the government had closed down rural breweries, in order to better control the quality. Therefore, enormous quantities of beer were imported from Hamburg. In an attempt to reverse the tide, entrepreneurs in Holland and Utrecht started with a new technology in beer brewing by producing 'hopper', which did not only push aside the imported beer from Germany and England, but also gave birth to a significant expansion in the export of Dutch beer. Even at the time when the Germans and British also had adopted the brewing of *'hopbier'* around 1400, Dutch entrepreneurs remained competitive, as they again developed a new process by brewing beer, using different raw materials. In the latter part of the 15th century the number of breweries in Delft and Harlem alone arrived at approximately 200 each and in Gouda, there were as many as 157 breweries. A comparative advantage of the brewery industry was the good quality water and an abundant supply of peat, an indispensable requirement, as one hl. of beer required approximately 20 kilograms of peat, a source of energy that was readily available in the delta.[317] Technological change was a hallmark of entrepreneurs active in the brewing industry. The application of new brewing processes spread throughout Holland, the declining unit cost of brewing beer and the types of beer that were brewed increased, were indeed dramatic developments. Brewing also became much more capital intensive, as both fixed and working capital requirements grew. Increased fixed capital investment embodied technological change, allowing brewers to profit from economies of scale. Thus, changes in the

---

316 The other types of entrepreneurship Schumpeter distinguished were "the conquest of a new source of supply of raw materials or half manufactured goods" and "the carrying out of a new organisation of any industry" , see: J.A. Schumpeter, The Theory of Economic Development. Leipzig: Duncker and Huymbold, 1912. English ed. Cambridge, MA: Harvard Univ. Press, cited in Baumol, 'Entrepreneurship', p. 5
317 R. van Uytven, p. 39-40

production process, scale of production, types of beer produced, marketing strategies, capital requirements and, not in the least, institutional and legal changes, were inextricably intertwined. A very modern cast, indeed. The conclusion in this respect is that changes brought about by entrepreneurs in both product- and processing techniques (quality improvement, lower unit cost, markets, economies of scale) were important aspects in entrepreneurial economic thinking in the 20th century as well, as was identified by Schumpeter. Much of this led to a form of what Schumpeter termed 'creative destruction'. By introducing new combinations (or innovations), successful entrepreneurs earned profits, hence reduced the earnings of their international competitors, possibly even driving them out of business. Entrepreneurs who did not, or could not adopt the latest innovations, typically opposed the change. Sometimes they even attempted to have the innovations outlawed. Thus the brewing industry's transformation from a small scale, 'medieval' undertaking into a larger and more capitalistic industry was bitterly opposed by the micro entrepreneurs in that specific trade, whose livelihood and income were threatened. The protests and laws around 1550 that sought to turn back the development of large scale capitalistic brewing, demonstrated the extent to which innovative entrepreneurs had been transforming the industry.[318]

Other entrepreneurial innovations, which had a dramatic impact on the expansion of the market, can be observed in the fishery and related shipbuilding sectors of this period. Next to the herring in the Baltic, the so-called North-Sea-herring - at the latter part of the 14th century - gradually captured the market. A first entrepreneurial innovation, which would alter the fishing industry drastically, was the process of salting the fish at sea, which could conserve the product for a considerably longer time. Secondly, this in its turn pushed other entrepreneurs in the development and construction of larger fishing vessels, which could hold many more tons of processed herring on board during an extending fishing period, resulting in increased productivity, lowered prices, improved quality and

---

318 R.J. Yntema, p. 194-201

strengthened market competitiveness.[319] This again resulted in an expanding market for entrepreneurs in the shipbuilding industry and other supplying industries, such as sailcloth- and cordage manufacturing. Thanks to this rapid expansion the merchant fleet experienced a tenfold increase in numbers and an even larger increase in tonnage between the beginning of the 16th century and the middle of the 17th century. At that time it was by far the largest fleet in Europe, three times larger than the English merchant fleet, which was second, and probably larger than all other countries combined. Considering the relatively short life of wooden sailing ships, this was translated into a large demand for cargo. To this demand entrepreneurs responded with a third innovation i.e. by rationalising their shipyards and to introduce elementary methods of mass production techniques. These entrepreneurs used mechanical saws and hoists actuated by windmills, and kept stores of interchangeable parts. Because of the efficiency of their enterprises and shipyards, they supplied not only to the domestic market, but to foreign markets as well, irrespective commercial rivalry. A fourth innovation had to do with the design of the ships. Entrepreneurs increased the size and improved the manoeuvrability of ships. Hence, the size of the ships in the Atlantic trade increased from 200 to 600 tons. Some warships needed for the protection of the commercial fleet even reached the unprecedented size of 1500 tons. But the most significant entrepreneurial innovation with the aim to improve productivity, hence lower the cost per transported unit, was the '*fluyt*' ship, or flyboat as the English called it, a specialised commercial carrier introduced at the end of the sixteenth century. The equivalent in some respect of the tanker in our times, it was specifically designed for bulky, low value cargoes such as grain and timber, and operated with smaller crews than conventional ships.[320] In the wake of these developments market innovation and expansion took place as well, since entrepreneurs not only manufactured or processed products, but also in providing services for carrying goods on behalf of other nations, lacking the required transport

---

319 Around 1477 herring fisheries was already one of the most important industries, with a fleet estimated as large as 250 ships and a crew as large as 6.250; R.van Uytven, p. 35;
320 R. Cameron, p. 117

facilities. This was the start of Dutch entrepreneurs becoming the transporters of Europe.

And 'Schumpeter' was neither absent in the labour intensive textile manufacturing, which underwent a similar development. The drapery and cloth industry in the delta in the 14th and 15th century brought also the development and expansion of the dying industry. Entrepreneurs imported not only much of the raw material from the Mediterranean, France and Germany, but they also developed new colours, particularly the red dye. This product came from the province of Zeeland and was exported to foreign cloth- and drapery manufacturers all over Europe. In fact, entrepreneurs in the city of Zierikzee (in Zeeland) succeeded in establishing dyeing centres for cloth coming from Flanders and England[321]. This again is a good example of entrepreneurial innovation, resulting in an expansion of the market. Research carried out by Gelderblom shows, in addition, that in this period a remarkable diversification in product development took place in that industry. In order to capture larger parts of the markets, entrepreneurs developed approximately 50 different qualities in unfinished and woven silk.[322] These innovations were in a large measure attributable to Flemish drapery weavers, who moved in the mid-14th century to Middelburg and Dordrecht, when the wool-staple market got established in these cities. Actually, Dutch entrepreneurs could not compete with the refined luxury cloth products manufactured in England and Flanders, but concentrated therefore their production at another segment of the international market by manufacturing semi luxury products for the Eastern European markets. And although the Hanseatic League tried to protect the English and Flemish products in the Eastern part of Europe, the commercial entrepreneurial spirit of the Dutch in combination with Flemish technology was stronger than that; subsequently, a considerable quantity of that cloth was exported to Russia, Finland and the Baltic states.

---

321 R. van Uytven, p. 42
322 O.Gelderblom, p.105; Also spices contained more that 40 different qualities, sugar and syrups 17, fruits 11 and wool and linen products as many as 21 varieties.

An imported side effect of the international trade, as a result of the expanding innovative orientation of Dutch entrepreneurs, was their travelling abroad, which provided new input for more expansion and more innovation. This was an excellent tool for diversifying markets for their products. Not only for sea faring and trade people, who made the journeys, but also for the merchants, shipbuilders, insurance agencies, and not to forget the young potential entrepreneurs, who were often sent to these regions to gain business experience. Another effect that may not be neglected is that it fed the entrepreneurs with the force of inventiveness, which highly stimulated their business and trade. They drew ideas from the contacts they had with other countries, regions or continents and adopted these successfully to a vast variety of uses. Examples include not only industrial applications, such as farm equipment, textile machinery, mills for grinding, operating bellows, navigation instruments, and paper making, but also cultivated imported products such as cotton, sugar and silk. Also an appropriate use was made of the ideas about business tools, including *commenda* contracts, sea loans and maritime insurances, as well as the bill of exchange, promissory note and double-entry accounting.

Expansion and innovation during economic supremacy (1580-1670)

As concluded before, a major characteristic of Dutch entrepreneurship was that is was able to perceive opportunities in a climate in which entrepreneurship had a positive cultural connotation. Seizing opportunities and expansion/innovation are, in fact, two sides of the same coin. An example, that does not stand on its own, is that of Louis de Geer, representing the successful entrepreneurs during the Dutch economic supremacy in Europe. De Geer arrived as a child in 1611 in the Netherlands as the son of a Flemish immigrant. Through his family in law (the famous indigenous Trip family) he came into contact with the Swedish copper and ore industries and got so much entrenched in this business and its industrial development, that it earned him the title: 'Father of Swedish industry'. Louis de Geer was extremely active in the process of continuously negotiating deals and agreements involving consortia of ever changing composition. Through this type of dealing and the connection he had with the Swedish copper and iron/ore industries, he made Amsterdam a major international staple market for military supplies after the outbreak of the Thirty Years' War in 1618. In the contacts he had with the Swedish crown he continuously tried to safeguard monopoly rights in his dealings, in order to reduce risk, as well as to optimise good perspectives on profits. Monopolies and licenses from foreign rulers was a powerful and attractive instrument in the hands of Dutch entrepreneurs, who were doing business in foreign markets. It prevented full competition and in that manner gave protection to the investments made by these entrepreneurs. However, foreign licences were scarce and could not be reckoned to be standard instruments of running businesses abroad. Nonetheless, licenses never played a decisive role in the emergence of economic of the Netherlands. It seem to be more likely, that the successful world-economic position was achieved because of the advantages the Dutch had in expertise, experience, capital provision, relations and initiatives, in short being competitive. They could do things that others apparently could not, reason why - just like De Geer - they were in quite a number of countries attracted by licenses. Investments did not follow the licences, but licences followed the investments.[323] Also diversification was vital in De Geer's business, since it implied both horizontal and vertical integration of activities. Scale economies in transport and financing were realised through expansion of production lines. That type of diversification, though, was only applied by a rather select group of entrepreneurs. The same can probably be said about his capabilities of manipulating the price formation in commodity markets.[324]

As discussed in the introduction to this study, entrepreneurship is not only geared towards societal processes that are regarded as 'elevated' or 'highly wanted'. In this respect, Baumol speaks about the entrepreneur as the one who ingeniously tries to find ways to add to his own wealth, power and prestige. Furthermore, according to

---
323 J.W. Veluwekamp (1996) p. 554-555
324 J. Th. Lindeblad, p. 77-84

Baumol, he will not be overtly concerned whether the activities that lead to these goals adds much, little, nothing at all, or even negatively to the social environment.[325] A case in point is piracy, which had a negative connotation. Nonetheless, quite a number of entrepreneurs saw opportunities in piracy. In a way, piracy, for them was a form of expanding, developing or at least safeguarding markets. The state even provided written approvals to selected entrepreneurs to exercise piracy, as a mean of waging war with the enemy and to expand their own markets. In doing so they did not only make profits from piracy and extended markets, but also contributed to policy formation of the Republic, as well as were supporting political aspirations.[326] However, a distinction should be made between the entrepreneurial activity of piracy, as carried out by groups in Algeria, Dunkirk or Bulgaria for personal or group gain and profits on the one hand, and piracy as an act of war on the other hand, e.g. when Piet Heyn captured a Spanish fleet loaded with silver coming from South America. Piracy as an act of war was indeed recognised as a respected entrepreneurial activity.

Productivity improvement through *innovation* was in the Dutch Republic regarded as the winning business approach in their competition with international businesses from France, Spain, Britain, Portugal and others. The fifty or so shipyards in Zaandam for instance were able to build more than 300 ships per year, which taken into consideration severe winter conditions took approximately 5 weeks -as an average- to construct a ship. This productivity resulted in a price per ship, which was in the middle of the 17th century nearly 50% cheaper as compared to similar type of ships made in England. Moreover, the ships were designed in such a way that they were able to load larger cargoes. The fluytship, as described in previous sections of this chapter, was an excellent example of such innovation: relatively large floating spacious ship-holds without any fringe, which could be navigated by a relatively small crew. There were no cannons on board and all technical simplifications were

---

325 Dealing in drugs, for instance, is an entrepreneurial activity, however does not have a positive effect on society.
326 C. Lesger & L. Noordergraaf, (1999), p. 17

designed to lower the cost of transportation. Therefore, ship-owners could charge a price for transporting cargo, which was thirty to 50% lower as compared to their English counterparts. Small wonder that the total fleet of ships coming from the Republic, navigating all world-seas. The Amsterdam harbour alone could accommodate four thousand small and larger vessels. Contrary to Fernand Braudel, who assessed this superiority by the plainness of the Dutch sailor and the shipbuilding technology, Méchoulan emphasised the specific entrepreneurship of the Dutch. As was the case by the development of the Amsterdam Exchange Bank - as Méchoulan reasons - there was money to be earned with commercial adventures at sea, by entrepreneurs who had some money and who dared to undertake hazardous actions. They could buy merchandise and transport that by vessel, could hire a ship for the cargo to be sold in another country and was able to get sufficient back-loads in order to guarantee the profits of such a venture. Apart from the natural ship-owners, there were also ship-owners who bought shares in other ships. These shares, in its turn, became a new commodity in which also smaller entrepreneurs started to trade. Hence, this attracted savings for investments in productive activities. The profits from sea trade therefore resulted in a closely-knit bond among entrepreneurs representing big capital and industry. But also artisans and small savers were part of that great adventure, which importance can only be understood looking at the import and export trade that ultimately emerged. In the mid 17th century, for example, the Republic was importing from France 28 different products and exported 72 products to the same country; only four of these products were produced in The Netherlands, whereas the remaining products were imported from other countries and stored in Amsterdam[327]. Such innovative type of trade led to another key element in the economic supremacy of the Netherlands in the 17th century, i.e. the organised storage of merchandise. Wherever there was scarcity, a conflict or even wars, Dutch entrepreneurs served each customer, as long as they paid the bill. The Amsterdam warehouses attracted capital

---

327   H. Méchoulan, p. 119 . This was also the reason why the British introduced the Navigation Acts, entailing that the transport of merchandise to England was only allowed to be done by ships from the country of origin or else English ships and this of course resulted in war.

from both local and foreign entrepreneurs with orders to buy and sell and because of the rapidity with which theses orders were executed, thanks to many commissionaires, the entrepôt became one of the most preferential places to conduct trade and business. This innovate entrepreneurial activity was furthermore stimulating the development of lots of new financial products as we have seen in the previous chapter. Credits were made available to the buyers and also the improved bill of exchange stimulated more buying and selling. The result of these transactions was an abundance of money, which lowered the interest rate to a point far below that of other competing nations. A final *innovation* in this respect was the fact that the Dutch entrepreneur was satisfied with relatively low profits against a high turnover of the merchandise. Percentage-wise profits were low, however due to the volume of the trade the money-income was very high.[328] In short, low profit margins and high turnover, as so many mass-merchandising companies of the 20th and 21st century currently do.

And also during this period *innovations* in the fishery sector took place. The herring fisheries became again more productive, when entrepreneurs developed new techniques in the transportation of the herring to the coastal cities. The herring busses became smaller, which decreased the crew from 18-30 men to 12-14, whereby the catch from these busses was rapidly brought on land by other very fast sailing transport ships. Obviously, this resulted in a further division of labour whereby the busses only had to undertake 3 trips of 4 weeks each per year to sea. [329] Likewise, in the whale fishery entrepreneurs made *innovations* by applying new fishing techniques of Whales in open sea, which increased the yield between 1643 and 1660 ten times. In addition, new working methodologies were applied, resulting in a smaller crew that was necessary for the catch. The whale fisheries, which remained a growing entrepreneurial activity during the second part of the 17th century, became the biggest employer in the fish industry. It produced oil that was cheaper than the vegetable oils and was used for candles and soap. In addition, it

---

328 H. Méchoulan, p. 121
329 P.W. Klein in Stuyvenberg, p. 94

supported a lot of other entrepreneurial activities, such try-houses for boiling the whale oil, the trade in oil and oil products, shipbuilding, sail cloth manufacturing, cordage, etc.[330]

The chain of *innovative activities* was the result of a high level of entrepreneurial activities, which had its foundation in the quality of human resources. Skills that had been developed over many centuries (navigation, shipbuilding, fishing and trading) were sufficiently developed to recognise and perceive opportunities in a changing world (discoveries of new worlds, information dissemination through printing techniques, nation-state building, money economy). In addition, financial means of the bourgeois were available as a result of their trading practices and absence of an exploiting and money-extracting nobility; entrepreneurs could do business and through their involvement in numerous city councils - the building blocks of the Republic - they could promulgate measures, which maximised a favourable entrepreneurial climate. So skills, opportunities and money were there to sustain innovative entrepreneurial activities and the one innovation often led to another as a result of both on-going technology development and the need to improve entrepreneurial competitiveness.

Expansion and innovation during economic decline (1670-1815)

During the latter part of the 17th century, Dutch entrepreneurs were still very much focused on expansion of production, specifically by diversifying the product range. International competition had been fierce, in particular in the textile industry, as the bigger countries, either through mercantilist policies or improved skills and lower wages, were able to compete successfully in the international market. So in the second part of the 17th century, the Leyden cloth manufacturers experienced fierce competition in finished products from England, at that time also the main supplier of raw material. The Leyden entrepreneurs developed an adequate answer to this commercial threat and the way they did this may be seen as ex-

---
330 P.W. Klein inn Stuyvenberg, p. 95

emplary for the commercial alertness of the Dutch entrepreneurial class. They worked out two ways to deal with that competition effectively. First, by manufacturing a specific kind of camelot, which was a mixture of camel- and goat hair with wool and silk. This product was very much wanted for men clothes to which English competition could not respond quickly. Secondly, they started to produce fine woollen fabrics, which could only be possible because of both the monopoly supply of Spanish wool and a large market in the Levant.[331] Obviously, this was not a one-time solution to try to remain dominant in the expanding world market. Time and again, international competition was able to absorb the new techniques and treatment of raw material as developed by Dutch entrepreneurs, so the name of the game was *'constant innovation'*, in particular to circumvent the disadvantage of the higher wages in The Netherlands. This, indeed, took place up to a point at which England and later France started to apply modern mechanised production techniques (large scale factory production), which required raw material (coal and ore) that were not available in the Netherlands. Hence, during the 18th century, Dutch entrepreneurs increasingly lost their international markets as a result of not being able to renovate their industrial sectors. The situation became even worse when internationally produced products – particularly textile - found their way into the Dutch regional markets. Generally, the decline was no longer relative, but in the last quarter of the 18th century absolute as well. The decline did not come all of a sudden; it was gradual and differed from sector to sector. Entrepreneurs in the sugar-, tobacco- and construction industry as well as the trade in colonial products were, till far in the 18th century, in a leading position. Likewise were those in commercial shipping and financial services. But entrepreneurs in shipbuilding, fishing, brewing and textile industry, could not identify sufficient opportunities any more, hence their businesses suffered heavily under the absence of applying innovative technologies.

The period of innovativeness and expansion came to an end. This was not the case though in the financial sector. In as far as finan-

---
331 J. de Vries & A.M. van der Woude, p. 342-343

cial services is concerned, Amsterdam, had been developed into the main financial centre of the world and had reached that position due to a) the existing freedom of import and export of precious metal, minted as well as un-minted, b) an excellent reputation of the in 1609 founded Exchange Bank and c) an abundance of capital and a low interest rate. New financial innovation kept on taking place till far in the 18th century, when new financial instruments were added to the existing ones, among these, the 'accept credit'. It meant that an Amsterdam merchant/banker with a high reputation (Clifford, Hoguer, Hope & Co., Pels en de Smeth) allowed in the case of, for example, a French exporter of wine to Hamburg, the Hamburg importer/creditor to draw a bill of exchange, which the Amsterdam merchant/banker accepted and by doing so guaranteed the payment. The merchant/banker, ran the risk of non-payment, which he tried to reduce, of course, by checking the reliability of the creditor. In fact it was a form of insurance for which the premium ran from one-third to half a percentage point. These bills of exchange then became tradable. The purchaser of a bill of exchange provided credit to the importer and the exporter received his money. With this form of credit, Dutch entrepreneurs financed an important part of the world trade. Also foreign traders made use of this facility and the capital wealth of the Republic, without making use of Dutch transportation and harbour facilities.[332] But this innovation, then, also worked as a dissolving factor for the position of the Amsterdam staple market, as various other "middle-men" functions were eliminated. Ultimately, this fitted the international trading system excellently as it produced less transactional cost for the importer.

8.3. Entrepreneurial traits

Specific traits during economic take-off (1350-1580)

The Jesuit Famiano Strada, author of the famous *Histoire de la Guerre de Pays-Bas*, a contemporary of the Eighty Years War and

---

[332] J.A. Faber, p. 149-150 and J.G. van Dillen, p. 348

a biased Spanish patriot, described the Dutch population, among them the entrepreneurs, as courageous and admired their diligence, the variety and quantity of their works, knowledge of navigation, inventions, integrity, as well as their perseverance in case of misfortune. The latter may indicate 'a need to achieve' (see chapter 3.2.4) - the ambition to win over misfortunes. However, Famiano Strada also recognised another personality trait, as he wrote *'they are more ardent then is necessary, when defending their liberties and, moreover, are of the opinion that it is to their honour to prefer these above all'*.[333] Obviously, the psychological *need for achievement* as well as the personal liberty was intertwined with the calvinistic belief system and gave to entrepreneurs an extra dimension in their drive to be successful and this gave access to a nearly inexhaustible source of positively oriented energy. And, obviously, because of their success, they were not short of quite an impressive dose of *self-confidence*.

However, in spite of that self-confidence, they were generally not over-courageous and therefore were trying to limit *risk-taking* as much as they could. The risks, which the entrepreneurs ran in that period, were not to be underestimated (acts of God, piracy, wars, unreliable business information, etc.). In this respect, the historian Kappelhof described an entrepreneur in the city of Breda, a certain Johan de Wyse, who did quite a lot of business with the local government headed by the Prince of Orange. Knowing the business risks he ran, de Wyse was eager in spreading his risks, by 1) trading in a large number of products, (thus reducing his financial dependency on the coincidental non-availability of a few products), and 2) marketed his products in both the city of Breda and the surrounding areas (thus reducing his financial dependency on a too small market). That was the way of doing business in those days. Risks could be brought even better under control, when there was a good network in which both the entrepreneur and those who were attached to the local government participated, as was also the case of Gerard de Wyse, father of the earlier mentioned Johan. Gerard

---

333 Ciitation taken from H. Méchoulan, Amsterdam ten tijde van Spinoza; Geld en Vrijheid (J. Noorman trans. Amsterdam au temps de Spinoza), Amsterdam 1992, p. 22

had developed contacts with two families who were in the service of the temporal lord in their territory and Johan (the son) - together with his brother - extended these ties through marriages.[334] The latter was about the best way to limit the risks in both carrying out the business operations as well as to expand the business. As described before, confidence and trust were dominant elements in business practices and marriage was such a bond, reducing the risks to acceptable proportions. For the same reason of risk evasion during these days, a number of new informal trading practices were introduced, with the aim to reduce the risks of being out of stock, or getting too low prices for their merchandise. Entrepreneurs in Amsterdam, for example, applied as early as 1550 early models of 'trading in futures'. They did this when concluding trading agreements for the supply of rye from the Baltic and the North-sea herring, before the rye was harvested and the herring caught.[335] In doing business, entrepreneurs were well aware that taking risks was an inseparable element of it, as it is to day. However, in taking risks, they calculated and assessed – mathematically or by intuition - the amount of risk they ran, comparing this risk with the possible result of the business activity and based on that they took the business decision.

Due to the fact that the legitimacy of entrepreneurship in the Netherlands was quite high, as we have seen before, entrepreneurs were not short of a *positive self-concept* either. Apparently, they were fully accepted in society, not in the least, as they were the major taxpayers, which provided the funds to defend and protect the religious and individual liberties against Spain. Moreover, they believed in their capabilities to control the seas and to successfully trade with other nations and, furthermore, they saw the results of their capabilities for technical innovations (ships, agriculture, textile), which again opened up markets and increased their success. And as we know from psychologists, the degree of success is normative for the level of a person's *positive self-concept*. And Dutch entrepreneurs were indeed successful. The resulting *positive self-concept* had a favourable radiation effects towards other entrepreneurial traits, such as 'an

---

334 A.C.M. Kappelhof, p. 318
335 J. de Vries & A.M. van der Woude, p. 186

independent stance'. Entrepreneurs in the Netherlands were independent from the government, as long as they paid their taxes and these taxes were to a large extent fixed by an elite composed of these same entrepreneurs, namely those who were members of city councils. Entrepreneurs had to follow the regulations, but again, these were to a large extent also proposed and approved by themselves in the city councils. In other words, entrepreneurs did not have the feeling, as in so many other countries, that government taxes and regulations were imposed on them. On the contrary, in the Republic it was a 'bottom-up' process. Indirectly, entrepreneurs designed business rules and regulations, as they felt these to be necessary for a regulated society, which again was imperative for a sound business climate. Entrepreneurs were also independent of religious castes. As long as the calvinistic religion was not challenged, everyone could exercise the religion of his or her own choice. In both cases, government and religion, entrepreneurs knew the borderlines in which they could do business and as they were relatively heavily involved in the two institutions, they did not feel dependent on the discretion of their leaders. This independent stance provided a climate of freedom, which proved to be very supportive for doing successful business, as well as fitted perfectly into the actual cultural trait of *'individualism'* as opposed to that of *'collectivism'*.

That was also reason why entrepreneurs were never shy to *take initiatives* in a wide range of business activities, as may be shown in the case of Claes Adriaensz. van Adrichem, a merchant from Delft. He was born in 1538 and took over the grain business in the sixties from his father, who became predominantly focused on domestically produced products using grain as a raw material. Claes invested the surplus of his earnings in real estate, life insurances and in short-term capital advances to farmers. He also started to invest in fisheries, when he took shares (parts) of ships, specifically in ships for the herring catch in the harbour of Delfzijl. After a while he possessed parts of four ships, involved in the Baltic trade. After each journey, the final account was made up and the investment partners of the ships, who carried out the trade, then decided how much of the revenues would remain in the business as a reinvestment, and how much would be paid to them in the form of dividend. By taking these *types of initiatives*, the entrepreneurs made themselves independent on only one market, or only one business activity. Another interesting example of showing *entrepreneurial initiative* was organising a better utilisation of the services of the captains of the ships. These started then to act as an intermediary between the entrepreneur and the factors (representatives) in the Baltic or Nordic countries, by transporting cash money for the trade and bringing back information about the growing demand of products or possibilities to supply new products and at what price. Letters of exchange, however, would soon replace this cash money.[336]

Another entrepreneurial characteristic, *'problem solving capability'* is very much linked to the level of creativity and innovation. Clearly, often innovations took place as a coincidental occurrence that all of a sudden proved to be a winner. It many cases it was also the result of technicians working with mechanical device. Their day-to-day activity in that work gave them an opportunity to improve production and processing techniques. However, there were also innovations taking place as a result of a business problem that was posed and efficiently tackled by the entrepreneur. So, if entrepreneurs experienced a problem with competition in sea transportation, they would try to find out what could be done in order to cope effectively with that situation. To try to solve that problem, they constructed a new ship model, which could hold more cargo and less crew (e.g. the fluytship), hence would decrease the unit cost price that in its turn would make them more competitive in the business. Problem solved! In addition, innovations were not the product of scientific research in laboratories; instead it was the product of strenuous trial-and-error methods.

Time bound planning of entrepreneurs was gradually coming up in this period, the more so as also sea transportation became more secure and reliable. Although not comparable with to-days entrepreneurial needs to be speedily on top of any new development, entrepreneurs during the 14th and 15th centuries saw increasingly

---

336   J. de Vries & A.M. van der Woude, p. 425

the importance of timely information, in order to optimise their business results. Reliable and timely information on the movements of goods and prices was also imperative for the prudently started trading in futures, as well as the developments of the Amsterdam staple market. Entrepreneurs, specifically those who were trading with foreign markets, were very sensitive with regard to the quality of information from these foreign markets. This was of importance in order to conclude lucrative deals with (foreign) buyers of merchandise. That was also reason why entrepreneurial families stationed family members as representatives abroad. The earlier the information reached the head office in the Netherlands, the better the Dutch entrepreneur was in the position to conclude a profitable deal. This worked also in the reverse. The representative abroad gave instructions to the head-office in Holland with regard to market opportunities in the country, to which he had been assigned. The sooner the information reached the head-office and were able to supply the merchandise, the better price could be made, due to absence of competition from either the French or British, who were also active in these far-away countries. This was specifically rampant among Portuguese jews, probably because of the many jewish settlements all over the world. The story goes - even at that time - that one of the richest jews in Amsterdam, Lopez Suasso, was bragging by saying that if he knew the Spanish king's death six hours before anybody else, he could earn a fortune. Apart from information gathering and its importance of accuracy and speed, entrepreneurial time-bound planning became also increasingly important in the issue of productivity. In the shipbuilding industry, for instance, cranes were introduced and also a form of standardisation took place, which shortened the construction time, took less labour, making the end product cheaper, hence improved the competitiveness of the business.

Finally, it is safe to assume that entrepreneurs during this period of *'Trade Capitalism'* (1350-1580), indeed, must have been very *hopeful about the future*. They specifically decided to make relatively large investments in new business ventures. Long term investments in the shipbuilding industry, land reclamation, beer brewing and in transport ventures for the importation of grain and timber, proved that entrepreneurs were indeed optimistic in assessing the chances for a good financial return in the distant future. Early successes in the money economy and not in the least the possibility to manage their own affairs, without interference of a foreign centralised power, made them undoubtedly '*hopeful about the future*' - being a distinct entrepreneurial trait, also nowadays. Dutch entrepreneurs were powerful at sea, possessing the largest fleet in Europe. Subsequently, they had defeated the German Hanse and the British in nearly all forms of trade during this era. They had made technological innovations, which improved the business results even more and, furthermore, they received entrepreneurial immigrants with lots of new business experiences, which were added to the ones the Dutch had developed themselves. In other words, Europe (and more than that) was a captive market to them. No wonder entrepreneurs were hopeful about the future, which activated them to look for new business opportunities. This inquisitive nature could find a way-out because of the existence of plenty of experienced skippers and tradespeople in the Republic. This, coupled to an increase of energy and entrepreneurial behaviour, gave rise to a search for new opportunities through discovery voyages, the establishment of trading companies, as well as to a large number of technical innovations that took place in society (fluytship, timber mill, ribbon weaving machines, the application of the elsewhere invented fulling mill, etc.). Entrepreneurs also saw hopeful signs for future developments, as a result of the increase of immigrants from the South Netherlands, Portugal, Germany and Poland. As we have seen in the previous chapters, they complemented Dutch business practices with their own business experiences and business network from their country of origin. What was still lacking, though, was to properly institutionalise all developed business methodologies and achievements realised so far. This would be the great challenge for the next period of 'Trade Capitalism' in the Republic (1580-1670), during which entrepreneurs made the Republic the undisputed economic supreme power of Europe and probably of the world.

Entrepreneurial traits during economic supremacy (1580-1670)

As elaborated before, local governments in the Republic were very active in attracting industries to their towns by offering attractive conditions and even subsidies. In that way they lured immigrants and capital of indigenous entrepreneurs to establish businesses in their cities. So during the initial period of this phase of both the increased urbanisation and the need to survive, the *'need for emerging entrepreneurs to achieve'* was very high. But as from the end of the war with Spain (1648), when business relations had been established and the dynamics of the first phase had increasingly produced wealth to entrepreneurs, the *'need to achieve'* became apparently less urgent, which led to a decline in pioneering mentality. In all layers of society a new generation emerged, who wanted to benefit from the advantages that the newly acquired wealth gave them. Apparently, among the new generation of entrepreneurs in this era, there was a growing number that possessed less *'need to achieve'* and was less interested in a thrifty life; but instead they were more interested in a form of conspicuous consumption, which, given the teachings in humanism and calvinism, was not allowed to be shown too abundantly. But still the majority of entrepreneurs during that period continued to invest productively in their business, rather than consume the profits.

As discussed in the introduction of this study, 'good entrepreneurship' and taking *'calculated risks'* are sides of the same coin. In practice Dutch successful entrepreneurship depended crucially on an elaborate and extensive system of protection against big risks. However, the historian P.W. Klein argues that 'the generally accepted idea of entrepreneurs as individuals who are always ready to take risks appear open to question. In reality they always made every effort to avoid unnecessary risks'[337] Risks, after all were built-in in the very circumstances of the entrepreneur's national existence. The perpetual effort to protect themselves from further hazards (floods, etc.) was deeply ingrained in Dutch mentality. For all the bravura

---
337   Quoted by Schama, S., p. 341

and exploratory ingenuity of the great mariners, navigators and colonisers, their work was firmly bound within the Dutch imperative to minimize risk as much as was possible. Risk evasion was definitely part of Dutch entrepreneurial life. This could vary from e.g. the issue of uprooting clove trees in the East Indies to the protection of prices in Amsterdam, to the down payment in hard specie for exclusive rights for an entire Norwegian forest. The objective was always to pre-empt competition, thus monopolise supply and control all conditions of trade from production of raw material to the terms of domestic or international sale. The famous Trip family was master of these kinds of arrangements. They managed to obtain exclusive rights to import Swedish tar by negotiating with a firm, which had the export monopoly. But that firm was again financed by the Trips, their major customer, who also organised the freight. The whole business, then, was more akin to an international cooperation trading between its own subsidiaries, than a business done between genuinely different parties. A further reduction of risks by banning competition even more effectively had to do with family loyalties. The marriage alliance between the families of the Trips and the de Geers, was meant to lock up the northern arms market even more tightly. Dutch commerce, then, ran smoothly, not from the spontaneous harmonisation of individual enterprises, but from a carefully and closely controlled system of regulated practices.[338] Nonetheless, business practices of this kind of trade formed exceptions to the rule and monopolisation was rarely achieved.[339] Monopoly in many cases just followed after entrepreneurs had been established risky business operations. Risk-avoidance behaviour of entrepreneurs, which has been noticed by some historians, has often been misinterpreted. Risk avoidance is probably misunderstood in relation to taking *calculated risks*, as was done e.g. by Hans Thijs, Louis de Geer, Pieter Litgens, Balthasar de Moucheron, Isaac Lemaire, Johan van Wely and other Amsterdam merchants. 'One of the striking features of Dutch entrepreneurship, was the high level of readiness to take risks at so many places at the same time throughout the world. Although confronted with losses and still

---

338 S. Schama, p. 341-343
339 J. Th. Lindblad (1995), p. 81

bigger insecurities, they increased their stakes and made even bigger amounts of money available'.[340]

An interesting case in dealing effectively with risks in distant places where entrepreneurs were active, were the family ties among the Dutch merchants of Archangel. Intermarriage and sons' succession to their fathers' businesses, were aspects of a strategy aimed at the commercial and social survival of the family. Commercial specialisation and steady business relations were two other basic mechanisms of this strategy. Specialisation gave them a competitive edge in market and commodity knowledge, whereas customer loyalty produced trust, credit, and stability of transactional conditions and volume of turn over. But these were not the only means to diminish risks. As we have seen in other chapters, expertise of the market and timely information were basic ingredients for the entrepreneur as well, to cope with risks. Méchoulan quotes Penso de la Vega when he writes that merchants working at the *Amsterdam Koopmansbeurs* (bourse) required a lot of expertise, which was necessary to make the fine-tuned calculations of the risks they were running. And by doing so they often knew by approximation what the result would be - a result that outsiders otherwise might describe as mere accidental. The entrepreneur was measuring the fluctuations of the world market and bought and sold according to rational criteria. He had to be profit-oriented and to be on the alert for all events around him that might affect his business.

The successful entrepreneur was someone who had specific skills at his disposal in order to function optimally, such as being a good cartographer in order to check the information about the route of the ships and the time they required returning to their home-base. He needed knowledge of mathematics in order to make the right type of price calculations, entailing overheads and assessments of risks to be included in the sales price. He needed to possess a certain level of eloquence, which was required in order to promote his product in the contacts he had with local and foreign trade partners. Furthermore he had to be familiar with legal affairs and even more so

---
340   J. de Vries & A.M. van der Woude, p. 474

be informed about the political situation abroad. In addition he had to be able to build up the network all over the world, which was required to inform him timely and regularly about new economic and/or political developments taking place in Asia and other regions in Europe, including information about the movements of traffic and cargos and expectations about the arrival in their home country. Next, the entrepreneur had to be able to handle rumours adequately. In circles of speculators in shares, there were often great disturbances, due to all sorts of rumours, plot and intrigue. Finally, the merchant had to be on his guard for manipulations in the market place. Penso de la Vega mentions in this connection the emergence of cartels, who were flooding the market with large quantities of shares, causing a drop in prices which, subsequently, were rapidly corrected with large purchases of these shares, resulting in favourable consequences for the speculating merchants. So what is happening nowadays in Wall Street, London, Frankfurt or Paris was, albeit at a more modest level, the day-to-day practice in the Amsterdam of the mid-17th century.[341] In conclusion entrepreneurs had to cope with risks, which they tried to limit and calculate as much as possible through forms of monopoly, inter-marriage, gaining expertise of international markets, getting access to information, diversifying their products and insuring their cargoes.

Conventional wisdom holds that successful entrepreneurs generally have a strong *positive self-concept.* And, indeed, that was the case with entrepreneurs during the previous and this period of Trade Capitalism. They undertook actions that were risky and through smart entrepreneurship they had to cope with the uncertain and risky business environment. And given the strength of the Dutch economy and the mercantile and financial position that the Netherlands took in Europe, Asia, Africa and the Americas, they were apparently successful in doing so. That success did not come by itself. It required entrepreneurs with *initiative and independence,* which was a characteristic of the Dutch in their century long struggle against the water and the sea, in which they could only depend on their own in order to survive. But also many of the immigrants possessed

---
341 H. Méchoulan, p. 101-102

this characteristic. They were not the faint at heart. They had the guts and courage to leave established ties behind and build up a new existence in a - for many - completely different environment. They were creatively trying to find a niche in the new markets of the new country they went to. Many of them loved the adventure, the unknown, the challenge to build up a new existence and also they had a healthy *self-confidence* and a properly developed *need-achievement* drive. Next to these characteristics entrepreneurs also required a god deal of *problem-solving capabilities.* Time and again it was necessary to be inventive when new unexpected situations arose when, for example Spain, after the truce in 1621, issued a new embargo on all ships of the Republic. Solution had to be found by the Dutch business communities to circumvent this embargo and to keep on trading with the Iberia Peninsular. Subsequently, entrepreneurs continued to safeguard a good deal of their business by sailing under the flag of convenience. In addition, because of their many contacts abroad, such as friends, family members and reliable agents alike, Dutch entrepreneurs were always able to get the merchandise they wanted from Spain and Portugal through harbours like Antwerp, Hamburg and various other French harbours.[342] But also on the domestic front problems had to be solved, since Amsterdam - for reasons of competition - was trying to exclude the Zaan region from exporting timber into the city of Amsterdam. The regents were never able to close the gates entirely, as smart Amsterdam entrepreneurs, who were not able to obtain an import license, were still able to import under the pretext that the timber was either sawn elsewhere or was destined for re-export to other places.[343] Also in these days, entrepreneurs were not easily to be beaten by just raising barriers.

A striking feature of Dutch entrepreneurs active in overseas business was that they were not always the first to start businesses in new foreign markets. These were in quite some cases, the English, who started the business with the Nordic Trade, with Russia, the Levant, South-America and even with whale hunting. Dutch entrepreneurs came in a bit later, though, with superior trading techniques, higher

---

342 O. Gelderblom, p. 236
343 D. Aten, p. 75

quality merchandise[344], better technical means of navigation and transportation, as well as financial means and therefore were very successful in capturing these new markets from the British. This characteristic in actively *searching the environment* and then to penetrate into these existing upcoming markets with superior techniques, created in the end a lot of tension among the English, which ultimately resulted in outright sea wars with the Netherlands.[345]

Next to the better techniques and finance, entrepreneur had to learn foreign languages and also be familiar with different costumes and habits in the various countries. In order to establish personal contacts with these foreign markets, entrepreneurs often established offices in these countries. At the same time this was also a good learning school for young entrepreneurial talent in terms of international businesses practices, knowledge of languages and a better understanding of different cultures. That type of *inquisitiveness or searching the environment* for chances was not limited to foreign trade only. It also happened in domestic trade, when entrepreneurs in the western part of the country discovered the class of peasants in the southern and eastern less industrialised provinces. So, in the middle of the 17th century these entrepreneurs utilised this reservoir of labour (small commodity producers). The cloth manufacturers in Leyden transferred, for instance, part of their production to Tilburg and its immediate environment. In another case, merchant/entrepreneurs from Haarlem switched the production of spinning linen thread to the Meierij region and the city of Den Bosch. And even around 1620 Amsterdam entrepreneurs transferred the processing of tobacco to the provinces of Utrecht and the city of Amersfoort. This *search of the environment* served two purposes: first, it made use of available manpower, which was difficult to obtain in the scarce

---

344 In the 17th century various observers noticed that entrepreneurs were exporting the high quality butter to various European markets, and imported the lesser quality and cheaper Irish and Brabant butter for domestic consumption. The balance was an influx of earnings. This was made possible because of both low transportation/trading cost, a simple life style, and above all in a strong market-oriented; see J. de Vries & A.M. van der Woude, p. 246; such approach was also followed in the Netherlands after the World War II, when the country had to build up its completely ruined economy.

345 J. de Vries & A.M. van der Woude, p. 402

labour market of Holland at that time and, secondly, it could produce a considerable part of the product at a lower price, hence were better able to meet international competition.[346] Constantly *searching the environment* by entrepreneurs was one of the determinants of capitalistic forms that could enfold in Dutch society.

Time bound planning as a characteristic of merchants and other business people in those days (in spite of the lack of electronic mail and information) was as pressing as in present day economic performances of entrepreneurs. This characteristic became during this period increasingly important, as 'marketization' increased, resulting in fixing prices based on supply and demand. Hence, the arrival of a certain ship-load a bit later or earlier than expected or timely information regarding wars, harvests, piracy and the like, had an immediate repercussion on commodity prices. Based on the timing of expected new supply, merchants could play with prices. This was done by either lowering their stock-pile as fast as possible at good prices before new supply would arrive, or not yet to sell and to wait till it became widely known that disasters had occurred and no supply of a certain commodity would arrive. In such a case, merchants would only start selling at the time when scarcity would be highest. Although, obviously, the speed of information in those days was less than in to-day's business, the alertness and nervousness regarding the issue of 'time' was probably not that much less as compared to the present time. Information from family members from far-away markets such as from Archangel, were very important and the earlier the information reached Amsterdam the better commercial use could be made of it.

---

346 J.de Vries & A.M. van der Woude, p. 252; Haarlem was known for its production of linen and had established a thriving export business in that commodity, however had to face severe competition. Hence, when wages in Holland rose, entrepreneurs from Haarlem were searching for alternative production areas where wages were lower. Zwolle was such an area, which had already business contacts with Haarlem since 1566 and involved in productions according to specifications of the Haarlem linen manufacturers. In order to reduce risks furthermore, a couple of marriages took place between members of the entrepreneurial families of Haarlem and Zwolle. In the 17th and 18th centuries also linen from German countries were transported via Zwolle to Haarlem in order to be bleached and, subsequently, to Amsterdam for further export trading of the commodity. (See also J. Streng, p. 78).

To the end of this period (around 1670) the political and economic environment had changed quite remarkably. Although Spain had officially recognised its loss of the Netherlands in 1648, France and England came up strongly and challenged the Dutch not only commercially, but also by simply waging trade wars. The latter over-extended the resources of the Netherlands. With approximately 2 million inhabitants it would never have been able to fight the British and French effectively which combined had a population of approximately 26 million. Nonetheless, Dutch entrepreneurs were still *hopeful about the future,* which is a trait considered to be indispensable in entrepreneurship. The VOC continued to produce big profits, international business in the Republic was at its zenith, art and culture flourished and money for investments was abundantly available. So when gradually the tide changed around 1660, the combination of the two entrepreneurial traits '*hopefulness about the future*' and '*searching the environment*' for new chances, brought entrepreneurs to invest specifically in foreign economies, rather than in their own country, as investment opportunities in the Republic gradually diminished.

Entrepreneurial traits during economic decline (1670-1815)

Also during this period calculated *risk-taking* was still a current personal trait of Dutch entrepreneurs, certainly as far as international trade was concerned. This was specifically true for purchasing products, which still had to be harvested, as was the case with e.g. wine from France. An interesting example, which was not always appreciated by the exporter, was what the French Father Mathias reported in the 17th century as the '*merciless practices, which was disheartening for the poor French nation*'.[347] The situation he referred to was that Dutch entrepreneurs ordered wine and brandy for later supply in big quantities by paying advance money. The city of Nantes, where the wines from Orléans, Bois-geny, Blois, Tours, Anjou and Bretagne flowed together, had become such an important trading junction, that more and more vineyards were established, reason why the cultivation of rye in that area dangerously decreased.

---

347 F. Braudel, p. 391

The surplus of wine necessitated the farmers to produce brandy, which required a lot of firewood, resulting in depletion of wood in the neighbouring forests, which for the population increased the price of fuel. In spite of these difficult local circumstances, Dutch entrepreneurs bought large quantities of wine production before it was harvested.

In this sub-period (1670-1815) many changes and shifts took place, which affected the level of entrepreneurial *initiative and independence* decisively. To the many countries to which the Netherlands exported, entrepreneurs now decided to go and collect the merchandise themselves and, circumventing the Amsterdam staple market, transported the merchandise directly to the buyer in whatever country. This was an autonomous development, which was strengthened by the 'Commission Trade'. Also these forms of commission trade were indeed *risky* and required *initiative and independence*. The fact that the Dutch share of the world trade constantly dwindled was the natural consequence of the fact that foreign entrepreneurs were catching up with the leeway they had in their competition with their Dutch counterparts. Apart from their advantage of human resources, England was also very rich in deposits, such as coal and ore. In addition, the increase of their fleet was strongly accelerated as a result of the well-known 'Acts of Navigation'. Finally, the protectionist trade policies of France led to a further decrease not only of the function of Amsterdam as the world staple market, but in the industry as well. The textile industry, particularly that of the city of Leyden suffered a lot. Protectionist policies of the Dutch would not have helped, as the Dutch market was far too small. Obviously, the level of successful entrepreneurship in a small countries like that of the Netherlands can only take place under a regime of free trade, as is also proven in the late 20th and 21st centuries by city-states like for instance Singapore and Hong Kong. However, that does not mean that the Netherlands in the 18th century – as an answer to mercantilist policies – did not try to introduce protectionist measures. As a matter of fact, Dutch entrepreneurs took the initiative in convincing the government to introduce measures to block the transition of raw material to the German Rhineland. The idea was to complicate industrial development in that region, in favour of the industrial development in the Republic, in particular as regards the refinery- and processing industries. To that end, high tariffs for the importation of finished products from that region were levied, for example, of refined sugar. Similarly, high export tariffs were levied for the exportation of raw sugar to that region.[348]

But, in spite of the declining economic situation in the country, entrepreneurs still had a *positive self-concept* of their existence. Until 1763, if not till the French Revolution, it was materially and without doubt also morally very satisfying to be a Dutch bourgeois and entrepreneur. The 'decay' that followed thereafter can only be explained in terms such as 'the rise' of others within the framework of an effective pursuit of profit.[349]

During these difficult times of declining economic importance of the Dutch Republic, the *problem solving* capacity of entrepreneurs was a valuable personal trait. So, when during the fourth English Sea War (1780-84), Dutch ships were targets, hundreds of ship owners changed the Dutch flag into the 'flag of convenience'. Documents made up by notaries show the 'sales' of more than 500 ships to a foreign merchants, who lent their name as so-called owners in exchange of 2% commission of the sales value of the ships and a same percentage of the income of the transportation.[350] However, the biggest challenge for Dutch entrepreneurs came when they could no longer invest that much in European goods, due to changes in policies of competing nations (mercantilism) and the subsequently changed position of the staple market. Instead, entrepreneurs started as from 1650 to concentrate relatively more on the supply of colonial goods from both the West and East Indies. Specifically during the period 1680 to 1720 they switched large amounts of investments to enlarge the trade volume of both Indies.[351] Thus, when investment opportunities for European products gradually decreased, entrepreneurs were able to mitigate that problem by seizing opportunities to invest increasingly in colonial products,

---

348 J.A. Faber, p. 136
349 I. Wallerstein, p. 45
350 J. de Vries & A.M. van der Woude, p. 568
351 J. de Vries & A.M. van der Woude, p. 499

which ultimately emerged in a new Dutch trade system, in which colonial goods took a central position. But not all entrepreneurs got the opportunity to increase their trade with the East, due to the strong monopoly position of the VOC. These entrepreneurs solved their problem by providing capital for the establishment of other competing companies in France, Denmark, Sweden and Toscana[352]. Indeed, Dutch entrepreneurs were not necessarily looking for investments for the sake of the nation; they were interested in their own sake, hence directed their capital to these places which brought them the highest return. This of course created economically and socially for the country a very undesirable and lob-sided situation as the investors and merchants who brought their capital to England, France, Germany and other countries, got in return very high amounts of interests without doing much, whereas it extracted at the same time these investments from the Dutch productive sectors of the economy, which led to increased unemployment and outright poverty for a relatively large chunk of the population.

There has been much historical debate about the alleged decay of the commercial spirit of entrepreneurs that seem to have been so obvious in this period. Business speculation, for instance, was considered to be a weakness of character and so were easy investments in foreign economies considered to be an escape for undertaking risky commercial ventures in their own economy. However, these critical sounds at that time were in fact the result of the self-interest of the merchant, banker and entrepreneur. And as a matter of fact, that same self-interest that had brought great economic results in the 16th and 17th century. However, when the Dutch economy declined, there was hardly any other opportunity - seen from the point view of the entrepreneur - but to invest in foreign economies. This was the way Dutch entrepreneurs were looking at the problem of optimising their business ventures and they resolved that by choosing investments, which would sustain or improve their wealth. Obviously, that personal trait of *problem solving,* is of course closely related to recognise the right type of opportunities. And in order to recognise opportunities, entrepreneurs had to be alert in constant-

---

352 F. Braudel, p. 425

ly *searching the environment* so as to see their commercial chances. These entrepreneurial characteristics were not only present during the two sub-periods prior to the decline of the Dutch economy, but during the latter as well. Research carried out by De Jong Keesing[353], who went through elaborate correspondence of entrepreneurs and merchants in Haarlem and Amsterdam in the 18th century, shows that no traces could be found of indolence of entrepreneurs. On the contrary, her impression is that they were hard working merchants, who did not lack energy and lived a relatively sober life. Charles Wilson also confirms this image, in quotes from correspondence between Dutch and English entrepreneurs. In conclusion there was hardly any other choice but to invest in foreign economies.

How did entrepreneurs look upon the future? How *hopeful about the future* were they? Obviously, the decline of the economy could no longer be stopped by also introducing protectionist measures in the Netherlands as the competing powers, England and France had done. The Dutch market was simply too small. This led to flexible answers on the part of the entrepreneurs to keep on hoping on a good business future. One of these answers was detaching trade from domestic production, or introducing more specialization. This was in a way the same process that took place earlier in the century, when ties were cut between trading on the one hand and the transportation and financing of transactions on the other, which before were all taken care of in the one person of the "merchant old style". Now, possessing and exploiting the ships became increasingly separated from the purchase and sale of goods. In addition, also the 'financing element' of business ventures developed in an independent activity. The 17th century entrepreneur from the harbour cities of the Republic, who united all these functions, had to leave a considerable part of his activities to specialised ship-owners, who transported merchandise that was not their property as it was before. The merchants in their turn often became trade agents, who specialized in selling merchandise on behalf of the real owner (supplier) at the payment of a commission. Capitalistic entrepreneurs were ready to finance a trade in which they themselves did not play

---

353 Quoted in J.G. van Dillen, p. 351-352

any role. As we have seen above, they were even ready to finance foreign traders, whose merchandise never went to the Republic. Obviously, this trend contributed to the disintegration of the trading system that was already in decline.[354] New trading systems were developed in order to satisfy the new demands of that time. But that was not sufficient to reverse the tide. Also the increased focus to the East-West trade and the newly developed attention to exploit the increasingly important German hinterland could no longer change that situation either.

---

354 J. de Vries & A.M. van der Woude, p. 582

9. ENTREPRENEURSHIP DEVELOPMENT DURING TRADE CAPITALISM AND ITS CONTRIBUTION TO MODERN TIMES

9.1 Evaluative remarks on entrepreneurship during Trade Capitalism

9.1.1 General

In previous chapters we have described the dealing and wheeling of Dutch entrepreneurs during the sub-periods of Trade Capitalism, i.e. the period of economic takeoff, the period of economic supremacy and finally during the period of economic stagnation and the ultimate decline. As shown in the introduction to these chapters the idea was to analyze Dutch entrepreneurship by making use of four different dimensions, which might shed light on entrepreneurial performance (see figure 5 below). These four dimensions and its 30 sub-factors, as mentioned in chapter 2, were based on both the mainstream of theories related to entrepreneurship and three identified orientations of entrepreneurs in general.

Figure 5: Research focus of the previous chapters 5, 6, 7 and 8

At this junction it may be helpful to realize how many entrepreneurs were really active during the heydays of trade capitalism, at the time that the Dutch Republic was the economic powerhouse of Europe. According to de Vries & Van der Woude, 6 to 8% of the professional labour around 1650 belonged to the elite bourgeois, which included; merchants, manufacturers, notary staff, clergy, doctors, civil servants, high army officers and later also persons living on interest income. Merchants represented the vast majority and together with the manufacturers the total number of entrepreneurs, disregarding shop owners and market people, may not have exceeded 3.5 to 4% of professional labour[355]. Taken into consideration a population of the country in 1650 of about 1,9 million, including a professional labour force of 1.140.000, it means that the number of people giving shape to Dutch trade capitalism hovered around a mere 45.600.[356]

It is altogether quite remarkable that such a small group of people (3% to 4% of professional labour) were able to generate that much energy that could bring the Republic to the very heights of the European economy could establish the first modern economy in the world as well. An important spin-off of the small number of entrepreneurs was the issue of 'trust'. In the relatively small-scale urban societies where they were active they knew each other quite well and this opened opportunities to start joint projects or to lend each other money for investments. This all resulted in acquiring wealth that allowed them to pay the required amounts of taxes which enabled the Estates General to defend the country's economic position by responding to trade wars with France and Britain and to become an independent state, liberating itself from the biggest military power at that time, catholic Spain.

---

355   De Vries & Van der Woude, p 650. See also p. 661 to 675 where taxable entrepreneurs represent 4.6% of all heads of families

356   The calculation is made as follows: the number of families representing 1.9 million inhabitants represent, taken into consideration a family size of 5, 380.000 families. Considering that the average number of professional labour per family is 3, the professional labour force of the Netherlands arrives then at 1.140.000. Hence, if 4 % of the professional labour force is involved in Dutch trade capitalism, the number arrives at 45.600 individuals. (See also De Vries & Van der Woude, p.597-605). A rough estimate as made by O. Gelderblom arrives at 11.356 entrepreneurs for Amsterdam only, i.e. 5.475 in manufacturing, transportation, retail trade and services) and 4.881 in wholesale trade (Gelderblom, O., 2008, appendix)

In evaluating entrepreneurship during the period of '*Trade Capitalism*' a summary of the four dimensions as discussed in the previous chapters will be dealt with. These are: a) opportunity conditions (chapter 5), b) institution development (chapter 6), c) socio-cultural aspects of the society, influencing entrepreneurship (chapter 7) and d) entrepreneurial characteristics (chapter 8).

9.1.2 Opportunity conditions for entrepreneurship

Within the context of increased European business activity during the latter part of the Middle Ages, the Dutch (emerging) entrepreneurial class with age-long expertise in navigation and shipbuilding was met with very favourable opportunity conditions.

The very first was the geographical situation of the Netherlands along the relatively busy navigable North Sea at the crossroads North-South (from Baltic Sea to the Mediterranean, v.v.) and East-West (from the German hinterland to the British isles, v.v.). In addition the Netherlands was a delta area with very well navigable rivers as the Rhine, Scheldt, Meuse and Yssel, which highly favoured safe transportation of merchandise over large parts in Europe. Another geographical opportunity condition was that the country was subject to the natural contracting of agricultural land which then was no longer fit to cultivate grain, which forced farmers to go into animal husbandry and entrepreneurs to import large quantities of grain from elsewhere, initially from France but later from the Baltic. In order to decrease transportation cost over a longer distance, hence to remain competitive, the imported volumes had to be large. Therefore, entrepreneurs designed newer, larger, types of ships so as to benefit from economies of scale. The large volumes of imported grain from the Baltic made it, next to feeding the population, also possible to start the processing of beer to be exported to many other places in Europe. This went together with animal husbandry products such as for instance cheese, which came from the Dutch rural areas, after the so-called contraction of agricultural land. Finally, the size of the country proved to be another opportunity condition for entrepreneurs, as communication among them and between markets, investors and financiers in a smaller country like that of the Netherlands went faster and more intense as compared to large nation states like France, England or Spain. The Netherlands at that time could be seen as the 20th century economically successful city-states, like Singapore or Hong Kong: compact, business-like, outwardly-oriented and mutually strengthening business services.

A second opportunity condition was the specific nautical skills that had been developed over a long period of time and were very much connected to the geographical situation of the Netherlands. Obviously, shipbuilding techniques in the country were relatively highly developed. It was, indeed, a very natural proto-industrial activity in a delta area with not that many land roads and where people were very much dependent on their navigation skills for reason of survival (floods), communication (food distribution, marketing products) and food production (fishing). All this stimulated shipbuilding techniques for both inland navigation and open sea transportation for fishing, as well as for regional trade. Luckily the money market came up and more international trader in this part of the world sharply increased.

A third opportunity condition was the availability of energy sources to entrepreneurs. The windy climate in the country made it possible to deploy effectively windmill technology, which was not only utilised for draining purposes and land reclamation, but for proto-industrial activities as well, such as processing of food products, producing paint and for the shipbuilding industry (saw-mills). An additional energy source was the abundance of peat in the country, which was an excellent and relatively cheap energy source to be used for warmth technology resulting in productive activities (manufacturing bricks, tiles, ceramics, casting iron). In addition, peat exploitation required the construction of canals for transporting the raw material, which – in its turn – was then also used to open up domestic markets in the peat digging areas.

Next, a fourth opportunity condition proved to be the proximity of large international 'captive' markets, specifically in the south (Antwerp, Bruges, Ghent, Ypres), but also in the East, for example, in the city of Cologne, which had a population with considerable purchasing power. Apart from profitable trade activities, it provided entrepreneurs information on new business developments and opportunities in these places, which stimulated them to constantly innovate their production means at home, for instance in the textile industries, which subsequently led to increased productivity. This then had a lowering effect on the cost price, which made their production internationally more competitive.

Finally, the fifth opportunity condition, which was highly favourable for Dutch entrepreneurs, was the 'Good Governance', or better – at least for that time - 'Appropriate Governance'. Although this opportunity condition is actually part of the 'Institution Development' dimension, which will be discussed below in greater detail, it is also appropriate to mention this factor at this place, since 'Appropriate Governance' was the umbrella under which entrepreneurs could make an effective use of all other opportunity conditions and thus were provided with an 'enabling environment' that made their actions successful. The Estates General was a democratically composed body of representatives from the 58 cities in the Republic, whose councils had many entrepreneurs in their midst. Hence, the influence of entrepreneurs into government circles was quite high, which led to the creation of an enabling legal and institutional environment for emerging and (increasingly growing) existing entrepreneurship. In addition, both ends – government and entrepreneurs - understood that their relationship was based on mutual dependency. The government collected funds through taxation, which was needed in order to secure freedom from Spain and to defend itself against trade wars with England and France. After all, entrepreneurs could only be successful in doing international business in an area that was free from suppression or war and were therefore prepared to pay for it through taxes.

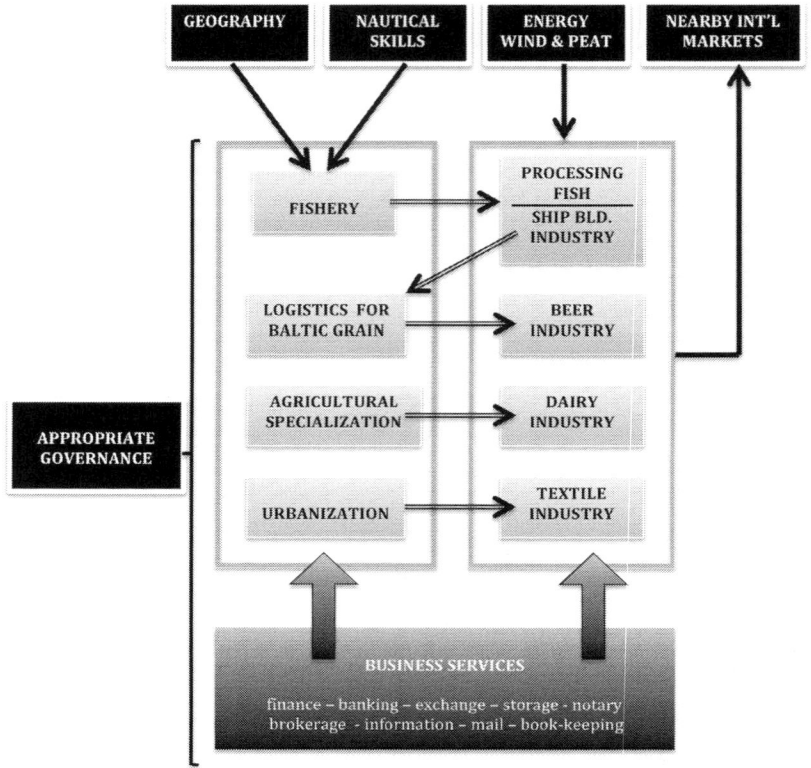

Figure 6: Relationship of opportunity conditions with entrepreneurial actions

The combination of these five opportunity conditions (see figure 6 above) was a very strong basis for entrepreneurs to build an economy, which during the period 1580 to 1670 became probably the strongest in the world and marked the beginning of globalised capitalism. Dutch entrepreneurs were indeed alert in making use of these opportunities at a larger, more international scale then they used to do before. It ignited the emergence of many other supporting industries, such as the manufacturing of sails, cordage, paint and in addition stimulated the importation of timber. This, together with the Baltic trade, attracted capital to both finance shipbuilding and for providing cash for the purchase of merchandise (timber and grain). Profits were, apart from basic needs, not consumed but largely re-invested. Not only investments in existing proto-industrial activities as wind-mill technology, shipbuilding and warmth technologies, but also in relatively new business projects like land reclamation and the labour intensive textile industry. This also attracted relatively cheap labour to the cities who had become redundant in the rural areas as a result of the less labour-intensive animal husbandry compared to the previous grain cultivation. It was indeed, a stimulating environment for international marketing and competitive export production and, not in the least, entrepreneurship development.

In the initial phase of identifying and employing the 'static' opportunity conditions (geographical position of the country, availability of energy sources and prosperous nearby markets) as well as the development of the 'dynamic' opportunity condition (nautical skills and shipbuilding techniques), this all led to a supposedly strong demographic growth. This provided unheard possibilities for entrepreneurial activities. It meant a gradual change from subsistence economy to production for very specific markets or target groups and, finally, to the production for the impersonal market (marketization). This was the start of an increasing commercialisation of the economy. The expansion of the cities was supported by the fact that also the rural areas increasingly started to produce export products and international services (transport), of which the trade and organisation came in the hands of entrepreneurs in the cities. There was a productive use of the marginal farmers in the economy as well, as they complemented agricultural specialised production (dairy production) with sweet-water fishing, peat production, duck breeding, improvements of drainage and water-management, as well as with the production of semi-finished products for the manufacturing of textile goods for the cities. In summary, around the year 1500 entrepreneurs had clearly identified the opportunity conditions and made great use of these to achieve wealth, power and prestige. The resulting proto-capitalistic structure as developed between 1350 and 1500, or as Van Zanden puts it, 'the proto-industrial reproduction pattern', laid the foundation of a strong entrepreneurial class and made the subsequent emergence of the great economic power of Holland, in the period after 1580, plausible.

By then the scene was set for the next period of economic growth leading to the economic powerhouse position of the Netherlands, which ran from approximately 1580 to the early 1700s. International trade brought a lot of raw materials to the country. Furthermore, there was still ample peat to take care for the required energy of both processing and proto-industrial activities (casting, bricks, tiles, ceramics, etc.). Sufficient and relatively high quality labour was - due to the waves of immigration specifically from the South after the fall of Antwerp - not a real problem either. Export markets were growing and again entrepreneurs in the shipbuilding industry took care for sufficient capacity for transporting the finished products to the various overseas-markets. The same was applicable with the shipbuilding industry, which also during the heydays of economic supremacy remained dependent on overseas imports (timber). Linked to the shipbuilding, entrepreneurs were instrumental in continuously differentiating the production patron. This development was strengthened by technology improvement and the innovative capacity of entrepreneurs in shipbuilding, which stimulated the building industry in Zaandam. The city of Zaandam was situated at a flat windy area, where a lot of sawing mills were erected for extensive construction of ships. In 1630 Zaandam counted 128 industrial mills, which number increased to nearly 600 in 1731 with a production of approximately 300 ships per year.[357] In this particular industry Dutch entrepreneurs were even that much competitive that quite a number of ships – and even warships - for British ship-owners, were manufactured in Zaandam, in spite of the animosity between the two countries. This is confirming Baumol's findings that entrepreneurs are not necessarily working for the good of the nation, but are strongly motivated by increasing their own power, status and wealth. Significant technical innovations at the end of the 16th and the beginning of the 17th century proved to be the engine for economic growth, for which money was amply available. Zaandam and the surrounding area became one of the strongest - if not the strongest - differentiated industrial area of Europe.

---

357 P.W. Klein, *De Zeventiende Eeuw*, p. 99/100

As from the end of the 17th century economic decline started to take place. In spite of enormous amounts of capital investment capabilities that were availlable, entrepreneurs in general, could no longer initiate new business activities at home. International competition, trade wars with France and Britain and highly protective measures of these countries resulted of course in far less commercial opportunities. There was such an abundance of money in the economy that entrepreneurs and investors did not really know what to do with the repayment of the redemptions of government-bonds and even resisted amortisation as much as possible. This was a clear indication of the scarcity of investment opportunities. Why was it not possible for Dutch entrepreneurs, who were in the forefront of all economic aspects in the world at that time, to produce sufficient business opportunities and not to be able to keep on developing the economy to even a higher level of sophistication? What prevented entrepreneurs in the domestic industry and the service sector to introduce new technologies so as to be at least as competitive as English-, France- or German entrepreneurs and to stay abreast of them? The question is important, as entrepreneurs in the 17th century in the Republic had indeed been very technology-oriented and innovative, hence, had created ample business opportunities for which funding was not that much of a problem. The reason, as worked out, lies in the sphere of weighing the advantages and disadvantages of divestments of current production means and instead to invest in new technologies.[358] The advantages of transferring to new production techniques (driven by steam and coal) were less big for the pioneers in business development (the Dutch entrepreneurs), because the latter had already a relatively high standard of production with the then current opportunity conditions, among them the energy sources (wind and peat). The cost in re-investment in new technologies and divesting in the current (old) ones was very high, whereas also the profitability of these new technologies was at that time still questionable. Moreover, the new techniques did not correspond that well with the stock of natural deposits of the Republic, such as ore and coal, which were abundantly available in other competing countries.

---

358 JL. van Zanden & A. van Riel, p43-46

An additional reason was that of the institutional rigidity, i.e. the growing gap between the economic and political elite, particularly as the regents in the cities – the former highly successful entrepreneurs - increasingly withdrew from business and insulated themselves from newcomers from outside. In the 16th and 17th century these two groups fell, to a certain extent, together but when the regents and the newly emerging entrepreneurs moved into different directions the institutions got stiffened and lost its previous flexibility. As a result, the *quality of factor inputs* into the economy and society diminished in this period. The resulting decline of the economy was even aggravated, due to competition of foreign entrepreneurs in other, larger, countries. Moreover, governments of these countries assisted their entrepreneurs either through protective measures (Navigation Acts), or outright trade wars (France and England). Increasing competition, foreign protectionist policies, and the lack of relevant deposits (coal and iron) killed the trading system of the country. Instead of a shortage of labour before, it had now an abundance of labour getting unemployed. Another way of looking at the decline of the Republic was the fact that France and England had become centrally guided states with strong armies, whereas the Republic could no longer defend itself sufficiently, due to its decentralized government system (58 cities), and relatively small army.

9.1.3   Institution development

There were two main reasons why city governments decided to keep on *promoting, protecting* and on taking *corrective* action as regards the business communities in their towns. The first was material in nature. By protecting the small commodity production city governments *promoted* employment and as a consequence they could reduce the financial pressure on the care for supporting the proletariat. That was also the reason why administrators of the city governments tried to exercise control of prices of foodstuffs and grains for bread baking so as to reduce public spending on the issue of the poor. This made money available to financially attract entrepreneurs from outside the country, who were active in new industries for domestic- or export trade. These, in turn, could employ idle workers and at the same time could increase taxable income for the cities. A second reason was ideologically tinted. The city council members and – later – the regents in the Republic, did not want to evade their moral obligations to the poor inhabitants of their own cities.[359]

The close connection between foreign and domestic markets made sure that the explosive increase of trade capital in the Republic after 1580 would result in a bigger demand for investments in capital goods. stimulated the development of institutions, specifically as regards structuring the emerging banking sector and organising commercial trading practices. These institutional improvements resulted in reduced *transactional cost* of trade. Likewise, it offered opportunities to profitable investments in technological innovations in the shipbuilding industry (fluytship, sawing technology), in the textile industry (new drapery, dyeing, etc.) and in a good number of processing industries (through windmill technologies). The number of patents, which was registered at the Estates General, reached its peak in the Republic around 1620.[360]

Further domestic growth was achieved by competing succesfully in international markets, which resulted in larger market shares. So, capital accumulation of the years between 1580 and 1621 coincided with a growth in the domestic market, which provoked depth-investments, strongly *promoted* by central and city governments. These investments ranged from infra-structural works, agrarian improvements, city expansion, increased exploitation of peat including transportation means (canals), to the construction of windmills for industrial purposes. Subsequently, against the middle of the 17th century, the Amsterdam staple market was solidly anchored in a specialised domestic economy, which was favoured with great capital wealth, employing the most advanced technology of its time. Labour productivity was the highest in Europe.

---

359 C. Davids, Kapitaal 108-111
360 J. de Vries en A.M. van der Woude, p 408; 60 in 1600, which annually increased to 125 in 1620 after which the number of patens sharply decreased.

As we have seen from studies of D.C. North[361] on the relationship between institutions and economic performance, the early part of the 17th century in the Dutch Republic seems to have been a confirmation of that positive relationship. As by nowadays standards, the more sophisticated the institutional structures are, the lower the transactional cost for businesses and the more competitive the economy as a whole will be. In addition, the more transparent the legal system is, the more secure entrepreneurs feel, which has a positive effect on their business transactions. As we have seen, there was a very close relationship between the governments and the private sector, as is shown in the figure 7 below.

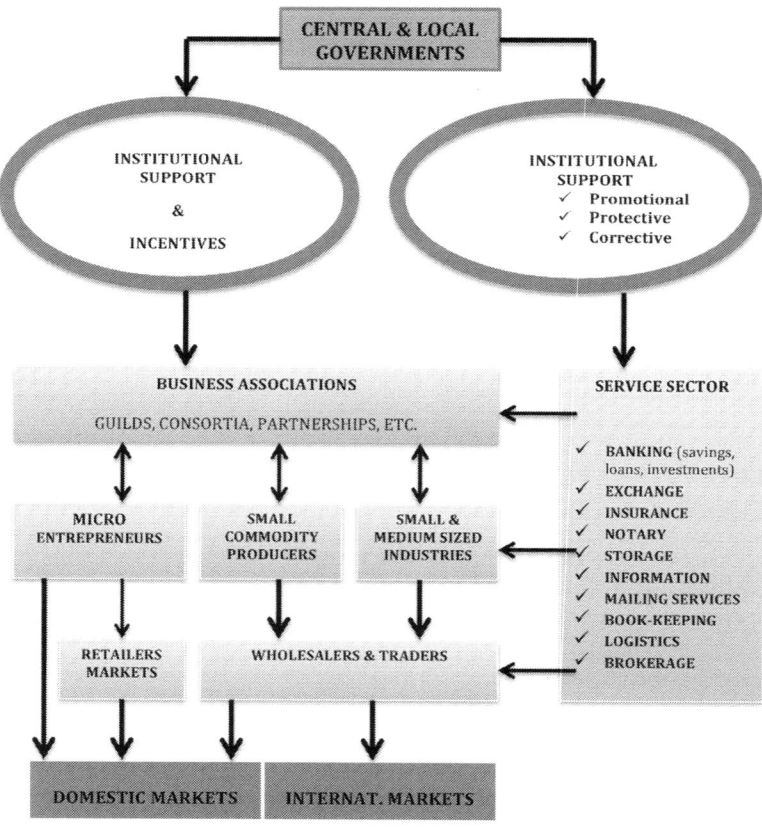

Figure 7: Overall institutional structure as a result of private sector development and government support

361 C.D. North, p78

As described before the Estates General was composed of members from the 58 city councils in the country. And these councils were mostly staffed with quite a number of members from the business community in these cities. Hence, institution development was at the heart of both the central and local governments and through these institutions all sorts of support and incentives were channelled to entrepreneurs.

Examples of *promotional institution development* included: the provision of monopolies (whale fishing); providing licenses and bounties; luring entrepreneurs to start new types of businesses in the cities offering them freedom of rent, cheap loans, tax exemption, the free use of equipment (business incubation); combining initiatives of various Chambers (e.g. in the case of the foundation of the VOC); building and maintaining infrastructure for trade purposes. As regards measures related to *protective institution development* the government was serious in reforming the administration by strengthening the legal structure, establishing property rights and developing business regulations concerning both markets (opening hours, days, place) and the financial sector. Furthermore it exercised supervision (*corrective action*) on business sectors (guilds), protected the rights of inventions by registering these, hence *protecting* patents and carried out control of standards and the quality of products. Concerning the measures taken by the central and local governments in *corrective institution development* it took action to regulate the bourse operations when things went out of control. Likewise, it intervened and took *corrective measures* when a financial crisis occurred as for instance happened in the dealing in futures of tulip bulbs (the so-called "tulpmania"). And because of the strong ties between government and private sector there was the required enforcement of the rules and regulations in order to prevent unfair competition among entrepreneurs. Finally, the government was in the forefront of providing all sorts of assistance to the business community in the various trade wars with England and France. As a matter of fact many of the city council members were entrepreneurs and to them it was quite obvious that not only the country or the state should be protected, but also their businesses. Hence, many investments were made in building warships and in the reorganization and strengthening of the army (Stadholder Maurits), so as to protect their markets. However, given the size of the country and the population (not even 2 million), the Republic would never be able to cope with the mercantile British and France trade wars. Ultimately it brought the Republic to the brink of bankruptcy.

Also the private sector was very keen in developing institutional structures, which would strengthen their business operations and would lower their transactional cost. Associations were set up in the form of guilds, consortia, partnerships or other forms of cooperation, either to *protect* their businesses or *promote* it by bringing together sufficient investments and expertise. To that end, a relatively strong service sector had been build up to effectively and efficiently support the economy: banking services, notary, brokerage, publications of journals for business information, insurances, shipping, etc. Without a thriving service sector entrepreneurs would never have been able to gradually set up and strengthen the Amsterdam staple market, which by itself was a major ingredient for strong economic development. In addition, there was a healthy cooperation in institution development between the private sector and both local- and central governments. Examples were the construction of halls, the roofed trading places, which of course stimulated trade. Another example was allowing cartels or monopolies in- or outside Europe (WIC, VOC), if and when opportune. The big difference with other trading nations such as Spain and Portugal in this respect was that monopolies in these countries were regarded as "royal" monopolies, whereas in the Netherlands the monopolies were provided to the private sector, which provided the required investments for establishing the first joint stock company in the world, in which everyone with money could buy shares.

9.1.4 Socio-cultural aspects of society affecting entrepreneurship

As discussed before, culture has been defined as the 'collective mental programming', which distinguishes one group from another. It influences patterns of thinking and acting in a given society. As any other group in society, also entrepreneurs are part of the norms- and value systems of a given culture, but in turn also provide input in framing the cultural identity of a society. Below follows a summary of the cultural aspects in the Dutch society, which affected entrepreneurship, vice versa.

Legitimacy of entrepreneurship

Entrepreneurship was a very legitimate activity in the Netherlands, more or less evoked by the fact that it produced the taxes, which were necessary to liberate the population from Spanish rule, heavy Spanish taxation and suppression of religious freedom. Furthermore, it brought full employment to the country, subsequently leading to more income for the labour force, hence an increase in purchasing power. All of this created a lot of support from local and central government circles, in which entrepreneurs themselves were often part of it. This symbiosis produced the right type of business climate, as it was in the interest of all parties to constantly improve the enabling environment for domestic and international business. For the entrepreneurs it increased their wealth, power and status and for the regents it produced the needed tax income, which was required to fight their independence struggle against Spain and the various trade wars in which the country was embroiled. The resulting economic growth and the positive attitude in the country towards entrepreneurship, attracted nascent and existing entrepreneurs from Flanders, France, Portugal, Germany and even a few from England. Their integration into Dutch society developed quite nicely, as a good number of them contributed very positively to the then constantly growing economy and prosperity of the country.

Social mobility

There were ample opportunities for successful entrepreneurship and this, in turn, resulted also in a high social mobility for both indigenous and exogenous entrepreneurs. Irrespective their descent they could climb the ladder from small entrepreneurs to the position of highly respected big international wholesalers, bankers and even mayors of the big cities. Similarly as in the 'American Dream' of the 19th and the first half of the 20th century, anyone, wherever they came from, could achieve whatever anyone of them could dream of!

This very open socio-cultural climate changed over time. Once the regents, around the 1700s, became a class in itself and less connected to the real economy, social mobility was decreasing. This trend went together with economic stagnation and a declining economy in the course of the 18th century. Due to heavy international competition and international protective measures to which Dutch entrepreneurs had no appropriate response, they started to invest their monies in foreign countries with better financial results than in their own country. Ideology and need-achievement were still features in existence, but entrepreneurs were no longer able to give it shape in the real economy.

Marginality

Because of the high legitimacy, both Dutch and minority groups in the country exercised entrepreneurship. All immigrant groups, those from the southern Netherlands, jews from Spain and Portugal and later from eastern Europe (Ashkenazim), the French huguenots, Germans and Scandinavians, were in the position to adopt the entrepreneurial role, often in close cooperation with indigenous Dutch entrepreneurs. The same was applicable to minority groups with a different religion than the dominant calvinism. Catholics, Jews, mennonites, lutherans, were free to exercise their belief as long as they did not do it too openly and specifically, as long as their partisans contributed to the economy. In short, descent or religious belief was never an issue of marginality in the sense that these groups were forced into entrepreneurship. As entrepreneurs they earned the same respect and legitimacy in society as compared to their indigenous Dutch counterparts.

Social integration and security

There may have been roughly 200.000 immigrants in the Republic at around 1650, which was 10.5% of the entire population[362]. There

---

362 The precise number of immigrants is not known and historians differ widely as regards the numbers per each immigrant group. Combining the various calculations,

was social acceptance, rather than integration. Acceptance existed, mainly as the immigrant groups contributed considerably to the economy. They were welcome entities, as the indigenous population (not even 2 million) was very small, certainly in relation to competing large powers as France and Britain, which had an approximate population at that time of 26 million in total. Ships to the East- and West Indies, to the Baltic- and Mediterranean seas had to be staffed; business people had to be sent to the colonies and outstations such as the East Indies, Caribbean, New Amsterdam (Manhattan), Archangel, Levant, South Africa, Ceylon and many other places. Processing and manufacturing activities in the Republic had to be carried out for export, such as beer brewing, cheese making, shipbuilding, textile, tiles, bricks, etc. Also the service sector, such as banking, insurance, notary, storage, bookkeeping, mailing serves, transport, etc. required a lot of people. And finally, the wars against Spain, France and Britain, required an army and a fleet, which had to be staffed as well. Hence, immigrant groups were generally very much welcomed.

Integration went far slower. Most of the immigrants remained very close to their own kin. Marriages were conducted in their own ethnical group, certainly during the first two to three generations. This gave them psychological ethnical security amidst another - for them - strange (Dutch) culture. In addition, 'trust' in those relatively uncertain days was a very much-needed commodity when running a business. Overseas contact in the export- or transport business included sending merchandise and/or money from one part of the globe to another, with the risk of being subject to criminal acts. So, whom could one trust better than their own family members or people from the same ethnic group?

Ideology and need achievement

The socio-cultural climate consisted of another important element, which was related to ideology and '*need-achievement*. The calvinistic

---

we arrive at a number of 150.000 immigrants from the Southern Netherlands, 8.000 Jew from Portugal and Spain, 27.000 Germans, which totals to 185.000. Add to these Scandinavian immigrants and huguenots, then the total immigrant population in the Netherlands around 1650 hovers around 200.000, which is 10.5% of a population of 1.9 million at that time.

ethic was certainly a support in developing modern capitalistic features, however, these features were already largely in place prior to calvinism, as can clearly be observed at the end of the Middle Ages, when the money economy was already about to start. However, it is quite obvious that capitalistic development went very well together with the calvinistic ethic, meaning that entrepreneurs were not only or primarily motivated by monetary incentives, but that money rewards constituted a symbol of achievement (status) and a proof of a divine affection.

9.1.5 Entrepreneurial characteristics

"*The*" entrepreneur - as such - does of course not exist. There is, indeed, a wide variety of entrepreneurs: the way they give form to their enterprises, equip it and finance it, differs considerably from one sector to the other and from the one entrepreneur to another. At this junction one cannot escape the notion that diversity and heterogeneity in entrepreneurship were manifestly present in set up and depth. Whether we are looking at capital wealth, the nature of the capital, creditworthiness and financing possibilities, or at the nature and volume of investments, the production activities, or at the modalities of production and its corresponding technology, organisation of enterprise and labour relations: the differences in terms of quality and quantity were immense. So, if we do justice to the 'rich' reality, the design of a differentiating image of the entrepreneur is hardly possible. Nonetheless, for the purpose of this study an effort is made to identity common entrepreneurial characteristics, which – in its diversity - were dominant during the greater part of *Trade Capitalism* in the Netherlands, running from 1350 to 1815.

Identity

Looking at this characteristic a few observations can be made, which were quite dominant manifestations in the 'land of entrepreneurship'. The Dutch entrepreneur in this period was *individually oriented*, which can be traced back to the very nature of the Dutch population in their fight against the sea and floods, which could not be won if one had to wait for local or central governments to help them. In spite of their individualism, they knew when to conclude consortia or other forms of cooperation, e.g. when they needed capital, or to spread risks. These forms of cooperation had a provisional character. This individualism had something to do with religion as well. The calvinistic ethic held the individual responsible for his deeds and personal success; this meant for many of them to strive for some sort of divine approval. This, in turn, explains the relatively high level of need-achievement among Dutch entrepreneurs as well.

But the same was also true for immigrants, or outsider entrepreneurs. Many of them fled because of religious freedom they lacked in their country of origin, hence Flemish, Portuguese, German and French immigrants felt 'at home', or at least at ease with the existing calvinistic ethic and were fully accepted among indigenous entrepreneurs and city councils. Many business coalitions were concluded among indigenous and exogenous entrepreneurs, irrespective belief. In as far as business is concerned there was practically hardly any difference between *mainstream and outsider*.

That was different as regards *family life in business*. Most of the exogenous entrepreneurs were – for a number of generations - sticking together with their own countrymen and family, which was a natural reaction for people arriving in a country with a different culture and in some cases a different religion. Hence, there were at that time quite a number of entrepreneurs who made a case of it to specifically employ family members in their business and, through intermarriage, were also able to build up relatively large family businesses. In addition, family businesses made it also possible to train younger members of the family to become seasoned business people. After basic education quite a number of these youngsters were sent abroad as representatives of their father's businesses and to run these factories overseas. Although extensive literature suggests that entrepreneurs belonging to the same family are likely to be less expansive and innovative, this study does not support that view in this period of trade capitalism. Quite a number of businesses in this period developed even into trade houses, which lasted a couple of centuries and some of them even into the 21st century.

The *socio-economic origin* in entrepreneurship was quite important in strengthening their identity and making use of the same. As from the 15th century, indigenous Dutch entrepreneurs had built up their network in the Baltic Sea. That network could be used in conjunction with the network in eastern and southern Europe, which the Flemish immigrants brought with them when they fled to the Republic. The same was applicable when jews from Portugal and Spain fled to the Netherlands. Their network in South America (Brazil) was very important for the diamond and sugar industry. All these separate networks were inter-actively used to the benefit of all entrepreneurs. Obviously, those that had been at the forefront of developing these networks knew better than anyone else the needs of the markets. So in quite a number of cases, those merchants, who also had the capital requirements, became proto-industrialist as they knew which products at what prices were needed in these markets. In fact, the merchant/entrepreneur made use of a favourable 'networking opportunity condition' when intensifying his business.

As we have seen in the previous chapters, the *religious orientation* of entrepreneurs in the Republic was quite strong. The calvinistic belief system was very dominant, not only as a religion, which appealed to the Dutch because it fitted nicely into existing cultural traits. In addition, calvinism was also seen as manifestation of opposition to Spanish rule that was considered to be the worldly leader of catholicism. Opposition to Spanish rule was not so much ignited by foreign occupation and suppression of the Dutch nobility, but more so because of heavy taxation of the population. So, to be a calvinist meant to be against heavy taxation from the Habsburgs in Spain, and therefore against catholicism. Understandably, calvinism was therefore very dominant in the Republic, although entrepreneurs understood that religion should never be a barrier to do business. And to be successful in business automatically meant to be a good calvinist, as success was considered to be an earthly reward of god. And above all, calvinist preachers understood that the taxes to fight catholic Spain had to come from entrepreneurs, whether or not they were calvinists. Altogether there was a handsome coalition between entrepreneurial goals and calvinistic principles.

As regards *old versus new entrepreneurs*, there have been discussions that old entrepreneurs were less expansive than the newly emerging entrepreneurs. The study of this period does not support that view. On the contrary, we have seen quite a number of examples in which old entrepreneurs were expanding their businesses even to a point that factories were set up abroad. Emerging entrepreneurs, in as far as these belonged to a business-family, were trained both domestically and abroad and were instrumental in expanding the business to a further level of profitability. In addition there was sufficient scope for newly emerging 'stand-alone' entrepreneurs to start and expand their small scale business; the required capital most of the time came from the wholesale merchant, which in return needed higher volumes of production for the export market.

Businesses were all privately owned and run, although in one case one could speak of a public-private business venture, i.e. the VOC (United East-Indian company). It had many private-sector shareholders and entrepreneurs were involved in the commercial trading activities of that limited liability company. The government, however, provided the trade monopoly and took care of the military protection of the company in the East Indies. As regards the contrast '*public-private*' in business at that time, it should be noted that many of the public officers in the city councils and the Estate General, had a marked entrepreneurial background and were in quite some cases, next to their official function, also active as entrepreneurs.

Orientation of entrepreneurship

Innovation was the big thing during this period. This was not only applicable to make an innovative use of the then available sources of energy, such as peat and wind, but specifically in exploring international markets. There were ample innovations in trade (staple market, foundation of multi-national corporations, etc.), in the service sector (finance, notary, logistics, cartography, etc.) and in production (ships, beer, textile, paper, timber, cordage, sail cloth, etc.). Innovation was necessary to keep abreast of competitors. New ship models were developed and constructed, which allowed much more cargo, where faster and at the same time required less people on board, which had a decreasing effect on the price of the merchandise to be traded –a price which hardly could be met by foreign competitors. But foreign competitors quickly learned the tricks of also increasing their productivity, which – in its turn - forced Dutch entrepreneurs to find other ways and means to improve their competitiveness. In addition to improve existing products and services, entrepreneurs also developed completely new ones, specifically in services; Amsterdam the staplemarket of serivces. Interestingly, entrepreneurs also developed new products for the domestic market in order to substitute imports. An example of it is beer, which was initially imported from Germany, but then Dutch entrepreneurs developed their own beer with grain coming from the Baltic and could then supply the captive domestic market. And when the beer-brewers later on started to apply a different processing methodology as compared to the Germans, they were then even able to develop the product into a profitable export product.

The most important innovation may have been the 'marketization' of the economy itself, which meant the production of goods not for specific target groups as was the case in the final period of the Middle Ages (around 1500), but for the 'impersonal' markets, wherever these markets might be. This was heavily supported by innovations in the fields as mentioned above, specifically when taken into consideration the proto-industrial mode of production technologies in the shipbuilding-, fisheries-, textile- and warmth industries. This, as a matter of fact, marked the beginning of the modern capitalistic economy which opened the way for the industrial revolution that later took place in England as from approximately 1750 onwards.

'Marketization' of the economy, was the direct consequence of a strong focus of entrepreneurs on *'expansion of commercial activities'*. It was quite obvious that taken into consideration the size of the country and its population, the Netherlands could only survive when active in international trade. At around 1650 the number of Dutch ships outnumbered the total number of ships of France and Britain together. Actually, it was the world at large that was the market place for Dutch entrepreneurs for both the purchasing of the raw material and the sales of finished products. Expansion and innovation were the key factors in the rise of the economy. Given the seize of the country it was a commercial survival mechanism, which worked as long as there was free trade.

When economic stagnation and decline set in at around the 1700's, the younger generations were far more relaxed as regards the further development of their businesses. That stagnation was partly due to both protectionist foreign policies, which resulted in trade wars and a far stronger competition from Britain and France in particular. In addition, theses countries were able to produce large scale productions at lower cost because of the use of new forms of energy - coal and iron, which were absent in the Netherlands. Hence, instead of continuing to invest in businesses at home, Dutch entrepreneurs at that time started to invest large sums in businesses abroad so as to benefit from a higher return on investments. This resulted in supporting foreign businesses in innovating and expanding their commercial activities, which strengthened their competiveness at the disadvantage of the Dutch economy.

Entrepreneurial traits

In section 3.2.4 of this study we have identified a number of characteristics, which were the outcome of various other studies concerning personal characteristics of the entrepreneur (Gibb, Patel, EIM). Below we will relate to each of these eight characteristics and to assess – based on historical evidence - in what way these traits were appplied during the period of research.

Looking at the specific entrepreneurial traits, the conclusion can be drawn, that Dutch entrepreneurs had *a very positive self-concept*. It started when they recognised and seized the opportunity conditions (geography, energy sources, nautical skills and nearby markets), which were of importance in a constantly increasing international money economy that emerged at the end of the Middle Ages. No wonder that in such an economic climate, whilst making use of the available opportunity conditions, activities in international business became extremely successful which strengthened their positive self-concept. In addition, entrepreneurship had a high status and legitimacy in the country, which was not on the least due to the fact that they were also financing the government through pretty high tax payments, which were needed for the independence struggle against Spain. And as discussed above, quite a number of entrepreneurs were represented in the government of the Republic, either in city councils or in the Estate General, which of course added positively to their status and self concept as well.

This entrepreneurial trait stimulated them to take *initiatives* and they did that *independently of others,* with the possible exception of colleague-entrepreneurs with whom they worked together in some commercial venture on a project-basis. They were more individually- rather than collectively oriented. Their initiatives led to innovations in the development of supporting services to both trade and proto-industry. In addition, it also led to product development, which gave their products a unique feature, which was necessary to improve their competitiveness. In addition, their initiatives also stimulated expansion in businesses. Entrepreneurs were eager in exploring new markets, wherever these were situated. Likewise, they expanded in product range. New or other products were added to the ones in which entrepreneurs were already dealing with. In short, to them it was some sort of a '*Sturm und Drang*' period, with ample opportunities and/or capital.

Taking initiatives includes *taking risks*. The business risks, which entrepreneurs took were not the risks of gamblers. They took calculated risks, either in terms of mathematical calculations or by business intuition. Obviously, in a period of starting capitalism at global level, there was no (international) regulating framework that could protect entrepreneurs effectively against forms of fraud and swindle, even in the cases where contracts existed. Likewise, there were hardly agreements with foreign governments on taking corrective actions when things went wrong. Risks in doing business were indeed quite considerable. Also the degree of risk could hardly be assessed properly. In an era of the emergence of 'marketization' of the economy, it was very hard for entrepreneurs to find out what the reaction of the (international) market to their offered products would be and how local and international competitors would react to it. However, to reduce these types of risks, representatives of the entrepreneurs were stationed in the various markets abroad, so that these could build up commercial and reliable networks of buyers in these places (Archangel, Levant, Aleppo, Bordeaux, etc.). Another way of coping with risks was by trying to get monopolies from the central- or local governments in the Republic, or from rulers in foreign markets (for example de Geer who got a monopoly from the Swedish king) with which one worked.

Taking initiatives is by its very nature strongly related to *problem solving capabilities* of entrepreneurs, which includes: *'fluency'*, defined as the ability to produce alternative solutions; *'originality'*, the ability to produce uncommon new solutions; *'flexibility'*, the ability to shift from one approach to another and finally *'innovation'*, the ability to define or perceive in a way that is different from the usual way. In the period under research there was really no lack of problems. These ranged from cultural differences when doing business in international markets, to increased international competition, to piracy, to fraud in an relatively poorly regulated foreign environment, to trade wars which hampered international business a lot and the protection of ships and storage places abroad. A case in point was e.g. when the Spanish throne forbid Dutch ships to tie up in Spanish harbours to get products from Asia which were collected and transported by Arabs. Dutch entrepreneurs decided then to collect these products directly from Asia and to transport these to Amsterdam. These direct business linkages with Asia (East Indies), circumventing Arab and Spanish middlemen. This led to a robust and profiable business for many Dutch entrepreneurs.

Social mobility was high. Born in rural areas or in a poor family did not necessarily mean to stay at that low social level. Chances for success in a strongly expanding economy were all over. Even immigrants could become mayors of large Dutch cities. This social mobility contributed considerably to a growing economy and the then acquired wealth and prestige made entrepreneurs very *hopeful about the future*. Looking at the expanding economy the future was indeed looking bright: the number of industrial windmills in the Zaan area increased from a mere 128 in 1630 to 584 in 1731; the number of sawing mills, mainly used for ship building, increased in the same period with approximately 500%[363]. Employment in international shipping rose around 1610 in 20 years time with 40%[364], which is an indication of intensity of international trade. But that 'hope' became less at the end of the 17th century and gradually evaporated in the course of the 18thy century, due to economic stagnation and decline. Obviously, this took place very gradually, whereby one sector felt the increased international competition stronger than another. Although the economy changed, it did not change the entrepreneurial character or the socio-cultural society, which was build up over a period of many centuries. The problem of course was that the existing opportunity conditions at the start of the economic take-off (1350 to 1580) were no longer appropriate in the further development of the capitalistic economy, taken into consideration the developments of the newly developed technologies and energy sources. In spite of the innovative capacity of the entrepreneurial class, it was no longer possible to compete effectively with countries like France and Britain. However, as there was no shortage of money, it is understandable that entrepreneurs in the 18th century became interested in prestigious government jobs and in making investments in ventures, which gave them a good return, if not in their own country than in other upcoming economic powers, such as France, Britain and later the United States of America. After Great Britain, the Dutch were for many centuries the biggest investors in the USA.

As regards the trait of *opportunity seeking* we have already elaborately discussed the issue of the seizing of opportunity conditions during the pre-trade capitalistic period and the period thereafter (see figure 7). Once these specific opportunity conditions were no longer sufficient to deal effectively with competing powers and protectionism, entrepreneurs had to identify other opportunities in order to continue their business or to keep their wealth intact. In spite of these negative developments, though, Dutch entrepreneurs were still able to do international trade till far in the 18th

---

363 De Vies & Van der Woude, p 406
364 Ibid. p. 472

century. In 1770 international trade was even 20% higher as compared to 1720, although their share in international business was considerably lower in comparison to the century before.[365] However, those who were not able to identify trade- or manufacturing opportunities at home, did indeed identify other opportunities, i.e. investing capital with a handsome return in business ventures abroad.

Time–bound planning whilst setting goals is definitely an entrepreneurial trait in modern times, where issues like time-management leading to higher productivity are getting a lot of attention. But time-bound planning was a big thing in the trade capitalistic period as well. Apart from being a staple market for merchandise, Amsterdam established a European central information centre for trade, - in the words of the historian Lesger - 'a great staple of news'.[366] That staple of news consisted of the newest sea maps made by cartographers, printed price journals, sea guides with text and coast profiles, printing study books related to trade (accounting, interest tables, etc.), and of an international fast mailing system. In short, international trade information in Amsterdam was collected from all over the world, exchanged and categorised, after which it was stored and analysed and, subsequently, disseminated all over the world. In other words, business was not done at random. Entrepreneurs established these information services to plan their actions and setting their goals.

9.1.6   Final remarks

The period of *Trade Capitalism* is presented in a bell curve, as shown on next page. During the upcoming period between 1350 to 1500 opportunity conditions were identified and subsequently developed. Entrepreneurs grabbed these opportunities and created commercial growth through 'marketization', which in its nature was fundamentally different from commerce in the later part of the Middle Ages. With these opportunities in place Dutch entrepreneurs laid the foundation for a modern globalized capitalistic economy as from

---
365   Jonker, J., K. Sluyterman, p. 81, table 2.1
366   Lesger, C., Handel in Amsterdam the tijde van de Opstand, Hilversum, 2001, p. 210

approximately 1580, which lasted till about 1700, being the zenith of the bell-curve. Thereafter stagnation and economic decline took place, which lasted till the end of the Napoleonic period (1815), at which the bell curve reaches the absolute zero point. At its zenith, though, entrepreneurs of other countries gradually took over the lead from their Dutch counterparts, as these had different opportunity conditions at their disposal which were more appropriate for large scale production and higher productivity, hence lower prices.

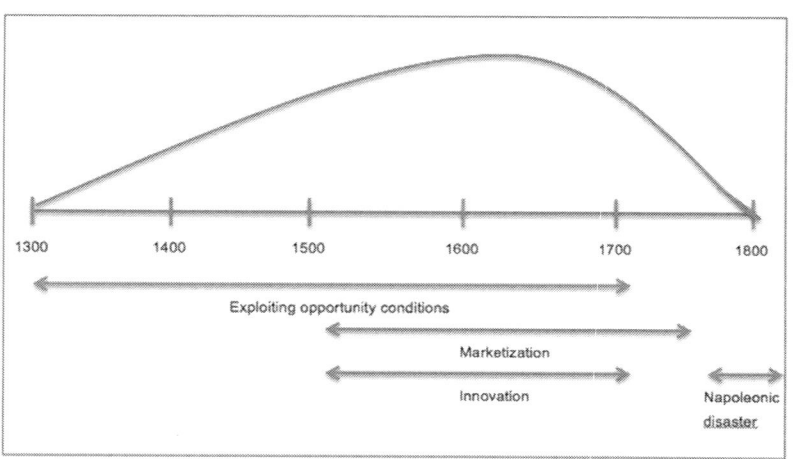

Figure 8: Bell curve Trade Capitalism

In conclusion, one cannot escape the notion that Dutch entrepreneurs created the very foundation of the modern economy. We will try to make clear in section 9.3, which deals with the period of '*Total Capitalism*' (1970-2000) that, although social, political and economic circumstances and entrepreneurial instruments were very different, there is not that much difference between Dutch entrepreneurs from the 17th century as compared to those of the 21st century. Prior to that section a summarizing view will be given in section 9.2 on entrepreneurship during '*Manufacture Capitalism*' (1815-1900) and '*Industrial Capitalism*' (1900-1970)

9.2. Entrepreneurship during Manufacture- and Industrial Capitalism

9.2.1 The start of the new kingdom of The Netherlands

At the end of *Trade Capitalism* in the Netherlands in 1815, the new kingdom of the Netherlands was created, which comprised the delta area (the former Dutch Republic) and the area, which is now Belgium. The idea to create a buffer state north of France, as was decided after the Napoleonic wars at the Vienna Congress, was to contain the natural expansion drift of the French. British diplomats specifically negotiated this buffer state. Obviously, Britain was not that much interested in a repetition of a Napoleonic adventure, since it had also been subject at that time to a possible invasion by France.

As mentioned before, the Dutch economy in 1815 was completely bankrupt, because of a form of ransacking by the French during their occupation of the country from 1806-1815. In addition, the Dutch trading system (to the Mediterranean and the East) – due to the Continental System – was completely disrupted. And to make things worse, the VOC (United East-Indian Company) went bankrupt during that period as well. However, the creation of a new kingdom in 1815 brought new chances. The Southern part of the country was rich of deposits (coal, iron, ore), whereas the Northern part of the country had a rich financing– and trading tradition, stemming from the *Trade Capitalistic* period. In addition, it also had colonies in Asia and in the Caribbean, although a number of these had been conquered from the Dutch and incorporated into the British colonial system (South Africa, Formosa, Sri Lanka). The combination: deposits, trade- and finance expertise, as well as colonies (raw materials), was an ideal mix to embrace and explore the newly developed technologies. The new kingdom was in fact the first country on the continent to introduce the spin-offs of the Industrial Revolution that had already started in England.

However, religious differences (the North was calvinistic whereas the South was catholic), the very high national debt of the Northern Netherlands and a not appropriate representation of important government posts resulted in 1830 in a revolt of the Southern Netherlands, which was politically supported by France, but was soon supressed by the Dutch army. When the French army threatened to assist the insurrectionists with the force of the French army, a stalemate was imposed, which lasted nine years, after which the Southern part of the country became with the support of France and the UK an independent state with the name Belgium. The large buffer state was gone. Although the configuration of the buffer state - north of France - was very much wanted by the British politicians in 1815, Britain changed its opinion, as it realised that the new political configuration of the Netherlands appeared to be become a staunch economic competitor of England, specifically considering the strength of the Dutch economy in previous centuries. Hence, it supported the independence movement and put someone on the throne, Leopold von Saxe Cobourg (married to Charlotte of Wales), who had been living in England for a relatively long period of time, with close ties to the British royal family. A friend on the Belgian throne was for the British after all better than a strong potential economic competitor. And France did not make any complaint either as the buffer state, to contain their expansionist drives, was dissolved. The official foundation of Belgium took place in 1839, which meant that a Dutch standing army was mobilised between 1830 and 1839. This was due to the fact that the Dutch government did not agree with the independency of the Southern Netherlands, as was advocated by both Great Britain and France. The financial consequences were grave. In 1815 the treasury was empty, because of French occupation and it remained empty because of the cost of the mobilization of the army up until 1839.

Below follows a description of entrepreneurship during the periods of '*Manufacture Capitalism*' (9.2.2) and '*Industrial Capitalism*' (9.2.3). During the period of '*Manufacture Capitalism*' (1815-1900) the main focus of the economy and entrepreneurs, was on manufacturing goods, rather than on international trading activities, which was the focus during the period prior to 1815, as described in chapters 5 to 8. During that period of 'Manufacture Capitalism' a prudent start was made with applying newly developed technologies, which was a spin-off of the British Industrial Revolution. However, the sorry state of the Netherlands at that time prevented a full-scale industrialization as took place in other surrounding countries. It was only around the 1900's when *'Industrial Capitalism*' in the country modestly came off the ground. Actually, both *'Manufacture- and Industrial Capitalism'* can be considered as a transfer period between *'Trade Capitalism'*, which produced the first Golden Age and *'Total Capitalism'* - also called the period of the *'Entrepreneurial Economy'* - which produced the second Golden Age. This is reason why a more in-depth analysis is made of the period of *'Total Capitalism'* (as from 1970) in chapter 9.3 in order to assess the contribution of entrepreneurs active during the period of *'Trade Capitalism'* to those active in the knowledge-based economy of *'Total Capitalism'*.

9.2.2 Manufacture capitalism (1815-1900)

The economy of the Dutch, with a territory as nearly as small as the previous Republic of the Seven United Provinces, was at that time very much agriculturally focussed, reason why the industrialization in the Netherlands proper started relatively late. Initially, industrialization in the Netherlands during *'Manufacture Capitalism'* hardly took place and in fact began more of less at the end of that period around the late 1800s. Clearly, the period of *Manufacture Capitalism* is therefore considered to be a preamble to the period of *'Industrial Capitalism'*, which ran from approximately 1900 to 1960/70.

During the period of *Manufacture Capitalism* (1815-1900), we see that international trading was more or less reduced to the still existing Baltic Trade, i.e. the import of grain and wood and export of agricultural products from and to Sweden, Russia, Denmark and Prussia. Agriculture and fishery were the sectors, which generated the biggest part of the income for entrepreneurs, including the artisan activities around these sectors, such as, cordage, shipbuilding, sawing mills, sail- and fishnet making, etc. In addition there were manufacture activities related to paper- and oil mills, tile- and brick making, chocolate, pins, earthenware, cigars, pipes, candles, beer and gin. But all these activities were in fact more artisan- than industrially-oriented In 1816 the city of Amsterdam counted 774 micro enterprises with not more than 3.200 employees (an average of 4,2 employees per enterprise).[367] To become a big manufacturer, was for those who lived off one's investments not attractive, as this was assessed as being too risky, whereas profits from investments from abroad were higher and less risky, in particular investment in the USA.

In order to revive the colonial business as was done before by the bankrupted VOC, king William I of the Netherlands founded in 1824 the '*Nederlandse Handels Maatschappij (NHM)*' (Dutch Trading Society). However, individual entrepreneurs could not participate in the venture, as it was a state monopoly. The NHM started to finance the trading in coffee, sugar, spices, tobacco, indigo and other colonial goods from the Netherlands-Indies (the later Indonesia). A great support to the profitability of the trade was the forced introduction in the Netherlands-Indies of the so-called 'Culture System'. This was a kind of taxation, which forced local farmers in the Indies to cultivate one-fifth of their land with a specific product as prescribed by the colonial Dutch government. This system engendered a lot of income for the state, as these products fetched high prices in the international market. In addition, many of these products had to be processed to final products in the Netherlands, which stimulated entrepreneurs to run a somewhat more industrial production. The NHM did not only import products from the Indies, but also established there a market for the so-called '*katoentjes*' (cotton-ware). This led to the development of the textile industry in the Netherlands. Entrepreneurs established in the eastern region the country (Twente) quite a number of large factories, which became the first real industrial undertakings in the country. In other parts of the country the NHM stimulated the establishment of factories for cotton and woollen fabrics. Next, entrepreneurs got a lot of support from the NHM in the reconstruction of the Dutch shipbuilding industry and the founding of shipping companies. This stimulated the foundation of international shipping lines. Furthermore, it stimulated entrepreneurial activities to transport goods along the river Rhine from Germany to other parts in Europe, which was a boost for the development of Rotterdam, which later became the

---

367 Wennekes, A., De Aartsvaarders, p.31

busiest harbour in the world. The monopoly of the NHM came to an end in 1860, after which entrepreneurs started their own business in colonial products, in particular, tin, spices and tobacco with the financial support of the NHM.[368]

Entrepreneurship came to life again, although no progress was made in the heavy industry, as was seen in neighbouring countries. This was primarily due to the fear of wealthy merchants to invest in these type of ventures, since they assessed the risk of a low return on investment as being too high. Also financial institutions kept on concentrating on financing trade ventures because this required short-term capital with a relatively high return on investment. Quite obviously, industrial activities required lots of capital for the construction of factories as well as for investing in expensive machinery, whereas it was not sure whether these investments would at all bear fruit. Next, an additional reason for the lack of interest for fuller scale industrialization was the fact that there were hardly researchers and technicians in the Netherlands to support and work with the hi-tech of that time. (This was reason to establish as from 1843 technical universities, thereby following the examples of France and Prussia).

Finally, calvinism did not prove to be a staunch supporter of industrialization as well. Calvinistic support was perceived as a form of blessing, which was given to artisans who made their own small-scale production and also undertook themselves the marketing of the same. However, when it came to larger impersonal production processes in factories, then there was a lot of moral resistance, which was expressed in refusing to finance these activities, as well as to participate in it in any form. The general impression exits that during the previous period of '*Trade Capitalism*', there was indeed more room for entrepreneurs to manoeuver in a calvinistic society. Economic prosperity at that time was seen as a devine blessing, although it was realized that prosperity and richness also inhibited quite some

---

368 The independence of the NHM came to an end in 1964 when, as a financial institution it merged with the 'Twentsche Bank' into the 'Algemene Bank Nederland' (ABN), which merged again in 1991 with the 'AMRO Bank' to ABN-AMRO

dangers. The tension between the temptations of richness on the one hand and moral regulations of calvinism on the other hand was always present in those days. However, it should not be forgotten that calvinism then also meant fighting Spanish catholicism, which required taxes from businesses to defend both the religion and the liberty of the country. And these arguments were no longer valid during the period of '*Manufacture Capitalism*', reason why calvinism could be imposed more strictly. The cultural climate was indeed different during '*Manufacture Capitalism*' as compared to '*Trade Capitalism*'. As much as relatively large-scale production was allowed and supported during *Trade Capitalism* (shipbuilding, beer brewing, cheese-making, tile- and brick manufacturing, etc.), the less legitimacy there was for entrepreneurs to start industrial projects during the period of 'Manufacture Capitalism'. Although the '*Vereeniging voor den Effectenhandel*' (the bourse) was (re)founded in 1876, bankers in general, remained very reluctant to support entrepreneurs in establishing industrial enterprises. The only exception was the famous Banker Martin Mees, who invested monies of the wealthy bourgeois – those who were genuinely interested in risky but potentially profitable ventures - in industrial projects. In spite of all these difficulties (lack of finance, religion/culture, lack of technology) entrepreneurs were able to generate support for a number of industrially oriented business activities. In 1876 there were already 456 limited liability companies[369], among them companies which later became very large enterprises, such as Unilever, Heineken, Stork, Lips and a couple of others, of which a number of them merged with other companies. Other large and well-known companies who were founded a bit later (around 1900) were Philips, Shell, Fokker and KLM.

At the end of the 19th- and the beginning of the 20th century, many laws were initiated, which had to do with the emergence of the new society. That new society was the society of the big businesses, making use of new inventions and technologies and where mass production was the tune of the day. The subsequent increased urbanization resulted in the emergence of communism and social-

---
369 Wennekes, De Aartsvaders, p.41

ism, which forced the government to take protective measures for labourers including children (safety, housing, education, health, right of union, etc.).

9.2.3 Industrial Capitalism (1900-1970)

The period of *Industrial Capitalism* started around 1900 and lasted till about 1960/70. This was the period of the emergence of the so-called 'neo corporatism', with newly created political parties, as well as the start of negotiating labour conditions and later the emergence of the *National Social Economic Council*, an advisory body for the government. It was the time when a number of companies, which were founded at the end of the 19th beginning of 20th century, were able to grow into large multi national organizations. In his book *'De Aartsvaders'* the author describes the dealing and wheeling of the founding fathers of these large corporations. It also provides insight into the characters of these entrepreneurs. They were restless souls with an in-built mission and orientation to crate something for the longer term, hence were not that much interested in the 'quick buck'. They were all structural thinkers and able to convert their thinking and ideas into practical action. These entrepreneurs – according to the author's research – founded KLM. Shell, Unilever, Akzo-Nobel, Philips, etc. and were individualists, taking initiative, risks - though 'calculated risks' - and solved the many problems that cropped up as a result of introducing innovative production in their companies. A very strong orientation of these entrepreneurs was on *'opportunity seeking'*. The latter was activated as a result of the second industrial revolution around 1900, which included the application of gas, electricity, machines, engines and chemicals. The combination of these opportunity conditions and their entrepreneurial traits, were the building blocks of the many multi-national companies, which were founded at that time and still exist. A financial report of 1991 provides some insight in that growth, as is listed in the table below.

The report mentions that these companies and some other large ones, together with the Dutch banking sector in 1991, generated an annual turnover of € 380 billion (GDP of Spain in that year was

€ 443 billion) and created work for 957.000 employees.[370] These achievements, though, were reached in spite of the many difficulties these enterprises went through. During the early decades of the 20th century, the First World War broke out, which disrupted the sound development of businesses considerably, as did also the financial crises of the 1920s and 1930s. And just when businesses started to revive, the Second World War erupted. After this war it took another 15 to 20 years before the large companies revived their business and it was around 1960/70 when big businesses were growing more and more internationally. It was during that time that globalization became an important issue and gradually the capitalistic model of that time changed from 'Industrial Capitalism' to 'Total Capitalism'.

COMPANY	TURN-OVER IN BILLION €€	EMPOLYEES
Shell	87,133	133.000
Unilever	34,744	298.000
Philips	25,903	264.000
SHV (retail business)	8,170	34.600
Akzo/Nobel	7,659	67.200
Hoogovens (metal)	4,068	26.800
KLM	3,597	28.300
Fokker	1,733	12.600
Stork	1,627	16.500

Table 3: State of affairs of large Dutch MNCs in 1991, adapted and taken from Wennekes, p.547

---
370 Wennekes, W., De Aartsvaders, p.547

But what had been the nature of enterprise development during *'Industrial Capitalism'?* In chapter 2, we mentioned already that the economic growth of industrial nations of the world appeared to be driven by large industrial firms, whereas small firms were being driven into failure because of the economies of scale of large firms. Entrepreneurship seemed to be a dead or a dying phenomenon. Not the least of these pessimists was Schumpeter himself, who argued in his 1942 book *Capitalism, Socialism and Democracy* that entrepreneurship could not survive in the face of the ever-larger industrial firms that monopolised innovation through well funded and organised research and development-laboratories. This belief continued to flourish after World War II. Since simple observation of industrial activities in the 1940s through the 1970s showed industrial firms growing ever larger, even to such an extent that John Galbraith in 1967 proposed that capitalist societies would evolve into three powerful groups, i.e. big businesses, big governments and big labour unions. Galbraith's 'new industrial state' was in fact devoid of entrepreneurs.[371] Innovations came from the R&D laboratories of the large enterprises. And that was certainly also the case in the Netherlands. This large-scale development of businesses was not only the case in industry, but also in the retail business. We see for example that the number of retail shops in 1950 numbered approximately 190.000 and in 1973 the number went down to 153.000 - a decline in retail shops of 20%. At the same time the population during that period increased with 30% with a GNP in 1973, being eight times higher as compared to 1950.[372] This is partly explained by the fact that the number of branch companies increased, but also means that the number of 'independent entrepreneurs' (independent shop-owners) drastically went down at the expense of 'shop managers'. As a matter of fact, the professional choice after education of young people was more or less clear; a fixed job at a large organization, with the advantage of much leisure

---

371 Galbraith, J.K., The New Industrial State, New York, 1967, in: Bruce A. Kirchoff, 'The Dynamics of Ambitious Entrepreneurs' in EIM publication *Entrepreneurship in the Netherlands; Ambitious entrepreneurs: the driving force for the next millennium*, Zoetermeer, 1999, p. 4

372 Luijckx, R. Th. Het kleine detailhandelsbedrijf in de herkansing, in: Dreesmann, A.C.R., *Dynamiek in de distributie, 1975*, Amsterdam, p. 255

time and early retirement. In 1899 the share of independent entrepreneurship in the Netherlands was 25% of total employment; in 1981 this had gone down to 10%.[373]

9.3 Entrepreneurship during Total Capitalism (as from 1970)

As from the period of 'Total Capitalism' (approximately 1960/1970 till now), a reassessment took place as regards 'entrepreneurship'. Because of increased globalization and competition, many of the large businesses started to concentrate on their core business. Peripheral business activities were abolished, which meant that quite a number of staff had to be dismissed. Instead of getting unemployed, quite a number of dismissed persons started their own business. In addition, the economy in the Netherlands went through very difficult times, since international competitiveness, hence international trade, decreased considerably as a result of the creation of a social welfare state, which was made possible because of the exploitation of the newly found rich gasfields. The cost of the welfare state had gone up from 13% of GNP in 1965 to 24% in 1980, whereas other European countries were spending around 14% of GNP to their social security system. This affected competitiveness, hence international trade quite negatively, resulting in more bankruptcies and unemployment. Whereas the unemployment percentage in the 1970's was around 4%, it rose to 11.7% in 1983.[374] These were all *push-factors,* which led to a much higher birth rate of new small business enterprises. But there were also a couple of *pull-factors,* which stimulated entrepreneurship. One of these pull factors was the so-called 'Agreement of Wassenaar' in 1982, where the government, employers' organizations and labour unions came together in the city of Wassenaar to decide to work together by making mutual sacrifices to their respective

---

373 Wennekers, A.R.M., Maatschappelijke urgentie van ondernemerschap, Den Haag, 2005, p.15
374 Bruggeman J. & A. Camijn, Ondernemersverbonden; 100 jaar centrale ondernemersorganisaties in Nederland, Wormer, 1999, p.230 and 245

policies (consensus), in order to stimulate the economy. This was the birth of the '*Polder Model*', a way of cooperation among the three major economic forces to negotiate solutions acceptable to all, rather than applying a policy of confrontation. This included also financial support programs to the start-up of new enterprises, hence employment. Another *pull-factor* for entrepreneurs had to do with the negative experience a number of 'intrapreneurs' had when working at large enterprises. Situations they were confronted with were, among others, threatening unemployment, no sufficient opportunities to make internal promotion, relatively low payment, hardly any appreciation for the work done, to little autonomy and business-disagreements with the top management. A new class of entrepreneurs emerged. They were people who wanted to be on their own, who had a dream, who were looking for challenges and those who wanted to bring new products in the market.[375] Specifically with the younger people and graduates, entrepreneurship became very popular. Within a couple of years the number of entrepreneurs went up dramatically. On January 1st 1992 small- and medium sized enterprises (SMEs) generated 70% of all jobs in the country. It represented 98.5% of all enterprises; hence large businesses represented 1.5% only. From the 98.5%, 90% of the businesses had less than 10 employees. Below follows a more detailed analysis of the period of '*Total Capitalism*', following the methodology as used in the chapters 5 to 8.

9.3.1 Opportunity conditions for entrepreneurship

The opportunity conditions for entrepreneurship can be subdivided into two factors, i.e. 'static factors' and 'dynamic factors'. To the first category belongs the geographical position of the country, which is situated in North-western Europe at the North Sea, with excellent harbour facilities in both Amsterdam and Rotterdam. Given the position of Rotterdam, at the entrance of the river Rhine, with direct access to the German hinterland, its harbour has been developed to the biggest and busiest one in the world.

---

375 Wennekers, A.R.M., Maatschappelijke urgentie van ondernemerschap, Den Haag, 2005, p. 24. The percentages refer to research made by EIM

Next to the very favourable geographical position of the country, the presence of capital also belongs to that same category of basic factors that constitute good opportunities for entrepreneurship. The banking sector in the country has been very well developed with organizations as ABN/AMRO, ING, and RABO-bank, which have a longstanding experience. In addition there are quite a number of relatively newly erected banks like SNS-REEAL, ASN, Triodos and many more smaller banks and credit institutions. The financial infrastructure is as such that entrepreneurs are in the position to make an abundant use of the credit facilities they offer, of course against viable business plans.

Finally, in the 1960's the country was blessed with the discovery of a huge stock of gas in the north of the country (province of Groningen) and in the Dutch territory of the North Sea. The gas field in Groningen is the largest in Europe and together with the North Sea gas has already produced 2600 billion m3, whereas there is still 1900 billion m3 to be exploited.[376] Much of the natural gas is exported to surrounding countries, which generates substantial income for the government. Additionally, it provides entrepreneurs secured supply of a relatively cheap energy source for their industrial businesses or offices.

The 'dynamic factors' that constitute the opportunity conditions for entrepreneurship include: the infrastructure of telecommunication (ICT), a highly educated labour force and academic research organizations. As distinct from the 'static factors' mentioned above, the 'dynamic factors" are those that are subject to change and therefore requires to be constantly created and maintained.

As regards the ICT infrastructure, the Dutch government actively promoted the use of ICTs in several ways, facilitating access to broadband internet and government services. The number of subscriptions to digital cable and terrestrial television and use of mobile services were growing rapidly; presently there are 1.2 mobile subscriptions per inhabitant. The volume of internet traffic expanded dramatically and gave access to high-speed internet connections.

---

376 Ministry of Economic Affairs, *Gas production in the Netherlands,* publication code: 04ME18

Right now, the largest and fastest internet hub in the world is the Amsterdam Internet Exchange. Therefore the country is a key actor in the digital era. These facts have brought many advantages to both Dutch and foreign entrepreneurs. The Netherlands is a preferred location for many international enterprises that want to do business in Europe; a good ICT infrastructure and a highly skilled workforce have attracted more than 5,000 foreign companies, most of them major ICT corporations like Acer Computer, IBM, BenQ, Google, Oracle or Sun Microsystems. Today ICT represents 70% of the country's innovative activities and 10% of the value generated in the country. Dutch ICT exports nearly doubled between 1998 and 2008, being the world's fourth-largest exporter in the field.

The Netherlands features one of the most highly educated, multilingual, enterprising and motivated workforces in Europe: 40% of the workforce possesses either a college or university degree and 91 % of them speak English. This highly skilled labour force fits handsomely with the information as provided in table 4, in which, in which industrial business over the years went down from 36 % to 16 %, whereas entrepreneurial focus on the service sector dramatically increased from 64% to 84% of all businesses.

	1930	1950	1963	1978	1983	1993
Industry	36.0%	37.6%	34.4%	27.1%	19.1%	16.1%
Services	64.0%	62.4%	65.6%	72.9%	80.9%	83.9%

Table 4: Shares of industry and services in the number of establishments, 1930-1993[377]

This is part of the currently developed 'knowledge-based economy', which is fully embraced by the younger entrepreneurs and highly promoted by the Dutch government. The employment growth in the service sector was four times higher than in non-knowledge-based companies. Furthermore these businesses were twice as active

---

377 Wennekers & Folkeringa, The development of self-employment rate in the Netherlands 1899-1997, Zoetermeer 2002, p15

than others in launching new products in the marketplace. This is also due to the fact that 78% of these businesses perform R&D activities, whereas entrepreneurs of non knowledge-based companies score not higher than 12% in R&D. All of this contributes to quite a high extent to the dynamics of entrepreneurship in the country.[378] In order to strengthen this development the government together with the Netherlands Organization for Scientific Research (NOW) and a number of entrepreneurs representing some 1500 businesses (mainly small- and medium seized organizations) have come together in order to coordinate all necessary activities to stay in the top 5 of the most competitive knowledge-based economies of the world. This implies contacts and coordination of all R&D centres in the country, including thirteen universities and a number of stand-alone internationally reknown research insittutions such as TNO, RIVM and the like.[379]

But also internationally a number of developments took place which had a very positive effect on Dutch entrepreneurship, specifically taken into consideration the conditions that existed during the hey days of *Trade Capitalism*. As has been described in chapters 5 to 8, it was the openness of the international economy, which was of importance for Dutch economic supremacy at that time. And this all changed dramatically when mercantilism was applied by the big powers, subsequently leading to trade wars, ultimately resulting in an absolute decline in international trade, which was the life-line of the country. However in this period of *Total Capitalism* trade became globalized, as was also previously the case during the period of *Trade Capitalism*. This was strongly supported by the World Trade Organization (WTO), whose mission is to provide a forum for negotiating agreements aimed at reducing obstacles to international trade and ensuring a level playing field for all, thus contributing to economic growth and development. The WTO also provides a legal and institutional framework for the implementation and monitoring of these

---

378 Snijders, J., Elk, K. van, Some characteristics and Trends of Dutch Entrepreneurship, in: *Entrepreneurship in the Netherlands; New firms, the key to competitiveness and growth*, p. 17-33, Zoetermeer, 1998
379 Information to Parliament with letter 11.02.2013 by the Ministry of Economic Affairs

agreements, as well as for settling disputes arising from their interpretation and application. And a next international event – though at a completely different level - was the emergence and further development of the European Union (EU). This created an opportunity for Dutch entrepreneurs, with an inborn drive for going international, a toll-free area of an immense size in which they could do business. In other words their market potential was unlimited. And finally, when the Berlin Wall fell in 1991 and the Soviet Union imploded, fear for wars and political tensions, which impeded international trade, evaporated.

Opportunity conditions for Dutch entrepreneurs were excellent: 1) the country physically situated in the middle of European business dynamics, state of the art harbours in Rotterdam and Amsterdam, 2) abundant financial services available, 3) enormous gas deposits, 4) world leader in ICT infrastructure, 5) highly skilled labour available, 6) world-class research and development (R&D) organizations, 7) international free trade, 8) a large "domestic market" (EU) and, finally, 9) no more trade interruptions because of wars. The scene was set for a second Golden Age!

9.3.2 Institution development

Government initiatives

As described before, the 'Wassenaar Agreement' in 1982 was an important year for Dutch entrepreneurs. The highest representatives of the government, among them the Prime Minister, the head of the Dutch Employers Association and the chairman of the Labour Union, came together with the objective to work together in order to improve Dutch competitiveness, which had dramatically gone down due to a too heavy social legislation. This was more or less the result of the exploitation of a huge stock of gas with was found around the 1960's and '70's in the country and the North Sea–territory belonging to Dutch territory and was exploited not only for own use, but for export as well. This generated a lot of income for the government and the coalition parties in the various cabinets that were in power during the '60's and '70's decided to introduce social legislation that was so expensive that in the end it could no longer be financed by the extra income from gas revenues. The national debt position of the country aggravated, but even worse was that the situation for entrepreneurs had become very difficult. Because of the social legislation, wages of employee had gone up as well as the social charges to be paid for by entrepreneurs. Sales price went up and export stagnated. The Dutch had lost its competiveness: the British *Economist* framed this as the 'Dutch Decease'. In order to reverse that situation the three parties came together in 1982 in the city of Wassenaar to discuss ways and means to improve the economic position of the country, by improving the competitiveness of Dutch enterprises. It meant that the three parties, each with a completely different agenda, had to make reciprocal sacrifices. This became the start of the so-called 'Polder Model'. This means that these three parties, since then, are regularly coming together, in order to arrive at a consensus on taking the right economic decisions, taken into consideration both the interests of employers and employees, without confronting each other by means of strikes and like. This form of institutionalizing consultation and common decision taking on economic and social issues affecting entrepreneurs and their businesses, is thereby taking away a lot of disruptions in carrying out business practices. Obviously, this type of institution development has strongly improved the position of both the emerging and existing entrepreneurs. An important spin-off of the consultations was the awareness of the importance of small- and medium seized enterprises for the economy at large and for employment generation in particular – the job-motor of the society. This resulted, among others, in making government credit facilities available to the tune of € 1,5 billion annually.[380] This led to a number of down-to earth support programs for entrepreneurial development. An interesting example has been the set up of *'Business Incubation Centres'* for starting entrepreneurs. These centres are presently assisting emerging entrepreneurs to start a business based on a business plan. These centres will house, at a very low rent, various production and service businesses for a relatively short period of time, during which they will be assisted by

---

380 Ministry of Economic Affairs, *Naar De Top; Het bedrijvenbeleid in acties,* Den Haag, 13.09.2011

the management of the centres to conduct their business in a profitable way (production, marketing, pricing, book keeping, etc.). Other central services may include: secretarial support, computer and email facilities, etc.). After an initial period, in which the incubators have proven to be able to stand on their own feet they will have to move out and rent their own facilities, hence making room available for other nascent entrepreneurs.

The Ministry of Economic Affairs has developed a support structure for entrepreneurs to be specifically effective in foreign markets. To that end it has abolished during this period of *Total Capitalism* unnecessary regulations and has created a business-friendly fiscal policy. The ministry therefore has made available the so-called Export-Credit Insurance, which is meant for the export of capital goods or capital-intensive services to non-EU countries. The often high-risk sectors involved include shipbuilding, contracting, dredging, glasshouse construction, and medical equipment. A study of the Netherlands Central Bank (DNB) disclosed that each Euro spent on insured exports generates over €2.50 in total exports. The government is furthermore focusing on strengthening the international market position of Dutch entrepreneurs operating in the top sectors of energy, the creative industry, life sciences, logistics, horticulture and propagation materials, high-tech, water, agri-food and chemicals. This top sector approach is geared towards providing a solid exchange between businesses, knowledge institutes and the government (the so-called 'golden triangle'). The government does not make its own proposals for the sectors, but invites businesses and scientists to draw up their action plans. For each top sector a 'Top Team' has been put together, consisting of: an innovative SME entrepreneur, a scientist and a civil servant and a standard bearer for the sector. These teams have contacts with entrepreneurs and scientists in the respective sector, who are then mapping out the various opportunities and challenges. They present action plans detailing their ambitions. The government then responds in a policy document, which is meant to fleshing out the plans into concrete lines of action and creates an enabling environment for the entrepreneurs to take action so as to achieve their newly identified business goals.

Another form of governmental institution development has been the set up of Chambers of Commerce throughout the country. It has a mandatory mission to register all enterprises in the country. In addition, its mission is to provide entrepreneurs support related to starting a new business, or to provide information to entrepreneurs planning to go abroad with their company, or about new government regulations, and the like. It represents the interests of the business community at large, for example, by advising the government and carrying out projects in the field of regional business incentives. In addition to the regional Chambers of Commerce in the Netherlands, there is also the so-called bilateral Chambers of Commerce. These are Chambers, for entrepreneurs who do business with a country, which they also represent. Examples are the Dutch-French Chamber of Commerce, the Dutch-German Chamber of Commerce, etc. These bilateral Chambers focus mostly on trade. It organizes trade missions and seminars on doing business with, say, Germany or carry out country surveys for their members/entrepreneurs.

Private sector initiatives

Next to the 'government initiatives regarding institution development, we see in this period of *'Total Capitalism'* many initiatives of entrepreneurs in nearly all sectors of the economy. A first example in this area is the initiative among entrepreneurs in *'clustering and network development'*. This provides opportunities for entrepreneurs to benefit from efficiencies in working together in obtaining raw material, imports, the use of logistical means and in production technologies (quality and quantity), in order to serve larger markets including forward and backward linkages with multinational organization.

Clusters can be seen as a business relationship among a number enterprises to share business ideas and to cooperate in the execution of the same, in order to fetch a market share which otherwise could not be obtained by the individual enterprise. Cluster are, among others, geographically agglomerated industries, i.e. a high-density business activity and are characterized by the focus of one particular industrial activity and the fact that many small firms specialize in different phases of the production process. An example, in this respect, is the cluster on semiconductor companies of which there are many in the Arnhem-Nijmegen region of the country. These companies are clustered in a network called Business Cluster Semiconductors , which covers the whole of Eastern Netherlands. It is a regional network of multinationals, knowledge institutions and innovative small- and medium sized enterprises active in the whole value chain of development, production and application. Concrete projects within this cluster are: 1) the establishment of an advanced packaging center, 2) shared electronic design automation through a shared ICT infrastructure and 3) the establishment of a development and production facility. This has resulted in a continual improvement of the production, hence increasing its competitiveness in doing international business. Another interesting example may be seen in the flower business with its 3.770 growers and 693 exporting enterprises, represented in more than 20 business associations, councils, research centers, etc. These enterprises are trading in 20.000 varieties of flowers and plants. By clustering their activities they established an auction system and extensive logistical systems, resulting in selling to the domestic and international markets more than 40 million flowers, in 125.000 daily transactions (2009). In general one may conclude that clusters enhance the competitiveness of established small businesses. Clustering of businesses, which often also leads to forms of innovation, has become an essential phenomenon of the 'new economy'.

Another example is the participation of entrepreneurs in the so-called *'Science and Technology Parks'* and *'Business Innovation Centres'*. In these centres entrepreneurs are running their businesses in close consultation with various faculties of technical universities in the country. In that cooperation they exchange newly researched technologies and empirical findings of enterprises when applying these new technologies. The idea is to innovate the production and/or production methodologies, hence to be more competitive in the domestic market (import substitution) and exports. In a number of cases these centres also provide consulting services and operational business services (accounting, communication, power/energy, security, etc.), which has a decreasing effect on the cost price of the production.

At present there are approximately 800.000 enterprises in The Netherlands, of which half of these are family businesses. 80% of all entrepreneurs of small, medium or large companies are member of a *'Sectorial Business Support Organization'* (SBSO), supporting entrepreneurs in a specific industrial- or service sector. (In the EU the percentage of entrepreneurs belonging to such organizations is 55). There are approximately 520 different branch organizations active in looking after the interest of their members. They provide sector–specific services, such as information on innovation, export markets, collective imports of raw material, international competition, judicial services, entrepreneurial training, etc. These 520 local- or regional branch organizations are in their turn represented by two large umbrella organizations, that directly deal with government officials on issues related to taxation, collective labour agreements, lower administrative burden and other forms of fiscal support systems.[381] Obviously, this type of infrastructural institutionalization provides a lot of support to entrepreneurs, as well as to the government government as regards their legal rights of taking measures to improve the competitiveness of the Dutch entrepreneurs and through them to the economy at large. As a matter of fact this form of institution development has a close linkage to the *'Polder Model'* or *'Consultation Economy'* as described above.

9.3.3 Socio-cultural aspects of society affecting entrepreneurship

Dutch society is egalitarian, individualistic and modern. In general entrepreneurs tend to view themselves as independent and self-reliant. In the research, which was carried out by Hofstede, the country scored very high in *individuality* (80%). Entrepreneurs value ability over dependency. This means that the relationship between the entrepreneur and his or her staff is considered to be a contract based on mutual advantages, whereby promotion decisions are based on

---

381 www.overlegeconomie.nl; info NCW, MKB-NL

merit only. Social mobility in the country is therefore is quite high. The more someone can contribute to the economy or the profitability of the enterprise, the more the person can grow into top positions, irrespective his or her descent. This also counts for members of ethnic minority groups in the country.

The management function of the entrepreneur is the management of individuals. This is also the reason why the *power distance* in enterprises is relatively low in The Netherlands (38%), which means that hierarchy in a company is considered to be for convenience only, whereby the entrepreneur is supposed to facilitate his staff in getting the right type of output, rather than demanding it. Organization structures in enterprises are usually flat instead of having a strong hierarchical (pyramid) model. The entrepreneur must be accessible and his staff expects to be consulted; communication is direct and participative.

Entrepreneurs have an aversion to the non-essential. Ostentatious behavior is to be avoided. Accumulating money is fine, but public spending of large amounts of money is considered something of a vice and associated with being a show-off. A high lifestyle is considered wasteful by most people and sometimes meets with suspicion. To a certain extent, this has also to do with what we have seen during the period of *Trade Capitalism*, where calvinism was given one of the reasons of this thrifty way of life. Hence, this attitude seems to be part if the Dutch gene-structure. This cultural value is highly correlated with the relatively high score (67%) in Hofstede's research on the issue of *pragmatism*. It means among others that entrepreneurs have a strong propensity to save and invest, to thriftiness and perseverance in achieving results.

At the international scene, Dutch manners are often considered to be blunt as a spin-off of a no-nonsense attitude, which is part of the local culture. For the Dutch it is a form of informality combined with adherence to basic behavior. This might be perceived as impersonal and patronizing by other cultures, but is the norm in Dutch culture, which values '*openness*' quite highly. More or less in contradiction to this trait is the fact that the society has a very strong *feminine culture* (86%), which explains why entrepreneurs strive for consensus. Conflicts are resolved by compromise and negotiation. An effective entrepreneur is supportive to his or her staff and decision-making is achieved through involvement.

Entrepreneurship in The Netherlands is a very *legitimate* activity. 85% of the population considers entrepreneurship as a desirable career and 69% among them give entrepreneurs a high level of status.[382] The Dutch society understands that entrepreneurship is very important for both the national economy and employment generation. In particular the small- and medium sized businesses in the country provide approximately 70% of total employment. This is also reason why the ministry of Economic Affairs is very keen on taking all sorts of measures to promote business development. At the same time entrepreneurs understand that they cannot be successful if they cannot count on full cooperation of their staff. And this again is reason for all parties to arrive at consensus in case there are conflicting interests.

Social mobility in The Netherlands is high. Merit is the key word for personal growth for both entrepreneur and employee. Irrespective birth or income, education for everyone is open, specifically taken into consideration the financial support given by the ministry of Education for those who want to do academic studies. In the year 2000 there were 114.000 businesses run by ethnic minority entrepreneurs, which is 14% of the total number of enterprises in the country. It appears, however, that non-western ethnic minority groups of - in particular - Moroccan, Turkish or Surinam origin are far less represented in entrepreneurship (43.000) than western ethnic minorities (71.000).[383]

Looking at the *social integration* of, in particular the non-Western ethnic minorities in to-days enterprising sector in The Netherlands, a big difference can be observed in comparing the migration wave since the 1970's with those during the period of *Trade Capitalism*.

---

382 GEM, The hidden entrepreneurial forces of the Dutch economy, in: *Global Entrepreneurship Monitor 2008 The Netherlands,* p.12
383 CBS, statistics on ethnic minority groups in The Netherlands

As has been described at length in the previous chapters, ethnic minorities were at that time coming from Flanders, Portugal and Spain (jewish merchants), from France (huguenots) and from other surrounding countries like Germany and Scandinavia. The majority of these immigrants could without many problems be integrated into the Dutch production and trading systems. As a matter of fact the majority of these immigrants had a business experience in their country of origin. This is different as compared to the ethnic minority groups that came to The Netherlands as from the 1970's and '80's. Based on a population of approximately 17 million inhabitants there were roughly 10% immigrants from non-Western origin, mainly from Asia, Turkey, Morocco and Surinam/Antilles. Percentagewise this is approximately the same as compared to the immigrants during the *Trade Capitalistic* period. The new immigrants, however, often have a backward position in society because of difficulties with native behaviour, language, religion and attitudes. The participation rate of ethnic minorities in the labour markets stays behind and, when they do participate, these jobs are often situated within the 'secondary' labour market occupations. One way for immigrant to escape their backward position is to become an entrepreneur. As compared to native entrepreneurs, ethnic business owners are more likely to start business in the service- and retail sectors that are characterized by low entry barrier and high competition, which increases the failure rate of these enterprises. In general the ethnic minorities often have the tendency to serve their own community with products and/or services.

Out of the 800.000 businesses in The Netherlands, there were in the year 2000 114.000 businesses in the Netherlands run by ethnic minority entrepreneurs. In 2009, the number of these ethnic entrepreneurs had increased to about 155.000. Their profit level is approximately 85% of the level of their native counterparts. In this respect, the age structure of the population of ethnic entrepreneurs may also play a role. Their prevalent age group hovers between 25 to 45 year, whereas indigenous entrepreneurs generally fall in the age brackets of 45 and 65 years. In other words, the more business experience entrepreneurs have, the better the business results will be. The second generation of immigrants – often born in The

Netherlands - are better equipped in terms of education and specifically language as compared to their parents. Their share of ethnic entrepreneurship has gone up to 7%, which is almost double as compared to the first generation of ethnic entrepreneurs (4%). This share can grow steadily in the coming years. The second generation also changes the nature of ethnic entrepreneurship. There is less interest in doing business in the hospitality industry and more in sectors such as business services.[384]

Another historical marginal group in the country has been the position of women in entrepreneurship. However, in the period 2000 to 2009, the proportion of female start-ups grew from 25% to 35% of the total number of starters. In absolute terms, the number of women entrepreneurs increased from around 300.000 to 350.000. In seven out of ten cases female entrepreneurs have a profitable business, but is still laging behind their male colleagues in that respect. The average profit of the female entrepreneur is about 60 percent of what male entrepreneurs generally generate. According to the researchers, the lower profit levels may be associated with different aspects of women's entrepreneurship. Women often have businesses in a service sector, which generally generates lower profit margins, such as laundries, hair salons and solariums.[385] Women are more inclined to start a business in retailing and services, sectors with a relatively low capital investment and more possibilities for part-time entrepreneurship. Women often have other activities next to their business, paid or unpaid (family, children), leading to time constraints and restricting their entrepreneurial activities.[386]

As regards the level of *need-achievement* in the Dutch society, the following observation can be made. About half of the Dutch adults who set up a new business or own and manage a young firm are active in the services sector. Motives put forward most often for starting a business are 'being independent' (55%), as

---
384 EIM, *Monitor female and ethnic entrepreneurship*, Zoetermeer 24.02.2011
385 EIM, *Monitor female and ethnic entrepreneurship*, Zoetermeer 24.02.2011
386 Verheul, I., a.o., *An eclectic theory of entrepreneurship: policies, institutions and culture*, Zoetermeer 2001, p. 30-32

well as 'accepting a challenge' (27%). Necessity-based motives are hardly heard in The Netherlands.[387] The combination of 'independence' and 'challenge' determine to a great extent the level of *'need achievement'* as was discussed in chapter 3. Significant of that trait, is that in a society with a high level of *need-achievement*, there is a preference for moderate risks and a belief that one's personal efforts will be influential in the attainment of the set goals. Furthermore, a high level need-achievement is not primarily motivated by financial incentives; monetary rewards only constitute a symbol of achievement. Taken into consideration the high level of individualism and challenge (together 83%), and a relatively low level of financial motivation (17%), the Dutch society may be considered to be one with a high level of *need achievement*.[388]

9.3.4 Entrepreneurial characteristics

Identity & orientation

Who are the present-day entrepreneurs and what are their motives? Dutch entrepreneurs are no longer coming from the traditional entrepreneurial families. There is much diversity among them, such as ethnic minority groups, women, former employees of existing enterprises or those that went bankrupt, and - in particular – many young people. These are entrepreneurs from micro-, small- and medium sized businesses. In quite a number of cases entrepreneurs of micro and small businesses are those that can be termed as part-time entrepreneur and they often work as 'own-account' entrepreneurs without staff, however often making use of their network in getting their product and/or service to the marketplace. This latter is in particular popular among new start-ups in businesses. They may still be studying or may have a part-time job in another enterprise for either income security or as a try-out in starting their own business.

Entrepreneurship in The Netherlands is considered by 85% of

---

[387] Bosman, & Sander Wennekers, *Entrepreneurial Attitudes versus Entrepreneurial Activities; Global Entrepreneurship Monitor 2003, The Netherlands*, Zoetermeer 2004, p. 1-5
[388] idem, p. 33-40

the population as a desirable career and has among 69% a high level of status.[389] This may also be the reason why during this period of *Total Capitalism* an increasing number of relatively high-level educated people have become entrepreneur. A rough estimate is that out of the current 800.000 enterprises in the country, there are approximately 200.000 entrepreneurs who were found to be highly educated and that number increases with 13.000 per each year. One third of all starting entrepreneurs in 1995 had finished their study in either High Professional Education (HBO) or at the university.[390]

Next to the group as mentioned above there is of course also the group of the very seasoned entrepreneurs, i.e. those of the large and multinational companies, such as Philips, Akzo-Nobel, DSM, Volker-Stevin, Endemol, ING, Ahold, ASML, etc. In research carried out in 1999 it was postulated, that the quality of these Dutch entrepreneurs was internationally assessed as people having a good command of foreign languages and dispose of a well-developed common sense next to great business acumen and business finance. As mentioned before, the Dutch has an aversion to the non-essential, which of course is also applicable to the entrepreneurs active in international markets and is often an additional reason for foreign companies to do business with Dutch entrepreneurs. From the survey of 50 of these top entrepreneurs, 40 of them had an academic degree, of which 6 with an academic-plus degree. And very much in contradiction with the period of *Trade Capitalism*, only 5 of them were of calvinistic religion and 11 of them catholics.[391]

What about the motives for them to be an entrepreneur? In research carried out by EIM and the Global Entrepreneurship Monitor 2003, motives for the entrepreneur to manage an enterprise (more than one motive was mentioned) are listed in table 4, below. This

---

[389] GEM, The hidden entrepreneurial forces of the Dutch economy, in: *Global Entrepreneurship Monitor 2008 The Netherlands*, p.12

[390] Bartels, C.P.A., Veel weten kan somtijds baten; over het commercialiseren van kennis, in: *Economenblad*, 25.01.1995, p. 1-2

[391] Crooijmans, H., Wie is de Nederlandse topman?; profiel van 50 grote beursgenoteerde bedrijven, in: *Elsevier*, nr. 39, 25.09.1999

issue of motivation has very much to do with the cultural trait of *'individuality'* which scores in The Netherlands 80 out of 100, as we have seen above in the research of Hofstede. This again points into the direction of a relatively high *need-achievement* of Dutch entrepreneurs involved in exercising their business.

Motives	2002	2003
Being your 'own boss'	64	55
Challenge	27	27
Earning more money compared to wage-earning	22	17
Pursuing a perceived new market opportunity	7	2
(Threat of) unemployment	7	2
Better possibilities to combine labour and nurturing	3	7
Dissatisfaction with current job	5	3
Other	17	10

Table 5 : Percentages of individuals in early-stage entrepreneurial activity (more than one answer possible); Bosman, M. & Sander Wennekers)

Entrepreneurial traits

What we have seen from the above is the present-day relatively highly educated (academic) level of the entrepreneur, which is so very different as compared to the entrepreneur during the *Trade Capitalistic* period. Then entrepreneurs were people who learned in practice how business had to be exercised. Very often they learned the trade by working in the family enterprise, or were sent to offices abroad, or had a chance to travel to other countries to look around. As a matter of fact, entrepreneurial knowledge was accumulated through practical actions, as well as through trial and error. Indeed, trial and error is also part of present-day entrepreneurship. Feeling, intuition, failure, trial and error are still very important and – for many researchers – the basic ingredients or traits for someone to become a successful entrepreneur. On the other hand, apart form the issue of 'educating society' - the cornerstone of human development since the Enlightment - present-day Dutch entrepreneurs in this period of *Total Capitalism* were confronted with a completely new world as compared to ever before: globalization, technology development, information & communication technology, free-trade zones, network & clustering, flexible labour market, social security, etc. Taken this into consideration, together with the worldwide competition and the search for (rapid) innovation, produced a well educated stock of entrepreneurs, who were keen not only to strive for continuity of their businesses, but to expand these as well in this knowledge-based economy.

Dutch entrepreneurs have a *positive self-concept*. This is part of the national cultural heritage of striving for *individualism* and *independence*. To be their own boss is preferred above being one of the (important) managers of a company, even if this goes at the expense of less income. Furthermore, entrepreneurship in the country is highly appreciated in the Dutch society, which is an additional factor in strengthening their self-confidence.

Entrepreneurs are 'challenge-prone' (27%). This, together with their strong inclination for individualism, leads to taking *initiatives* in many areas. This may relate to innovation of production, searching for new markets, identifying market niches, establishing clusters, etc. Important in that respect is that – in general terms – entrepreneurs are more focussed on trying to be successful with their initiatives, rather than the monetary incentive. However, taking initiatives also includes *taking risks*. Dutch entrepreneurs are no gamblers. The risk they take is a calculated risk. As a matter of fact risk-avoidance behaviour among Dutch entrepreneurs is higher than risk-taking, which inhibits the fear of failure, or bankruptcy that may prevent potential entrepreneurs to go into business. Contrary to other countries, particularly in the USA, bankruptcy of business is considered by the Dutch society as a personal failure, not so much as an experience to do better next time.

In a knowledge-based economy, innovation is the lifeline for success. *Innovation* is partly *creativity*, partly *opportunity seeking*, partly *alertness for competition* and partly to avail of *problem-solving* capabilities. The position of Dutch entrepreneurs in the innovation sub-index of the World Economic Forum of the year 2000 was at place six of all countries in the world. Since the year 2000 there was a lull in innovative activity in the country, however, because of supportive activities of the government Dutch entrepreneurs managed to become again more innovative.[392] Dutch entrepreneurs managed to get the third place in the number of patents applications that were granted in Europe in 2001 and the 11th country for patent application in the USA.[393] In other words, the entrepreneurial traits of *innovation, opportunity seeking* and *problem-solving capabilities* are strongly developed, taken into consideration the international position the Dutch entrepreneurs take in as far as innovation is concerned.

Given both the dynamic and static opportunity conditions for enterprising sector, in particular 'free trade', entrepreneurs are very *hopeful about the future*. Obviously they understand that globalization and free trade also mean competition in the home-market. So far Dutch entrepreneurs were able to be flexible and adaptable to changing circumstances in the world economy. Quite a big advantage in this 'new economy' is the ICT infrastructure, which is considered to be one of the best in the world. Given the fact that the present-day economy is a '24 hours economy' with fast communication needs, Dutch entrepreneurs are in a very good position to be able to at least maintain their competitiveness for the time being, if not to improve on that issue.

Before elaborating on the modernity of early Dutch entrepreneurship (chapter 9.4), in which we will show the entrepreneurial instruments as were developed during the period of *Trade Capitalism* and still practiced by present-day entrepreneurs, it may be informative to indicate how an international organization as OECD is assessing the quality of life in The Netherlands as per 2014. Without exaggeration, entrepreneurs - to quite some extent - have contributed to a situation, which may be termed as the Second Dutch Golden Age.

---

392 In 2013 the Netherlands took the 4th position, just after Switzerland, Sweden and the United Kingdom (Global innovation index 2013)
393 Ministry of Economic Affairs, *Analysis of the Dutch innovation position,* The Hague, 2003

OECD Economic Surveys: Netherlands 2014

How's Life?

The Netherlands performs well many measures of well-being, as shown by the fact that it ranks among the top countries in a large number of topics in the Better Life Index.

Money, while it cannot buy happiness, is an important means to achieving higher living standards. In the Netherlands, **the average household net-adjusted disposable income per capita is 29 697 USD a year**, more than the OECD average of 23 938 USD a year. But there is a considerable gap between the richest and poorest – the top 20% of the population earn more than four times as much as the bottom 20%.

In terms of employment, nearly **75% of people aged 15 to 64 in the Netherlands have a paid job**, above the OECD employment average of 65%. Some 80% of men are in paid work, compared with 70% of women. **People in the Netherlands work 1 381 hours a year**, less than the OECD average of 1 765 hours. **Less than 1% of employees work very long hours,** much lower than the OECD average of 9%, with **1% of men working very long hours, compared with almost no women.**

Having a good education is an important requisite for finding a job. In the Netherlands, **72% of adults aged 25-64 have earned the equivalent of a high-school degree**, slightly lower than the OECD average of 75%. This is slightly truer of men than women, as 74% of men have successfully completed high-school compared with 71% of women. In terms of the quality of the education system, **the average student scored 522 in reading literacy, maths and science in the OECD's Programme for International Student Assessment (PISA).** This score is higher than the OECD average of 497, making the

Netherlands one of the strongest OECD countries in students' skills. **On average in the Netherlands, girls outperformed boys by 5 points**, less than the average OECD gap of 9 points.

In terms of health, **life expectancy at birth in the Netherlands is 81 years**, one year higher than the OECD average of 80 years. Life expectancy for women is 83 years, compared with 79 for men. **The level of atmospheric PM10** – tiny air pollutant particles small enough to enter and cause damage to the lungs – **is 30 micrograms per cubic meter**, considerably higher than the OECD average of 20.1 micrograms per cubic meter. The Netherlands perform better in terms of water quality, as **94% of people say they are satisfied with the quality of their water**, higher than the OECD average of 84%.

Concerning the public sphere, there is a strong sense of community and high levels of civic participation in the Netherlands, where **92% of people believe that they know someone they could rely on in time of need**, higher than the OECD average of 89%. **Voter turnout**, a measure of public trust in government and of citizens' participation in the political process, **was 75% during recent elections**; this figure is higher than the OECD average of 72%. Social and economic status can affect voting rates; voter turnout for the top 20% of the population is an estimated 84% and for the bottom 20% it is an estimated 65%. This 19-percentage point difference is much larger than the OECD average difference of 11 percentage points, and points to shortcomings in the political mobilisation of those of lower socio-economic status.

In general, **82% of people in the Netherlands say they have more positive experiences in an average day** (feelings of rest, pride in accomplishment, enjoyment, etc.) **than negative ones** (pain, worry, sadness, boredom, etc.), more than the OECD average of 76%.

9.4 Modernity of early Dutch entrepreneurship

What has been a striking phenomenon in this analysis is the modernity of entrepreneurship and its performance during the heydays of *'Trade Capitalism'* (1580-1670) when compared with today's performances of entrepreneurship. When applying the four dimensions, based on modern theories of entrepreneurship, to the beginnings of the modern world economy in The Netherlands, we see images of entrepreneurs, which - in essence - do not differ from nowadays entrepreneurs. The definition of modern entrepreneurship as adopted in chapter 2 of this study was *'the ability and willingness of individuals, both on their own and within organisations, to: a) perceive and create new economic opportunities; b) introduce their ideas in the market, in the face of uncertainty and other obstacles, by making decisions on location, form and the use of resources and institutions; c) compete with others for a share of that market'*. Looking at the three elements of this definition, which is based on 21st century entrepreneurship, and apply these to the 'early Dutch entrepreneurs', we see that also they *'perceived and created new economic opportunities, i.e. new products, new production methods, new organisational schemes and new product-market-combinations'*. These early Dutch entrepreneurs, indeed, developed new products, such as better quality beer, dairy products, newly designed ships, new textile products and a lot more, as is evidenced by the many registered inventions. Also new production methodologies were introduced, such as for instance the processing of herring, shipbuilding technologies which made use of separately manufactured spare parts, processing of many foods stuffs through wind-mill technologies, etc. They developed new organisational schemes, such as partnerships, but also introduced and set-up the first limited liability company in the world. In addition, they founded large multinational corporations (de Geer in Sweden), as well as trading houses, which survived until in the second part of the 20th century. And also in the case of creating PMCs (product-market-combinations) the early Dutch entrepreneur knew what products to manufacture and services to develop for specific markets and business groups. They diversified their textile production in terms of specific quality and price for certain markets (cloth from Leyden); for transportation of mass merchandise (grain) they designed and developed specific ships (large holds and less crew) for ship-owners so as to enable them to transport mass merchandise economically. And also in services, Dutch entrepreneurs developed new products for the international business community, such as cartography for sailors, insurances for ships and cargo, ship brokering, communication, information and financial services, etc.

As regards the second part of the definition, *'introducing their ideas in the market, in the face of uncertainty and other obstacles, by making decisions on location, form and the use of resources and institutions'*, the early Dutch entrepreneurs knew very well how to introduce their ideas in the market, given the many foreign markets where they were active, ranging from the north of Europe (Archangel, Baltic Sea) to the south in the Mediterranean (Venice, Levant, Aleppo). They did that in the face of a lot of uncertainty and obstacles, such as the confrontation of pirates and ships of warring nations (Spanish, British). There was hardly any weather forecast, so ships went out and had to deal with bad weather with ships that were far less fit to overcome severe weather conditions than the vessels we have nowadays. International law was non-existent, hence, the international businesses environment less secure, as regards payments, fraud and the like. Although the speed of the business transactions were so much less than at present times, also in these days quick decisions had to be made. As discussed before, a case in point was the sudden refusal of Spanish harbours to receive ships from the Republic to do business in Asian spices. This barrier ignited Dutch transporters and entrepreneurs to go directly to Asia for collecting spices themselves directly from the source, thereby eliminating both the Arabs and Spanish business people. Another example was that entrepreneurs, due to soil-contaction in agricultural areas, switched over to animal husbandry (dairy products) and the importation of large volumes of grain. Surplus of grain was than used for the production of high quality beer for the export market. Decisions also had to be made related to the form and use of resources and institutions. The way in which peat and wind as energy resources were used for proto-industrial purposes and the way these were institutionalised brought the Republic at its economic zenith. Entrepreneurs understood that in spite of their individualistic nature 'institution building' was an import ingredient for business continuity, which is so overwhelmingly proven by the decisions to establish the VOC, the WIC, the various chambers in the country, the various fishery directorates, associations of entrepreneurs, and the like. Also they knew, that the stronger the intermediate business support organisations and institutions were, the better they would be able to conduct their businesses profitably. These institutions, as by to-day's standards were able to lower transactional costs. This gave them a head-start in international competition.

The third component of the definition, *'competing with others for a share of that market'*, was an activity in which the early Dutch entrepreneur was very well versed. Because of their nautical skills and appropriate vessels, entrepreneurs navigated all over Europe and explored areas to do business with. In the 1650's they had so many foreign markets that it required a number of ships for transportation that was larger than all ships of Europe combined. However, competition was always luring around the corner from competing entrepreneurs in Spain and Portugal and in particular those from England and France. By doing smart business, Dutch entrepreneurs were able to keep ahead of international competition, specifically by regularly innovating their products and production techniques, as well as to make an optimum use of the dynamics and static opportunity conditions they had. However, when it came to military force as a result of protectionist measures, the Republic with a mere 1.9 million inhabitants was no match for England and France with a combined population of 26 million. Apart from the brute force of violence, competitiveness of these nations also increased, due to the new modalities in production techniques (coal, steam, iron), which allowed mass production of a – for that time - unprecedented level. This had a direct effect on the cost price of merchandise, which the Dutch could not meet. In addition, Dutch businesses also suffered from the the so-called *'inhibitory lead'*. This meant that switching over from old to new technologies (coal, iron, ore), was initially not profitable at all in comparison to existing production technologies based on peat, wind and wood.

When going over all the four dimensions of the research and comparing the modern definition of entrepreneurship with the early Dutch entrepreneur, we have seen behaviour and initiatives in setting up and developing associations and business services, as well as developed business techniques, which to-day are still extremely valid. In that sense, the present-day entrepreneurs stand on the shoulders of his counterparts of the 17th century. Most of these innovations are to be found in the dimension of 'Institution Development', specifically as regards the development of Business Services, Business Associations and government incentive programs. Below follows an inventory of the innovations as made by the 17th century entrepreneurs, which are still applicable in this era of '*Total Capitalism*'.

Business Services

Financial instruments

- Bill of Exchange (originally coming from the Italian city states, albeit refined by Dutch entrepreneurs)
- Promissory notes
- Founding the first Exchange Bank of Amsterdam for deposits and reimbursements
- Setting up the Bourse for attracting investments and speculation
- Dealing in futures, thereby reducing risks and safeguarding supplies
- Emission services for new business ventures to be founded
- Developing credit instruments:
    - Acceptance credit
    - Loans for micro entrepreneurs

Brokering services

- Agents for cargo space (identifying ships and cargo space for certain destinations and specific time)
- Agents for insurance of freight and/or ships
- Agents for storage of merchandise (places, prices, time)

Book keeping services

- Double entry book keeping as had already been developed in the Italian city states, however furthermore refined during *Trade Capitalism*

Notary services

- Determining legal contracts and arrangements for local and foreign entrepreneurs

Information services

- Daily pricelist of 205 commodities
- Establishing the very first newspaper with local and international news
- Collecting and processing incoming news from abroad and the dissemination thereof
- Establishing a European printing centre for books and other publications partly meant for improving business skills

Mailing services

- Domestically and abroad; related to commercial business activitiesBusiness associations

Business associations

- Branch organizations for employers (Guilds)
- Business clusters: business support organizations per branch for both employers and employees (Neringen), so as to promote the joint production for certain markets
- Consortia and partnerships as forms of short term cooperation among selected entrepreneurs for a certain commercial venture
- Public/private directorates (*Publiekrechtelijke Bedrijfs-Organisatie –PBO*)

- Collegae of Fisheries
- Levant Trade
- Nordic Company

Government incentive programs

Infrastructure

- Regulated market places
- Roofed halls for doing business
- Pawn shops for taking surplus of unsold merchandise
- Reclamation of land for business purposes
- Canal digging (in support of peat transportation and distribution of merchandise)

Support to nascent entrepreneurship

- Tax exemption
- Use of equipment free of cost or at a small fee
- Raw material provision for micro and small businesses
- Loan offices for micro and small entrepreneurs when shortage of cash at short term
- Making business localities available

Attracting new (proto-industrial) businesses

- Employment generation
- Poverty reduction
- Creating purchasing power

Finance

- Re-organising mint system (reducing number of mints and establishing fixed values per unit mint)
- Guaranteeing deposits at the Amsterdam Exchange Bank
- Regulating the operations of the Bourse and taking corrective action when developments run out of hand (tulpmania)

Protection

- Allowing monopolies when opportune (VOC, WIC, Whale fishery), so as to meet foreign competition
- Protecting free trade as a principle of doing business
- Registering patents submitted by entrepreneurs/innovators
- Arming ships for the protection of trading vessels when on a journey.
- Promotion
- A number of 20 consuls and diplomats were assigned in markets abroad in order to promote Dutch products and to build up a network of clients to be used by entrepreneurs for conducting business (the commercial attaché of the nowadays embassies abroad)

How did entrepreneurs create new business opportunities; how did they introduce their ideas in the market, when facing obstacles and uncertainties and how did they compete with their domestic and specifically their foreign competitors?

Some of the answers have been given above in listing the business services and government incentive programs, which were developed – often in close consultation with entrepreneurs, because of their seats in city councils. An additional answer may be the development of business techniques, which entrepreneurs developed and implemented - techniques that hardly differ from sophisticated entrepreneurship of the 21st century.

Business techniques

Marketisation

- Producing specific products to the needs of the various target groups in the world market
- Offering large quantities of merchandise at relatively low margins, hence safeguarding high profits (mass merchandising)
- Developing product-market-combinations (PMCs) in selected product lines

- Constant diversification and innovation of existing- or new products (beer, textile, ship building, etc.)

Productivity improvement

- Time management in production processes (herring buss)
- Mechanization by using:
  - windmills for production and/or processing purposes
  - peat for warmth technology in producing consumer- or construction goods (ceramics, tiles, bricks)
  - standardization in production by applying mechanized instruments (windmills) and using interchangeable components/parts (shipbuilding)

Competitiveness

- High quality merchandise through independent quality control (certification/seal by local governments)
- Applying economies of scale, thereby reducing cost price (grain, timber, fisheries)
- Constant innovation of products and transport means in order to keep abreast of competition

Setting up distribution channels

- Regulating weekly markets
- Shops to be established (initially in combination with manufacturing; later only for product ranges, processed or manufactured by others)
- Establishing trading houses (active till far in the 20th and 21st centuries)
- Setting up the Commission Trade; agents as intermediates between demand and supply of merchandise against a certain percentage (often around 2% to 3 %)
- Establishing offices for business representatives abroad
- Foreign offices taking care for the interest of a certain company they represented

- Offices in, among others, Archangel, Sweden. Levant, Aleppo, etc.

Advancing funds to suppliers or producers in order to secure raw material for the business, or for final product for sale

- For finished products, for example, advances in the textile business to small commodity producers (funds, and equipment)
- For raw material specifically in the agricultural sector to provide advances before the harvest would take place (wine, grain, timer, etc.)

Setting up Limited Liability Companies
(in close consultation with the government)

- Shareholding by private sector
- Generating investments which were too large for individuals

As by to-days standards, successful entrepreneurship is all about competitiveness. And that is exactly where also entrepreneurs in the 17th century were aiming at. And competitiveness was then achieved by making use of: 1) the static and dynamic opportunity conditions, 2) increasing productivity, 3) constant innovation of products, services, instruments and the like and 4) the development of supporting institutions.

The creation of the republic in the 16th century, the drive of independence, the creation of the nation state was to quite some extent the result of dynamic entrepreneurship. The creation of wealth as a consequence of international trade and the resulting strong economic development of the country made it possible to survive economically and politically. But there was more than that. Dutch entrepreneurship created a new modern economy, which was fundamentally different as compared to the period prior to 1500. That economy has led via the various revolutions (industrial, electronic) to to-days economy. Even, in our era, free trade has come back after the Dutch had to fight trade wars and to cope with protectionism of big economic powers. Free trade is indeed the world in which Dutch entrepreneurs, then and nowadays again, flourish. One might say that to-day's strength of Dutch entrepreneurship, resulting in the second Golden Age for the country, is to a very high extent the result of what earlier entrepreneurs from the first Golden Age indeed established.

BIBLIOGRAPHY

Abbink Spaink, J.J. , *IJsselstein; verleden en heden,* Municipality of IJsselstein, 1963.

Aten, D., Amsterdamse gilden en regenten contra de Zaanse nijverheid, in: Lesger, C. & l. Noordergraaf (eds.), *Ondernemers en Bestuurders; Economie en politiek in de noordelijke Nederlanden in de late Middeleeuwen en vroegmoderne tijd,* Amsterdam, 1999, p 61-76

Audretch, D.B. & A.R. Thurik, *The Knowledge Society, Entrepreneurship and Unemployment,* EIM Research Report 9801/E, Zoetermeer, 1998

Aymard, M. ed., Dutch Capitalism and World Capitalism, Cambridge, 1982

Baillien, H., *Tongeren, Belgie's oudste stad,* Tongeren, 1965.

Baumol, W.J., Entrepreneurship: Productive, Unproductive and Destructive, in: *Journal of Political Economy,* (1990) 98(5) 893-921.

Bautier, R.H., *The Economic Development of Medieval Europe,* London, 1971.

Beaud, M., *Geschiendenis van het kapitalisme; Van 1500 tot heden,* (A..Abeling, E. Van Empel, G. Papa, Trans. Histoire du capitalisme, de 1500 à nos jours, 1990/94), Utrecht, 1994.

Beekelaar, G..A. M., a.o. (ed), *Vaderlands Verleden in Veelvoud; 31 opstellen over de Nederlandse geschiedenis na 1500,* The Hague, 1975.

Berg, J.TH.J. van den & Molleman, H..A..A., *Crisis in de Nederlandse politiek,* Alphen aan de Rijn, 1975.

Boer, D. de, & J. de Vries, *Moderne Geschiedenis van Nederland,* Amsterdam, 1965.

Bosma, N., *The Long Road to the Entrpreneurial Society,* Zoetermeer, 2002

Bosma, N., Entrepreneurship unxer pressure, in: Global Entrepreneurship Monitor 2002 The Netherlands, Zoetermeer, 2002

Baut, J.K., *A Dutch approach for creating growth and employment,* Leusden, 1999

Braudel, F., *Beschaving, Economie en Kapitalisme (15de-18de eeuw); Het Spel van de Handel, Deel II,* (E. Gratama, K van Gulik, G. Rombach, Trans. Civilisation matérielle, Economie et Capitalisme XVe-XVIIIe siècle. Tom 2: Les Jeux de l'échange, 1979), Amsterdam, 1989.

Bruggeman, J. & A. Camijn, *Ondernemersverbonden; 100 jaar centrale ondernemersorganisaties in Nederland,* Wormer, 1999

Brugmans, I.J., *De arbeidende klasse in Nederland in de 19e eeuw 1813-1870,* Utrecht, 1978

Bruin, J.R., Scheepvaart en overheid omstreeks 1600, in: Lesger C. & L. Noordergraaf (eds), *Ondernemers en Bestuurders; Economie en politiek in de noordelijke Nederlanden in de late Middeleeuwen en vroegmoderne tijd,* Amsterdam, 1999, p 77-84

Bruijn, M.W.J. de, e.a., de Utrechters en hun nijverheid, and, de Utrechters en hun handel, in: *Ach Lieve Tijd; Dertien eeuwen Utrecht en de Utrechters,* numbers 4 and 11 resp., Zwolle, 1984.

Bruins, A., *Ondernemerschap na de eeuwwisseling; een strategische verkenning,* EIM/Algemeen Economisch Beleid, Zoetermeer, 1996.

Cameron, R., *A Concise Economic History of the World; From Palaeolithic Times to the Present,* Oxford, 1997

Cole, G.D.H., *Introduction to Economic History 1750-1950,* London, 1978.

Colenbrander, S., Haarlems stadbestuur in textiel, in: *Ondernemers en Bestuurders; Economie en politiek in de noordelijke Nederlanden in de late Middeleeuwen en vroegmoderne tijd,* Amsterdam, 1999, p 85-108

Crooijmans, H., Wie is de Nederlandse topman?; Profiel van de leiders van 50 grote beurtsgenoteerde bedrijven, in: *Elsevier,* 25.09.1999, p. 84-96

Cuppen, A.J., *Twintig jaar maatschappij en onderneming beleft door Frank Sweens,* SMO-boek, The Hague, 1990.

Curtin, P. D., *Cross-Cultural Trade in World History,* Cambridge, 1984.

Daalder, R. (ed.), Goud uit graan; Nederland en het Oostzee gebied 1600-1850, Zwolle, 1999

Dale, E. (ed.), *Readings in Management; Landmarks and new frontiers,* New York, 1965.

Davids, C.A., W. Fritschy, L.A. van der Valk (eds), *Kapitaal, Ondernemerschap en Beleid; Studies over Economie en Politiek in Nederland, Europa en Azië van 1500 tot Heden*, Amsterdam, 1996.

Davids, C.A., Neringen, hallen en gilden. Kapitalisten, kleine ondernemers en stedelijke overheid in de tijd van de Reupbliek, in: Davids, C.A. a.o. (eds), *Kapitaal, Ondernemerschap en Beleid; Studies over Economische Politiek in Nederland, Europe en Azië van1500 tot Heden,* Amsterdam, 1996, p 95-120

Davids, C.A., Deregulering in de stedelijke exportnijverheid in de vroegmoderne tijd. Beschouwingen over de Republiek in Europees perspectief, in: Lesger, C. & L. Noordergraaf (eds), *Ondernemers en Bestuurders; Economie en politiek in de noordelijke Nederlanden in de late Middeleeuwen en vroegmoderne tijd,* Amsterdam, 1999, p 109-129

De Soto, Hermando, The Mystery of Capital; why capitalism triumphs in the West and fails everywhere else, London, 2001

Deursen, A. Th. Van, *Mensen van klein vermogen; Het kopergeld van de gouden Eeuw,* Amsterdam, 1996.

Demey, J., *De Historische Twee-Eenheid Der Nederlanden,* Brugge, 1978.

Dillen, J.G. van, Omstandigheden en physische factoren in de economische geschiedenis van Nederland, in: Beekelaar, G.A.M., a.o. (eds) *Vaderlands Verleden iin Veelvoud, 31 opstellen over de Nederlandse geschiedenis na 1500,* Den Haag 1975, p 337-363

Dockum, C.G. van & E.J. van Ginkel, *Romeins Nederland; Archeologie & geschiedenis van een grensgebied,* Utrecht 1993.

Dollinger, P., *De Hanze; opkomst, bloei en ondergang van een handelsverbond,* Utrecht, 1967.

Donckels, R.T., Degadt, J, Dupont, B., *KMO's in België; sociaal-economische betekenis,* Leuven, 1988.

Dorren, G. Stadsbestuur en ambachtsgilden in Haarlem in de zeventiende eeuw, in: Lesger, C. & L. Noordergraaf (eds), *Ondernemers en Bestuurders; Economie en politiek in de noordelijke Nederlanden in de late Middeleeuwen en vroegmoderne tijd,* Amsterdam, 1999, p 129-138

Dorren, G., 'Want noijt gebeurt dat een vrouw meester is geworden...' Vrouwen en gilden in de zeventiende eeuwse Haarlem, in:

Lesger, C. & L. Noordergraaf (eds), *Ondernemers en Bestuurders; Economie en politiek in de noordelijke Nederlanden in de late Middeleeuwen en vroegmoderne tijd,* Amsterdam, 1999, p 139-152

Dreesmann, A.C.R., & E. van der Wolk, (eds), *Dynamiek in de Distributie,* parts 1 and 2, Amsterdam, 1975.

Driel, H. Van, *De Vorming en de Ontwikkeling van de Middenstand in Nederland tot 1940,* Erasmus University, Rotterdam, 1984.

Dijk, J. van & F. Boekema, (eds), *Innovatie in bedrijf en regio*, Assen, 1998

Drucker, Peter F., *The new markets ...and other essays*, London, 1971

Drucker, Peter F., *Management*, New York, 1977

Economist, *Manufacturing*, survey, London, June 20, 1998.

Economist, *Innovation in Industry*, survey, London, Feb.20, 1999.

Eerenbeemt, H.F.J.M. van den, De Patriotse-Bataafse-Franse tijd (1780-1813) in: Stuijvenberg, J.H. van (ed), *De economische geschiedenis van Nederland,* Groningen, 1977

Egmond, F., De strijd om het dagelijks bier. Brouwerijen, groothandel in bier en economische politiek in de noordelijke Nederlanden tijdens de zestiende eeuw, in: Lesger, C. & L. Noordergraaf (eds), *Ondernemers en Bestuurders; Economie en politiek in de noordelijke Nederlanden in de late Middeleeuwen en vroegmoderne tijd,* Amsterdam, 1999, p 153-194

EIM & Ministry of Economic Affairs, *Entrepreneurship in the Netherlands: Ambitious entrepreneurs; the driving force for the next millennium,* Zoetermeer, 1999.

EIM & Ministry of Economic Affiars, *Entrepreneurship in the Netherlands: New economy; new entrepreenurs!,* Zoermeer, 2001

EIM & Ministry of Economic Affairs, *Entrepreneurship in the Netherlands: Opportunities and threarts to nascent entrepreneurship,* Zoetermeer, 2002

EIM & Ministry of Economic Affiars, *Entrepreneurship in the Netherlands. Ten years entreprenruship policy: a global overview*, Zoetermeer, 2009

EIM, *Kleinschalig ondernemen 1991; trends in het midden- en kleinbedrijf,* Zoetermeer, 1991

EIM, *Kleinschalig ondernemen 1993; Dynamiek en ondernemersklimaat,* Zoetermeer, 1993

EIM, *Strategies and characteristics of SME entrepreneurs going international*, Zoetermeer 1997

EIM, *Ondernemen in de Sectoren*, Zoetermeer 2008

Elias, N., *Het Civilisatieproces; Sociogenetische en psychogenetische onderzoekingen*, Parts 1 and 2 (W. Kranendonk e.a. Transl. Über den Prozess der Zivilisation, Sociogenetishe und psychogenetische Untersuchungen), Utrecht, 1983.

Elliot, J.H., *Europe Devided 1559-1598,* London, 1976.

Engels, M.C., Kooplieden en politiek. Botsende belangen in de handel in ruwe zijde aan het begin van de zeventiende eeuw, in: Lesger, C. & L. Noordergraaf (eds), *Ondernemers en Bestuurders; Economie en politiek in de noordelijke Nederlanden in de late Middeleeuwen en vroegmoderne tijd,* Amsterdam, 1999, p 195-202

Enthoven, V., Een symbiose tussen koopman en regent. De tweetrapsraket van de opkomst van de Republiek en Zeeland, in: Lesger, C. & L. Noordergraaf (eds), *Ondernemers en Bestuurders; Economie en politiek in de noordelijke Nederlanden in de late Middeleeuwen en vroegmoderne tijd,* Amsterdam, 1999, p 203-236

Faber, J.A. , De achttiende eeuw, in: Stuijvenberg, J.H. van, (ed), *De economische geschiedenis van Nederland,* Groningen, 1977

Fayol, H., *General and Industrial Management*, London 1971 (translation of: Administration industrielle et générale, Paris, 1916

Fischer, E.J., *Geschiedenis van de Techniek; Inleiding, overzcht en thema's,* Den Haag, 1980.

Frijthof, W., Hollands identiteit in de vroegmoderne tijd, in: *Spiegel Historiael,* januari 2000, p 34-40

Fukuyama, F., *The End of History and the Last Man,* New York, 1992.

Fukuyama, F., *Trust: The Social Virtues and the Creation of Prosperity,* London, 1995.

Gelderblom, O., De deelname van de Zuid-Nederlandse kooplieden aan het openbare leven in Amsterdam (1578-1650), in: : Lesger, C. & L. Noordergraaf (eds), *Ondernemers en Bestuurders; Economie en politiek in de noordelijke Nederlanden in de late Middeleeuwen en vroegmoderne tijd,* Amsterdam, 1999, p 237-258

Gelderblom, O., *Zuid-Nederlandse kooplieden en de opkomst van de Amsterdamse stapelmarkt,* Utrecht, 1999 (Manuscript).

Gelderblom, O., The Political Economy of Foreign Trade in England and the Dutch Republic (1550-1650), Utrecht (UU), undated.

Gelderblom, O., *The golden Age of the Dutch Republic*, Utrecht (UU), 2008.

Gelderen, M.W. van, *Ontluikend ondernemerschap; een studie naar mensen die bezig zijn met het opzetten van een bedrijf (nascent entrepreneurs)*, Zoetermaar, 1999

Geyl, P., *Geschiedenis van de Nederlandse Stam,* part I to VI, Amsterdam, 1961.

Geyl, P., *Verzamelde opstellen,* parts 1 to 4, Utrecht, 1978.

Goff, J. Le, *De woekeraar en de Hel; Economie en Religie in de Middeleeuwen,* (L. Knippenberg Trans. La bourse et la vie; Economie et religion au Moyen Age), Amsterdam, 1996.

Goor, J. van, *Indië/Indonesië; Van Kolonie tot Natie,* Utrecht, 1987.

Goor, J. van, *De Nederlandse Koloniën; Geschiedenis van de Nederlandse expansie 1600-1975,* Den Haag 1994.

Goudsbloem, J., e.a. (eds), *Hoofdstukken uit de socioloogie,* Utrecht 1977.

Groenveld, S. Adriaen Pauw (1585-1653) een pragmatisch Hollands staatsman, in: *Spiegel Histotiael*, oktober 1985, p 432-439

Hamer, E., *Was ist ein Unternehmer?; Was verdanken ihm Betrieb und Gesellschaft?,* München, 2001

Hampson, H., *The First European Revolution 1776-1815,* London, 1970.

Hartwell, R.N., *The causes of the Industrial Revolution in England*, London 1967

Hébert, R.F. & A.N. Link, *The Entrepreneur; Mainstream Views and Radical Critiques,* New York, 1982

Hessels, J., Nieuw ondernemerschap in herstel, in: *Global entrepreneurship Monitor 2004 Nederland*

Hessels, J., The Hidden Entrepreneurial forces of the Dutch economy, in: *Global Entrepreneurship Monitor 2008 The Netherlands,* Zoetermeer 2009

Heuvel, D. van den, Women & entrepreneurship; Female traders in the Northern Netherlands, c. 1580-1815, Amsterdam 2007

Hobsbawn, E.J., *The Age of Revolution; Europe 1789-1848,* London, 1973.

Hoefnagels, H., *Een eeuw sociale problematiek; De Nederlandse Sociale ontwikkeling van 1850 tot 1940*, Alphen aan de Rijn, 1977.
Houtte, J..A. van, *Economische Geschiedenis; De Historische Wording van de Hedendaagsche Wereldeconomie*, Antwerpen, 1942.
Houtte, J.A., De zestiende eeuw (ca. 1485-ca 1585, in: Stuijvenberg, J.H. van, (ed.), *De economische geschiedenis van Nederland*, Groningen, 1977
Howell, R., *Cromwell*, London, 1977
Hughes, H. Stuart, *Consciousness and Society; The Reorientation of European Social Thought 1890-1930*, New York, 1977
Huisman, H. & W.J. de Ridder, *Vernieuwend Ondernemen; Een Analyse van de Relatie tussen Ondernemersklimaat en Economische Ontwikkeling*, The Hague, 1984
Huizinga, J., How Holland became a Nation, in: Beekelaar, G.A.M., a.o. (eds), *Vaderlands Verleden in Veelvoud; 31 opstellen over de Nederlandse geschiedenis na 1500*, The Hague, 1975.
Huizinga, J., *Herfstij Der Middeleeuwen; Studie over levens en gedachtenvormen der veertiende en vijftiende eeuw in Frankrijk en de Nederlanden*, Groningen, 1986
Hunt, E.S. & J.M. Murray, *A history of Business in Medieval Europe 1200-1550*, Cambridge 1999
ING, Internationale groeikansen vor het MKB, 2012
Israel, J.I., *Nederland als Centrum van de Wereldhandel, 1585-1740* (F. Van Meurs and R. Tersmette Transl. Dutch Primacy in World Trade, 1585-1740, 1989), Franeker, 1991
Israel, J.I., Dutch economy during the Thirty Years' War, in: Davids, C.A. a.o. (eds), *Kapitaal, Ondernemerschap en Beleid; Studies over Economische Politiek in Nederland, Europe en Azië van1500 tot Heden*, Amsterdam, 1996, p 77-94
Jacobs, D., *De economische kracht van Nederland*, Utrecht, 1990
Jacobs, E.M., *Koopman in Azië; De handel van de Verenigde Oost-Indische Compagnie tijdens de 18e eeuw*, Zutphen, 2000
Jansen, H.P.H., *Middeleeuwse Geschiedenis der Nederlanden*, Utrecht, 1979.
Jappe Alberts, W., *De Nederlandse Hanzesteden*, Haarlem, 1965.
Jappe Alberts, W., *De Middeleeuwse Stad*, Bussum, 1980.

Jones, J.R., *Britain and Europe in the Seventeenth Century*, London, 1976.

Jong, A.G.M. de, & C.W.A.M. van Paridon, *De economische geschiedenis van West-Europa in vogelvlucht; een speurtocht naar groeibepalende factoren*, Centraal Planbureau, Den Haag, 1989.

Jong, M., Kooplieden en hun belangen in overheidsfinancien van de Republiek: bilaterle subsidies en leningen als 'case study' 1615-1630, in: Lesger, C. & L. Noordergraaf (eds), *Ondernemers en Bestuurders; Economie en politiek in de noordelijke Nederlanden in de late Middeleeuwen en vroegmoderne tijd*, Amsterdam, 1999, p 277-298

Jonker, J. & K. Sluyterman, *Thuis op de wereldmarkt; Nederlandse handelshuizen door de eeuwen heen*, Den Haag, 2000

Junker, D., Over de legitimiteit van waardeoordelen in de sociale wetenschappen en de geschiedenis. In: *Boer, T. De & Kobben, A.J. (eds.), Waarden en wetenschap*, Bilthoven 1974, pp 172-199.

Kamerling, R.N.J., (ed), *Indonesië toen en nu*, Intermediair, Amsterdam, 1980.

Kappelhof, A.C.M., Twee Bredase ondernemers en hun verleden: Johan de Wyse (1635-1725) en Jacob Beens ((ca 1615-1673), in: Lesger, C. & L. Noordergraaf (eds), *Ondernemers en Bestuurders; Economie en politiek in de noordelijke Nederlanden in de late Middeleeuwen en vroegmoderne tijd*, Amsterdam, 1999, p 299-324

Kaptein, H., De Haarlemse overheid en de trasformatie van de lakennijverheid, 1516-1530, in: Lesger, C. & L. Noordergraaf (eds), *Ondernemers en Bestuurders; Economie en politiek in de noordelijke Nederlanden in de late Middeleeuwen en vroegmoderne tijd*, Amsterdam, 1999, p 325-348

Kastelein, T.J., *Groei naar industriele samenleving*, Groningen, 1984.

Kennedy, P., *The Rise and Fall of the Great Powers; Economic Change and Military Conflict from 1500 to 2000*, London, 1989.

Kerste, R., *Regionale clusters nader bekeken*. Zoetermeer, 2001

Keuning, D. & D.J. Eppink, *Management en Organisatie; Theorie en Toepassing*, Leiden, 1985

Klein, P.W., De Zeventiende Eeuw (1585-1700),in: Stuijvenberg, J.H. van, (ed), *De economische geschiedenis van Nederland*, Groningen, 1977

Klein, P.W. *Kapitaal en Pré-industriële Ontwikkeling in Nederland in de Factor Kapitaal;* Rotterdamse Monetaire Studies, nr. 4, Rotterdam, 1982

Klein, P.W., Kapitaal en stagnatie tijdens het hollandse vroegkapitalisme, in: Lesger, C. & L. Noordergraaf (eds), *Ondernemers en Bestuurders; Economie en politiek in de noordelijke Nederlanden in de late Middeleeuwen en vroegmoderne tijd,* Amsterdam, 1999, p 299-324

Kleinpenning, J.W.G., *Profiel van de derde wereld; een inleiding tot de geografie van de ontwikkeling,* Assen, 1978

Kooijmans, L., Risk and Reputation; On the Mentality of Merchants in the Early Modern Period, in: Lesger, C. & L. Noordergraaf (eds), *Entrepreneur and Entrepreneurship in Early Modern Times; Merchants and Industrialists* within *the Orbit of the Dutch Staple Market,* Den Haag, 1995

Korthals Altes, W., Valuta in de wissel van de tijd. De Nederlandse gulden in het internationaal betaalverkeer vanaf de zestiende eeuw, in: Spiegel Historiael Themanummer: *Van Elektron tot Euro. Geld en Geldpolitiek door de eeuwen heen,* juli/augustus 1999, p 334-343

Kossmann, E.H., *De Lage Landen 1780-1940; Anderhalve eeuw Nederland en België,* Amsterdam, 1976.

Kotler, Ph., *Marketing Management; Analysis, Planning and Control,* New Jersey, 1980

Kotler, Ph. & K. Cox, *Marketing Management and Strategy; A Reader,* New Jersey, 1984

Kranenburg, M, & K. van der Malen, *Het tijdperk Lubbers 1982-1994,* NRC Handelsblad, Rotterdam, 1994.

Kuip, I. Van der, *Early development of entrepreneurial qualities; the role of initial education,* EIM Strategic Study, Zoetermeer, 1998

Landes, D., *The Wealth And Poverty Of Nations,* London, 1999

Lesger, C., *Handel In Amsterdam ten tijde van de Opstand; Kooplieden, commerciële expansie en veranderingen in de ruimtelijke economie van de Nederlanden ca. 1550-ca.1630,* Hilversum, 2001

Lesger C & L. Noordegraaf, eds., *Entrepreneurs and Entrepreneurship in Early Modern Times: Merchants and Industrialists within the Orbit of the Dutch Staple Market,* Den Haag 1995

Lesger, C. & L. Noordergraaf (eds), *Ondernemers en Bestuurders; Economie en politiek in de noordelijke Nederlanden in de late Middeleeuwen en vroegmoderne tijd,* Amsterdam, 1999, p 299-324

Leymarie, J. *Die Holländische Malerei,* Genf, 1965

Lindblad, J. Th., *De* handel tussen Zweden en de Republiek in de 17e en 18e eeuw, in:*Spiegel Historiael,* mei 1986, p 238-244

Lindblad, J. Th., Louis de Geer (1587-1652. Dutch Entrepreneur and Father of Swedish Industry, in: Lesger, C. & L. Noordergraaf (eds), *Entrepreneur and Entrepreneurship in Early Modern Times; Merchants and Industrialists within the Orbit of the Dutch Staple Market,* Den Haag, 1995

Loo, I.J. van, Kaapvaart, handel en staatsbelang. Het gebruik van Kaapvaart als maritiem machtsmiddel en vorm van ondernemerschap tijdens de Nederlandse Opstand, 1568-1648, in: Lesger, C. & L. Noordergraaf (eds), *Ondernemers en Bestuurders; Economie en politiek in de noordelijke Nederlanden in de late Middeleeuwen en vroegmoderne tijd,* Amsterdam, 1999, p 349-368

Maassen, H.A.J., Onmisbare zondaars. Kerk, overheid en banken van lening, in: Lesger, C. & L. Noordergraaf (eds), *Ondernemers en Bestuurders; Economie en politiek in de noordelijke Nederlanden in de late Middeleeuwen en vroegmoderne tijd,* Amsterdam, 1999, p 299-324

Marx, K. Het Kapitaal; *een Kritsiche Beschouwing over de Economie; deel 1: Het Productieproces van het Kapitaal* (I. Lipschits, Trans. Das Kapital, 1867), Bussum, 1970.

Marx, K. & F. Engels, *Het Communistisch Manifest,* (W.C. Sieuwertz van Reesema, Trans. Das Manifest der Kommunistische Partei, 1848) Amsterdam, 1988 .

Mathias, P., (ed), *The Causes of the Industrial Revolution in England,* Norwich, 1977.

Mathias, P., Strategies for Reducing Risks by Entrepreneurs in the Early Modern Period, in: Lesger C & L. Noordegraaf, eds., *Entrepreneurs and Entrepreneurship in Early Modern Times: Merchants and Industrialists within the Orbit of the Dutch Staple Market,* Den Haag 1995

McLellan, D., *Marx,* Fontana, 1975.

Méchoulan, H., *Amsterdam ten tijde van Spinoza; Geld en vrijheid*

(J. Noordman, Trans. Amsterdam au Temps de Spinoza, 1990), Amsterdam, 1992

Meredith, G.G. , R.E. Nelson, P.A. Neck, (eds), *The practice of entrepreneurship*, ILO, Geneva, 1982

Ministerie van Economische Zaken, *Internationaal Ondernemen; Wat kan de overheid voor u doen?*, Den Haag, 1999

Muizer, A.P., *Industry clusters and SMEs*, Zoetermeer 1998

Neck, P.A. & R.E. Nelson, (eds), *Small enterprise development: Policies and programmes,* Management Development Series No. 14, ILO, Geneva, 1987.

North, D.C. & R.P. Thomas, *The Rise of the Western World; A New Economic History*, Cambridge, 1973

North, Douglass C., *Institutions, Institutional Change and Economic Performance*, Cambridge, 1990

NUTEK, *Creating Viable Business Firms; A Study in Enterprise Creation*, National Board for Industrial and Technical Development, Stockholm, 1992

OECD, *Promoting Private Enterprise in Developing Countries*, Paris 1990

Otten, A., *Alles te Koop; Geschiedenis van de Middenstand te Gemert,* Gemert, 1992.

Painter, S., *A History of the Middle Ages; 284-1500,* London, 1976.

Panhuysen, B., Bij uitstek toegankelijk. De gilderegulering van het kleermakers- en naaistersambacht in de Republiek, in: Lesger, C. & L. Noordergraaf (eds), *Ondernemers en Bestuurders; Economie en politiek in de noordelijke Nederlanden in de late Middeleeuwen en vroegmoderne tijd,* Amsterdam, 1999, p 387-416

Palmer, R.R. & J. Colton, *A History of the Modern World,* New York, 1971.

Poelwijk, A., Wet en regelgeving in de Amsterdamse zeepnijverheid, ca. 1500-1630, in: Lesger, C. & L. Noordergraaf (eds), *Ondernemers en Bestuurders; Economie en politiek in de noordelijke Nederlanden in de late Middeleeuwen en vroegmoderne tijd,* Amsterdam, 1999, p 417-432

Polak, M., Geld als water. Smeerolie voor de stapelmarkt, in: *Spiegel Historiael Themanummer: Van elektron tot Euro. Geld en Geldpolitiek door de eeuwen heen,* juli/augustus 1999, p 324-333

Polak, M.S., Monetaire politiek in de zeventiende eeuw, in: Lesger, C. & L. Noordergraaf (eds), *Ondernemers en Bestuurders; Economie en politiek in de noordelijke Nederlanden in de late Middeleeuwen en vroegmoderne tijd,* Amsterdam, 1999, p 433-444

Pors, H., *Kleine Geschiedenis van de Grote Middenstand,* Assen, 1993.

Presser, J., *De Tachtigjarige Oorlog,* parts 1 and 2, Amsterdam, 1980.

Prince, Y.M., *Factors influencing export development of Dutch manufactured products; An explorative study,* Zoetermeer, 2004

Retab, B., *The emergence of Ethnic Entrepreneurship: a conceptual framework,* Zoetermeer, 2001

Reynolds, P.D., (ed), *Global Entrepreneurship Monitor; 2000 Executive Report,* London, 2000

Rommes, R., De gilden , manufactuur en het stadsbestuur van Utrecht, ca. 1500-1800, in: Lesger, C. & L. Noordergraaf (eds), *Ondernemers en Bestuurders; Economie en politiek in de noordelijke Nederlanden in de late Middeleeuwen en vroegmoderne tijd,* Amsterdam, 1999, p 445-464

Roorda, D.J., De Regentenstand in Holland, in: Beekelaar, G..A. M., a.o. (ed), *Vaderlands Verleden in Veelvoud; 31 opstellen over de Nederlandse geschiedenis na 1500,* The Hague, 1975, p 232-251

Roos, H..A.M., *When The Saints Go Marching In,* (inauguration speech for accepting the appointment of Professor at the University of Brabant in social and economic questions related to small and medium enterprise), Tilburg, 1988.

Rostow, W.W., *The Stages of Economic Growth, a non-communist manifesto,* Cambridge, 1960

Rutte, g., & J. Koning, *De Supermarkt ; 50 jaar geschiedenis,* Baarn, 1998

Saget, M. Le, *Le Manager Intuitif; Une nouvelle force,* Paris, 1992.

Santen, H.W. van, *De Verenigde Oost-Indische Compagnie in Gujarat en Hindustan, 1620-1660,* not-published dissertation 1982 at the University of Leyden

Schaik, R. van, Marktbeheersing: overheidsbemoeienis met de levensmiddelenvoorziening in de Nederlanden (14e – 19e eeuw, in: Lesger, C. & L. Noordergraaf (eds), *Ondernemers en Bestuurders; Economie en politiek in de noordelijke Nederlanden in de late*

Middeleeuwen en vroegmoderne tijd, Amsterdam, 1999, p 445-464

Schama, S., *The Embarrassment of Riches; An Interpretation of Dutch Culture in the Golden Age,* New York, 1987.

Schöffer, I., G. Parker e.a., *De Algemene Crisis van de Zeventiende Eeuw,* Haarlem, 1976.

Schuurman, A., J de Vries, A. van der Woude, *Aards Geluk; De Nederlanders en hun Spullen van 1550 tot 1850,* Amsterdam, 1997.

Slicher van Bath, B., *Bijdragen tot de agrarische geschiedenis,* Utrecht,1978.

Smith, A., *An Inquiry into the Nature and Causes of the Wealth of Nations,* Edited edition, Toronto, 1973.

Smits, J.P., E. Horlings, J.L. van Zanden, *Dutch GNP and its components, 1800-1913,* Groningen 2000

Sprunger, M., Entrepreneurs and Ethics. Mennonites Merchants in Seventeenth Century Amsterdam, in: Lesger C & L. Noordegraaf, eds., *Entrepreneurs and Entrepreneurship in Early Modern Times: Merchants and Industrialists within the Orbit of the Dutch Staple Market,* Den Haag, 1995

Stevens, H., *Dutch Enterprise and the VOC; 1602-1799,* Amsterdam, 1998

Streng, H., *Stemmen in staat; De bestuurlijke elite in de stadsrepubliek Zwolle 1579-1795,* Hilversum, 1997

Stuart Hughes, H., *Conscious and Society; The Reorientation of European Social Thought 1890-1930,* New York, 1977.

Stuijvenberg, J.G.H. van (ed), *De Economische Geschiedenis van Nederland,* Groningen, 1977.

Suddle, K., *Entrepreneurial Culture as Determinant of Nascent Entrepreneurship,* Zoetermeer, 2006

Swartttouw, C.N.F., *De Textielvoorziening van Nederland Gedurende den Bezettingstijd 1940-1945,* Amsterdam, 1947.

Tielhof, M. van, Stedelijke regulering van diensten op de stapelmarkt: de Amsterdamse korengilden, in: Lesger, C. & L. Noordergraaf (eds), *Ondernemers en Bestuurders; Economie en politiek in de noordelijke Nederlanden in de late Middeleeuwen en vroegmoderne tijd,* Amsterdam, 1999, p 491-524

Todaro, M.P., *Economics for a Developing World; An introduction to principles, problems and policies for development,* London, 1977

Trompetter, C., De eerste schreden. De politieke aktiviteiten van Twentse textielondernemers in de Patriottentijd, in: Lesger, C. & L. Noordergraaf (eds), *Ondernemers en Bestuurders; Economie en politiek in de noordelijke Nederlanden in de late Middeleeuwen en vroegmoderne tijd,* Amsterdam, 1999, p 525-546

Tucker, R.C., *Karl Marx; Zijn Filisofie en de Mythe,* (S.C.J. Funneman Stevens, Trans. Philisophy and Myth in Karl Marx, 1961), Utrecht/Antwerpen, 1966.

Uniken Venema, C.A., *Enqueterecht en Ondernemerschap; Rechterlijke toetsing van ondernemersbeleid en ondernemrschap,* Den Haag, 1995.

Uytven, R. van, Oudheid en Middeleeuwen, in: Stuijvenberg, J.G.H. van (ed), *De Economische Geschiedenis van Nederland,* Groningen, 1977.

Veluwekamp, J.W., The Purchase and Export of Russian Commodities in 1741 by Dutch Merchants Established at Archangel, in: Lesger C & L. Noordegraaf, eds., *Entrepreneurs and Entrepreneurship in Early Modern Times: Merchants and Industrialists within the Orbit of the Dutch Staple Market,* Den Haag,1995

Veluwekamp, J.W., Buitenlandse octrooien en hun betekenis voor de ontwikkeling van het Nederlandse handelsstelsel in de zeventiende eeuw, in: Lesger, C. & L. Noordergraaf (eds), *Ondernemers en Bestuurders; Economie en politiek in de noordelijke Nederlanden in de late Middeleeuwen en vroegmoderne tijd,* Amsterdam, 1999, p 547-556

Veluwekamp, J.W., *Archangel; Nederlandse ondernemers in Rusland 1550-1785,* Amsterdam, 2000

Veluwekamp, J.W. Handel op Archangel; Nederlandse ondernemers in Rusland in de 17e eeuw, in: *Spiegel Historiael, nr. 3, 2001, p 127-132l*

Ven, F.J.H.M., van der, *Geschiedenis van de arbeid; part I: oudheid en vroege middeleeuwen; part II: hoge middeleeuwen en nieuwe tijd; part III: negentiende en twintigste eeuw,* Utrecht, 1968

Verheul, I., *An esclectic theory of entrepreneurship: policies, instiitutions and culture,* Zoetermeer, 2001

Verwey, G., *Op zoek naar het wezenlijke in de Nederlandse geschiedenis,* Amsterdam, 1980.
Vlessing, O., The Portuguese-Jewish Mercantile Community in Seventeenth-Century Amsterdam, in: Lesger C & L. Noordegraaf, eds., *Entrepreneurs and Entrepreneurship in Early Modern Times: Merchants and Industrialists within the Orbit of the Dutch Staple Market,* Den Haag, 1995
Voss, P., Community in Decline? The Dutch Merchants in Bordeaux, 1650-1715, in: Lesger C & L. Noordegraaf, eds., *Entrepreneurs and Entrepreneurship in Early Modern Times: Merchants and Industrialists within the Orbit of the Dutch Staple Market,* Den Haag, 1995
Vries, J. de, *De Nederlandse Economie Tijdens de 20ste eeuw,* Bussum, 1978.
Vries J. de & A. van der Woude, *Nederland 1500-1815; De eerste ronde van moderne economische groei,* Amsterdam, 1995
Wallerstein, I., *Mercantilisme en de Consolidatie van de Europese Wereld-Economie 1600-1750; het moderne wereld systeem II* (G. De Wit, Trans. The Modern World System II; Mercantilism and the Consolidation of the European World-Economy 1600-1750), New York, 1980.
Wansink, H., Holland en de Zes Bondgenoten: de Republiek der Zeven Verenigde Provincien, in: Beekelaar, G..A. M., a.o. (ed), *Vaderlands Verleden in Veelvoud; 31 opstellen over de Nederlandse geschiedenis na 1500,* The Hague, 1975.
Weber, M., De Kapitalistische Geest. In J. Goudsblom, B. Van Heerikhuizen, A. De Keyser, C.T. Marijnen, eds): *Hoofdstukken uit de Sociologie* (C. Cruson, Trans. Die protestantische Ethik und der Geist des Kapitalismus, 1904I), Utrecht/Antwerpen, 1977, pp 95-105.
Wegener Sleeswijk, A. Binnenlandse belastingen en internationale handel. De crisis in de wijnhandel van 1749-1751, in: Lesger, C. & L. Noordergraaf (eds), *Ondernemers en Bestuurders; Economie en politiek in de noordelijke Nederlanden in de late Middeleeuwen en vroegmoderne tijd,* Amsterdam, 1999, p 557-574
Wennekers, S., *Entreprenruship, Economimc Growth and What Links Them Together,* Zoetermeer, 1997

Wennekers, S., *Maatschappelijke Urgentie Van Ondernemerschap*, Zoetermeer, 2005

Wennekers, S., *Entrepreneurship at Country Level; Economic and Non-Economic Determinants,* Dissertation 2006

Wennekers, S., R. Thurik, F. Buis, *Entrepreneurship, Economic Growth and What Links Them Together*, EIM Strategic study, Zoetermeer 1997.

Wennekers, A.R.M., J. Meijaard, P.J.M. Vroonhof, N.S. Bosma, Maatschappelijke Urgentie Van Ondernemerschap, Den Haag, 2005

Wennekes, W., De aartsvaders; Grondleggers van het Nederlandse bedrijfsleven, Amsterdam, 2000

Wennekes, W., *Gouden handel: De eerste Nederlanders overzee en wat zij daar haalden,* Amsterdam, 2002

Westera, L.D., De geschutgieterij in de Republiek, in: Lesger, C. & L. Noordergraaf (eds), *Ondernemers en Bestuurders; Economie en politiek in de noordelijke Nederlanden in de late Middeleeuwen en vroegmoderne tijd,* Amsterdam, 1999, p 575-602

Wever, E., *Ondernemen in techniek*, Leusden 1992

Wijngaarden, H. van, Het Zwolse werkhuis: liefdadige instelling of onderneming?, in: Lesger, C. & L. Noordergraaf (eds), *Ondernemers en Bestuurders; Economie en politiek in de noordelijke Nederlanden in de late Middeleeuwen en vroegmoderne tijd,* Amsterdam, 1999, p 603-620

Wijnroks, E.H., 'Nationale' en religieuze instellingen in de Nederlandse Rusland handel, 1600-1630, in: Lesger, C. & L. Noordergraaf (eds), *Ondernemers en Bestuurders; Economie en politiek in de noordelijke Nederlanden in de late Middeleeuwen en vroegmoderne tijd,* Amsterdam, 1999, p 621-632

Wilken, P.H., *Entrepreneurship; A Comparative and Historical Study,* Norwood (NJ), 1979.

Windmuller, J.P. & C. de Galan, *Arbeidsverhoudingen in Nederland*, part 1 and 2, Utrecht, 1977.

Wit, A. de, Reders en regels. Visserij, overheid en ondernemerschap in het zeventiende eeuwse Maasmondgebied, in: Lesger, C. & L. Noordergraaf (eds), *Ondernemers en Bestuurders; Economie en politiek in de noordelijke Nederlanden in de late Middeleeuwen en vroegmoderne tijd,* Amsterdam, 1999, p 633-648

Wolf, E.R., *Europe and the People Without History*, Berkeley, 1982.
Wijst, D. van der & W.H.J. Verhoeven, *Financial aspects of firm growth*, EIM Strategic study, Zoetermeer, 1996.
Yamanaka, T., *The Small and Medium Business of the World*, Tokyo, 1981.
Yntema, R.J., Entrepreneurship and Technological Change in Holland's Brewery Industry, 1500-1580, in: Lesger C & L. Noordegraaf, eds., *Entrepreneurs and Entrepreneurship in Early Modern Times: Merchants and Industrialists within the Orbit of the Dutch Staple Market*, Den Haag 1995
Zanden, J.L. van, *Arbeid tijdens het handelskapitalisme; Opkomst en neergang van de Hollandse economie 1350-1850*, Bergen, 1991
Zanden, J.L. van, *Een klein land in de 20e eeuw; Economische geschiedenis van Nederland 1914-1995*, Utrecht, 1997
Zanden, J.L. van, De laatste ronde van de pre-moderne economische groei, in: *BMGN*, 112, (1997).
Zanden, J.L. & A. Van Riel, *Nederland 1780-1914; Staat, Instituties en Economische Ontwikkeling*, Utrecht, 2000
Zandvliet, K., (ed), De 250 rijksten van de Gouden Eeuw, Amsterdam 2006

--------, Keesings Historisch Archief, Amsterdam, 1918 till 2013

--------, Middeleeuwse en Nieuwere Geschiedenis, Reader, part III and V, Instituut voor Geschiedenis, Rijksuniversiteit Utrecht, 1979.

--------, Sociaal Economische Geschiedenis, Reader, part IV, Instituut voor Geschiedenis, Rijksuniversiteit Utrecht, 1979.

INDEX

A

Albany, 128
Amsterdam, 74, 84/5, 88, 92, 96, 98/101, 104, 107, 110/114, 118, 120, 123, 126/7, 129, 132, 135/177, 186/188, 191, 199/207, 210/226, 235, 238, 241, 246, 249, 251, 255, 263, 265, 267, 288, 290
Amsterdam Bourse, 138, 174, 288, 290
Amsterdam Exchange Bank, 136, 148, 177, 186
Antwerp, 11, 12, 64, 75, 82/85, 100, 113/115, 158, 167/169, 187/189, 216, 229, 232
Archangel, 85, 103, 108, 185, 214, 218, 241, 249, 286, 293

B

Baltic Sea, 72, 85, 145, 166, 227, 244, 286
Banning Cocq, F., 163/165
Baumol, W., 9, 31, 32, 37, 38, 98, 161, 175, 199, 200
Bicker, A., 163
Birch, D., 28
Bontemantel, H., 163/4
Bordeaux, 104, 169, 249, 309
Breda, 116, 206
Bruges, 11, 12, 65/68, 73/75, 99, 115, 189, 229

C

Cantillon, R., 13, 19, 20, 37
Charles V, 112/3
Colbert, J.B., 104, 125
College of the Fisheries, 128
Competition, 10, 29, 36, 43, 46, 65, 66, 78, 82, 103/109, 115/121, 126/129, 136, 146/149, 153, 1767, 182, 186, 199/204, 209/220, 233/237, 240, 247, 249, 250, 262, 272, 275, 281/2, 287/292
Coulomb, A., 26
Creative destruction, 23, 24, 30, 37, 195

D

Danzig, 168/9
De Geer, L., 198, 199
Delft, 82, 118, 126, 132/135, 147, 152, 194, 208
Deventer, 64, 65, 81, 120
De Vries J., & A.M. Van der Woude, 11, 83, 86, 92, 161
Dordrecht, 64, 66, 81, 82, 112, 119, 123, 131, 148, 197
Drucker, P.F., 28/30, 37

E

Edward I, 66
Egypt, 60, 104
EIM, 36, 38, 41, 42, 54, 247, 278
England, 11, 13, 34, 36, 60/66, 70, 72, 81/85, 92, 95, 105/115, 125/129, 138, 149, 176, 177, 194, 200/204, 219/223, 228/9, 234, 237, 239, 246, 253/4, 287
Enkhuizen, 126, 151/2
Erasmus, 161

F

Famiado Strada, 205/6
Fayol, H., 22
Flanders, 64/68, 76, 87, 158, 167, 190/1, 197, 239, 275
Floris V, 66
Flussing, 148

France, 11, 12, 24, 36, 62, 82/85, 92/95, 99/110, 115, 125, 129, 138, 149, 153, 165/169, 172/177, 184, 197, 200/204, 219/229, 234/241, 246/7, 250/257, 275, 287
Frederik Hendrik, 165

G
Galbraith, J., 27, 261
Gelderblom, O., 168/9, 197
Germany, 11, 39, 73, 76, 81, 84, 100, 105, 154, 169, 172, 184, 187, 192, 194, 197, 211, 222, 239, 246, 256, 270, 275
Gestner, F., 21
Gouda, 82, 118, 134, 194
Greece, 104
Guilds, 65, 74, 119, 120, 131/134, 156, 171, 176, 180, 185, 188

H
Haarlem, 82, 118, 131, 140, 217, 218, 223
Hagen, E.E., 51
Hébert, R.F., 40
Heyn, P., 107, 200
Hofstede, G., 272, 279
Holland, 66, 74, 82/84, 87/89, 99/105, 108, 110, 114/5, 126, 135, 145, 158, 163, 172, 184, 192/194, 210, 218, 231
Hoorn, 88, 126, 151, 152
Hope, A., 149, 150, 205
Hungary, 105
Hunt & Murray, 13, 70, 75, 76

I
ILO, 13, 19, 30, 31, 37, 39
Innovation, 10, 15, 23 27/31, 37, 41/47, 53, 55, 61, 71, 72, 89, 96, 97, 179, 182, 184, 193/209, 246/249, 261, 271, 272, 281/293

K
Kirzner, I.M., 29, 30, 37
Klein, P.W., 103, 212
Knight, F., 30, 37
Kondratieff, N., 24

L
La Rochelle, 169
Lesger, C., 29, 251
Levant, 101, 104, 129, 144/146, 166, 204, 216, 241, 249, 286, 290, 293
Leyden, 82, 89, 94, 106, 112, 118/9, 132, 140, 163, 165, 180, 203, 217, 220, 286
Link, N., 40
Louis of Male, 99
Lübeck, 66, 72/3, 169

M
Manhattan, 128, 241
Margaretha of Flanders, 66
McClelland, D., 26, 27, 38, 50
Méchoulan, H., 114, 171/173, 201, 214
Mees, M., 258
Mercantilism, 19, 109, 124, 221, 226
Middleburgh, 148, 169
M.I.T. , 28
Montpeliers, 169

N
New Amsterdam, 128, 241
Nordic Company, 146, 147
North, D. C., 33/38, 75, 113, 146

O
OECD, 40, 282, 283

P
Paris, 73, 169, 215
Philips II, 113, 114, 156
Portugal, 84, 99, 104, 126/7, 164, 167, 169, 177, 185, 187, 189,

200, 211, 216, 238/240, 244, 275, 287

R

Reformation, 8, 25, 26, 117, 156, 161, 183
Renselaer, 128
Roosevelt, 128
Rostow, W., 78
Rotterdam, 99, 126, 148, 149, 152, 165, 181, 256, 263, 267
Russia, 10, 36, 93, 101/104, 144/5, 169, 184, 197, 216, 255

S

Schama, S., 137/139, 160, 175, 188, 192, 212/3, 307
Schulze, M., 21
Schumpeter, J., 17, 23, 24, 27, 37, 43, 103, 193/197, 261
Silisia, 60, 105, 140
Smith, A., 20, 124
SMO, 38
Spain, 12, 18, 34, 62, 84, 92, 98, 104/107, 113/115, 126/129, 160, 164, 170, 173, 177, 185, 189, 200, 207, 212, 216, 219, 227/229, 238/244, 248, 259, 275, 287
Spinoza, B., 163, 173
Staple market, 82, 98, 101/103, 112, 123/4, 129, 140/143, 150, 153, 167, 186/7, 197/199, 205, 210, 220/1, 231, 238, 245, 251

T

Taylor, F., 21, 22
Thijs, H., 168/9, 213
Thijs, P., 169
Trip, E., 158, 162, 198, 213
Tulpmania, 138, 237, 290
Turkey, 104, 138, 275

U

Utrecht, 62/67, 74, 93, 114, 119, 139, 194, 217

V

Van der Meulen, A., 188, 190
Van Oldenbarneveldt, J., 126
Van Zanden, J.L., 151, 231
VOC, 89, 101, 103, 107, 126/128, 137, 141, 146, 151/153, 162/173, 191, 219, 222, 237/8, 245, 253, 256, 285, 291
Von Mises, 30, 37, 41

W

Warsaw, 168
Weber, M., 24/27, 38, 191, 192
WIC, 103, 127/8, 146, 238, 287, 291
Wilken, P., 35, 38, 40, 49
William of Orange, 114

Z

Zeeland, 82, 83, 100, 108, 152, 158, 197
Zwolle, 81, 135, 218

FIGURES

1.	Schumpeter's waves acceleration	24
2.	Research model	56
3.	Research focus on next chapters	79
4.	Simplified entrepreneurial relationships	142
5.	Research focus	225
6.	Relationship of opportunity conditions	230
7.	Overall institutional structure private sector/government	236
8.	Bell curve Trade Capitalism	252

TABLES

1.	Dimensions and factors	57
2.	Dutch international trade flow comparison 1720-1770	154
3.	State of affairs large Dutch MNCs 1991	260
4.	Share of industry and services 1930-1991	265
5.	Motives for starting entrepreneurs	279